'Sudjic explans how Foster helped transform his profession. When he started out, it was largely a gentlemanly, small-scale business, a sort of cottage industry with a strong emphasis on the handicraft of models and drawings. Projects outside an architect's country were the exception. Today, Foster's practice employs well over 1,000 people. The book tells this story clearly and it makes a good introduction to Foster' *Observer*

'Deyan Sudjic's discursive biography offers a portrait of a searcher, a man always exploring the limits of architecture, of whom one client pays the ultimate compliment: Foster "asked the right questions"' *Sunday Telegraph*

'It is an extraordinary story of a truly self-made man who seems a kickback to the great Victorians, the engineers and industrialists who made the Manchester he came from and conquered the world with their machines' *Financial Times*

'Deyan Sudjic has delivered meticulously researched and psychologically resonant insights into the conflicting forces of aspiration and outsider status that propelled Foster towards his breakthrough building, the amenities block for the Fred Olsen Line in Milwall in 1969 . . . Sudjic is particularly good at delineating Foster's astonishing ability to get clients to revise their expectations so that he could develop truly radical architecture' *Independent*

'The success of the book comes from its insights into the young Foster's life' *Scotsman*

'Deyan Sudjic has traced Foster's career since he mounted the now legendary Fosters Rogers Stirling Exhibition at the Royal Academy in 1986 . . . This book is a story about power that charts Foster's journey' *Daily Telegraph*

Deyan Sudjic studied architecture at the University of Edinburgh and has worked as a critic, editor and curator. Currently the director of the Design Museum, he helped establish *Blueprint* magazine, edited *Domus* in Milan for a number of years and was the director of the Venice architecture Biennale in 2002. He is a former architecture critic for the *Observer*, the *Guardian* and the *Sunday Times*.

Norman Foster
A life in architecture

DEYAN SUDJIC

PHOENIX

A PHOENIX PAPERBACK

First published in Great Britain in 2010
by Weidenfeld & Nicolson
This paperback edition published in 2012
by Phoenix,
an imprint of Orion Books Ltd,
Orion House, 5 Upper St Martin's Lane,
London WC2H 9EA

An Hachette UK company

10 9 8 7 6 5 4 3 2

A CIP catalogue record for this book
is available from the British Library.

ISBN 978-0-7538-2857-1

Typeset by Input Data Services Ltd, Bridgwater, Somerset

Printed and bound by CPI Group (UK) Ltd, Croydon CR0 4YY

The Orion Publishing Group's policy is to use papers that
are natural, renewable and recyclable products and
made from wood grown in sustainable forests. The logging
and manufacturing processes are expected to conform to
the environmental regulations of the country of origin.

www.orionbooks.co.uk

Contents

One
The view from the window   1

Two
I could have stayed in America   55

Three
How much does your building weigh?   104

Four
Reinventing the skyscraper   156

Five
Architecture and power   193

Six
The art of the juggler   247

ACKNOWLEDGEMENTS   294
REFERENCES   296
ILLUSTRATION CREDITS   297
INDEX   299

One

The view from the window

The Indonesian site foreman with an ikat headdress under his hard hat blows his whistle to push the tangle of construction workers back out of the way. They look expectantly across the concrete hulk, marooned in the flat, featureless sandscape that blows aimlessly around the outer edges of Abu Dhabi's airport, in what will one day be the heart of a new township with homes and jobs for 100,000 people. Minutes pass, then a slender, silver bubble glides silently into sight. From the front, its slit eye headlamps, and the rictus grin of its vestigial radiator grille give it the look of a slightly sinister alien species. It approaches, lights gleaming, draws level, and then, as it goes noiselessly on its way, its open doors briefly give a glimpse of the ghostly interior of a vehicle big enough to take four, but without driver or controls. It moves, steered by nothing more tangible than its digital intelligence, guided by invisible sensors buried in the concrete floor, and by counting the wheel revolutions that allow its computers to understand where it is. A single technician sits inside monitoring its performance on his laptop. This is the transport system that is taking shape to serve a new settlement planned by Norman Foster. On an artificial ground level, seven metres above, a network of pedestrian streets with all the usual architectural dreams of umbrella-shaded cafés, shops and apartments is planned. Down here, in the undercroft, will be a fleet of silver bubbles, descended from the prototype that has just slipped by. They will need no tracks, and no drivers, and they will abolish traffic jams and car parks.

There are tower cranes above, spreading out over air-conditioned site huts. Every day 6,000 labourers are bussed in. On the main site, concrete structures have risen eight and ten storeys high on some buildings. They have been herded together so as to create shaded lanes narrow enough to generate a cooling breeze, like a traditional walled city. This is Masdar, the Arab word for source. Construction workers moved on to the site three months after Foster won a competition to do the plan. It is called a city, but that is putting it perhaps too optimistically. Masdar is one of the string of settlements sprouting up between Abu Dhabi and Dubai. What makes Masdar different from what is around it – the airport compound that houses flight crews, next door, the golf course, or the Formula One track – is that this is an experimental laboratory for a world that is waking up to the fear that it might be making itself uninhabitable.

The first phase will include the home of the Masdar Institute of Science and Technology, a research centre dedicated to renewable energies linked to Imperial College London, MIT and New York University. It is being built by the same mix of migrant workers from across Asia that have been drawn to the Gulf over the last decade to build the glittering towers of Dubai, the artificial islands, the indoor ski slopes with real snow, the most extreme form of the architecture of irrational exuberance that evaporated on the day the credit finally ran out. This is a place in which oil is burned to desalinate the water which is used to grow the grass and the trees that fringe the highways: a process that is killing the mangroves that keep the Gulf alive at its choke point at the straits of Hormuz.

Masdar claims that it will be different. It aims to be carbon neutral, recycling all its own waste. Even during construction there are carefully sorted piles of waste stacked in colour-coded pens on the edge of the site. Most of the steel used for its reinforcing rods and structural frames comes from recycled sources. There is a 10-megawatt photovoltaic power station already operational. Later there will be larger solar farms and experimental plantations and attempts to harvest energy from algae blooms. The plan is for the entire area to be free of cars. The shaded streets are intended to encourage walking – no small ambition in the climate of the Gulf, where in August the temperature is a brutal fifty degrees.

In its optimism and its search for answers, Masdar is an echo of the first city of the future that Norman Foster explored with his adolescent imagination growing up in Manchester. Long before he met Buckminster Fuller, he never missed an instalment of *Dan Dare: Pilot of the Future*. As a young teenager Foster read the comic strip, with its intricate depiction of a world of atomic-powered monorails and levitating taxis (which look a lot like Masdar's personal rapid transits), every week in the *Eagle*, the comic aimed at middle-class adolescents in the England of the 1950s. Foster has been thinking about cities ever since.

If you have been fortunate enough to be engaged with so many extraordinary projects, with the passage of time you realise that the issues of sustainability are about density. If you have the luxury of having lived long enough to understand that, you realise that making cities is less about the individual buildings, and much more about the bigger picture. It takes me back to the thesis that I did on city spaces. It's not a new thing: it goes back to roaming the streets of Manchester.

The view from the front bedroom at 4 Crescent Grove in Levenshulme, a faded suburb washed up on Manchester's southern limits by the tide of Victorian development, has changed hardly at all since the day more than half a century ago that a twenty-one-year-old Norman Foster took out brush and poster colours to paint it. Neither a crescent nor a grove, Crescent Grove is a short, plain, terraced street just five houses long, caught between the mainline railway from London to Manchester and the road to the south. It looks as if it was built more by accident than as part of any rationally considered plan. Small factories, some workshops and a few yards have been scattered seemingly at random among the terraces of houses that frame Crescent Grove.

What was once Foster's home is at the end of one of these terraces. Its gable end has been sliced off at an awkward angle and a makeshift back extension tacked to one side. The front door is set inside an arched opening in an attempt at an architectural flourish. Like its neighbours, it has the bay window and front garden that serve to distinguish it from the slightly humbler houses in the surrounding streets. The moulded clay tiles around the eaves give it a vaguely gothic flavour, but not in a way that would have gladdened John Ruskin's heart. There is a modest walled yard at the back of the house that once had enough space for a coal shed and an outdoor privy. Beyond is the alley demanded by nineteenth-century health regulations. It was meant to be the route for the bin men who came every week to collect refuse. In fact it was universally used as the way into the house, opening directly into the kitchen. The front door was for special occasions only: funerals, Christmas, and visits from the doctor. Beyond the alley is the railway, hoisted up on an embankment. When Foster was sitting drawing at the table in his tiny bedroom, it was at eye level.

The house is still fragile enough to shake every time a train goes by. In the 1950s it was the soot-black steam locomotives of the state-owned British Railways that were doing the shaking as they hauled the passenger trains past Crescent Grove, spitting smoke, fire and cinders along the way. There is nothing quite so elemental to see now, just the wires of the overhead electric power lines, and the silvery grey skin of the Virgin Pendolino blasting past four times every hour.

Crescent Grove is unmistakably on the wrong side of the tracks. Duck down under the railway embankment, penetrated by an underpass finished a century and a half ago by the London & North Western Railway's engineers in hard purple engineering brick of infinitely better quality than anything that Levenshulme's penny-pinching housebuilders ever invested in, and you find yourself in an altogether primmer kind of suburbia than the rest of Levenshulme.

When I tell Foster that I have been to see the house that was once his home, he reaches for his pencil with his left hand and, without pausing, reproduces in his notebook exactly what I have seen for myself. More than twenty years after he was last there, he deftly delineates a blackened arch burrowing under the tracks like a mousehole. Five ill-assorted bollards of various sizes and shapes stand in the way to stop vehicles driving through. Unprompted, he scrawls a sentence that had already occurred to me: 'The tracks that divide one world from another.'

Foster's drawing gives a glimpse of the half-timbered early twentieth-century houses that I saw on the other side of the arch. They are relatively substantial and sit on wide, tree-lined streets, even if they look as though they have come down in the world a bit. To the other side of Crescent Grove lies Stockport Road, the main route which comes spooling out of the southside of Manchester, crawling through Longsight, and into Levenshulme. It is a continuous strip of Edwardian banks, pubs and shopping parades that have also seen better days. Beyond them are mosques, and Pakistani community centres.

A madrassa has slipped into the gap between the two-up, two-down houses of Prince Albert Avenue, where Foster's grandmother once lived, and the Crescent behind it. The Topkapi Turkish restaurant offers its customers an outdoor terrace with hookah pipes, while the old Palace Cinema on Farm Place is now the Al Waasi banqueting hall with an all-you-can-eat buffet at £5 a head. Back in the days when he was a student, Foster's mother got him a job next door in Robinson's bakery.

It was in Levenshulme in 2007 that a Shi'a preacher forced two local boys, aged thirteen and fifteen, to flagellate themselves with a ritual five-bladed rope and was subsequently convicted of child abuse. Norman Foster, meanwhile, has been invited by King Abdullah bin Abdul Aziz Al Saud, guardian of the two most holy sites of Islam, to discuss restructuring the approaches to Mecca.

Levenshulme is a place built mostly of harsh red brick, with the occasional ladylike neo-Georgian bank made up in faience and cream. One such specimen, formerly Martins Bank and now Barclays, sits opposite the Farmer's Inn around the corner from Crescent Grove.

The terraces on either side of Crescent Grove have been thinned out in an attempt to make it look like a place that people might want to live, rather than an essential but ultimately somewhat regrettable by-product of the Industrial Revolution. Foster describes the process that has reshaped Levenshulme since the time that he lived there as gentrification, but that is hardly the right word. There are still a few people here who say that they have lived in the area since they knew Foster as a child. They live alongside the occasional art student or folk musician and a vigorous community of migrants from Pakistan, along with their descendants. All of them have the electricity and the bathrooms that were luxuries during Foster's childhood, yet this still isn't a desirable address. A few streets in the area do show the occasional flash of architectural ambition. Some have a round arched doorway picked out in clay tiles. Others deploy a keystone or two, and some have decorated roof ridges. But the materials that were used to build them were so cheap that the pitted surface of the clay brick used widely throughout Levenshulme looks as if it has been peeled raw by some particularly aggressive skin disease over the years.

The original front doors and window frames have rotted away, to be replaced by flush panel hardboard and aluminium. There are telegraph poles at the street corners from which overhead telephone lines radiate like anorexic maypoles. The Crescent Grove of today, hemmed in by the railway, with McCosken's builder's yard immediately to the west of Foster's old house, and a scrap yard, is still recognisably the product of the provincial England of Foster's youth. It belongs to a country of granite cobbled city streets, of trams and trolley buses with conductors in barathea blazers and celluloid peaked caps, of concrete cooling towers, canals and factory chimneys, of smogs and dance halls.

Even when Foster was a pale young adolescent, it was already a world overshadowed by signs of an aggressive modernity. Manchester's boundaries were defined for him by his bicycle rides into Derbyshire and Cheshire. He pedalled all the way to the Lake District, and back: 130 miles in a single day. He went south to Jodrell Bank to see the Lovell steerable radio telescope when it was unveiled in 1957. In the British context it was as startling a vision of the future as the final assembly building of Cape Canaveral was for America.

Sitting in his bedroom in 1955, Foster was working on a set of drawings for the portfolio that would propel him out of Levenshulme for good. He needed them to apply for a place on the architecture course at Manchester University as a mature student. His drawings were inspired in equal parts by the industrial landscapes of L.S. Lowry and the cutaway drawings of the aircraft carriers and delta-winged Vulcan bombers that filled the china-clay-coated photogravure-printed centre pages of the *Eagle*.

Half a century later, Foster has one of Lowry's paintings hanging on his wall. It's a gift from his wife, Elena. It shows a landscape not so different from the one that Foster would have seen from his window: the unforgiving industrial Manchester of the 1930s. Until the day that he retired as chief cashier of the Pall Mall Property Company, Lowry would personally tour those streets collecting rents on behalf of his employer.

The *Eagle* was essential weekly reading for adolescent boys from aspirational families in the 1950s. It was started by Marcus Morris, a Methodist minister from Lancashire, who was worried both about the morale-sapping effect of what he saw as dubious imported American comics, and the home-grown anarchy of the *Beano*. There was a strong religious streak to the *Eagle*, exemplified by a long-running strip outlining the life of Jesus. But far from providing a bulwark against the permissive society of the 1960s, which was already gathering momentum, the *Eagle* had the unintended and entirely unexpected consequence of breeding a generation of high-tech architects. This was certainly true in Foster's case; the *Eagle* offered both a refuge from his isolation as an only child and an introduction to contemporary architecture.

The cover of each issue featured the unmistakable lantern jaw and improbable eyebrows of Dan Dare. Against a backdrop of monorails running down the middle of the Thames and space ports that faithfully reproduced late-period Frank Lloyd Wright urbanism, the hero of Frank Hampson's science-fiction strip – armed with little more than pluck and a self-sealing space suit – would engage in weekly battle with the evil Mekon and his green-complexioned Treen followers. The *Eagle*'s centre spread was always devoted to an intricate cutaway drawing that would lay out the complexities of one engineering triumph after another. In 1951, the magazine published an exploded view of the Dome of Discovery, built for the Festival of Britain, designed by 'the young British architect' Ralph Tubbs. This was the closest that Foster ever got to actually seeing the Festival for himself – it had been demolished by the time that he finally reached London. A rallying point for the generation of architects and designers who worked on its various pavilions, the Festival marked the first occasion that contemporary architecture got a real audience in Britain. In a later issue, the *Eagle* showed another key British building of the 1950s, Basil Spence's design for Coventry Cathedral, describing it as 'The Cathedral of the Space Age'.

To the impressionable young, the *Eagle* was highly effective propaganda, not just for modern architecture but for technology. There were images of nuclear-powered ships and gas turbine-engined cars that the *Eagle* predicted would be the personal transport of the very near future. As portrayed by the *Eagle*'s artists, these vehicles bear a close resemblance to Buckminster Fuller's Dymaxion car, shaped like tear drops and driven on three invisible wheels. The cities of the future were going to look like modular collections of pods. One issue had a cutaway drawing of an American Antarctic base that had been clipped together from a series of units half-buried in snow and ice. Ten years later, that drawing would not have been out of place on the pages of an avant-garde architectural magazine.

Foster was, and still is, charmed by these images. Both by the look of the drawings, that in his eyes are artworks in their own right, and by the insight into the world of design that they offered. Studying those carefully rendered images that sliced away the layers of the fuselage to show the underlying geodesic structure of a Wellington bomber, designed to be tough enough to survive a direct hit in the air, or that laid bare the construction techniques used to build the Forth Railway Bridge, it's easy to see why they would have ignited a spark of curiosity in the mind of a young James Dyson or a Norman Foster about the way the world worked.

Years later, Foster tracked down John Batchelor, the artist responsible for some of the later cutaways, and asked him to make a drawing to analyse the vivid yellow steel masts that he had designed to support the roof of the Renault parts warehouse that he built outside Swindon. Despite their charm, these cutaways seem to lack the authority of the cross-section through a Cunarder that Le Corbusier cited as a precedent for his apartment slab in Marseilles, the Unité d'Habitation. As a source of inspiration, anonymous popular culture is one thing, but the kind of imagery that has never entirely succeeded in escaping beyond the tastes of adolescent males is quite another. Frank Lloyd Wright admitted to having played with Froebel blocks as a child, and acknowledged their impact on his architecture. Roy Lichtenstein's transfiguration of the conventions of the American comic strips changed the direction of contemporary art in the 1960s. But few architects have the innocence to admit that their eyes to the modern world were opened by the most wide-eyed kind of science fiction in the way that Foster does.

Number 4 Crescent Grove was the house to which Norman Robert Foster, the only child of Robert and Lillian Foster, moved shortly after his birth in Reddish, near Stockport on 1 June 1935. Foster's parents had married two years earlier, in 1933, at St Luke's Church in Levenshulme. His mother's maiden name was Smith. She was twenty-seven at the time of their marriage, Foster's father was thirty-three.

Foster has no recollection of Reddish; but when he was introduced into the House of Lords as a life peer in the summer of 1999, by Lord Weidenfeld and Lord Sainsbury, taking the title Baron Foster of Thames Bank, he was described in Hansard as 'of Reddish in the county of Greater Manchester'. The crest that Foster later adopted has at the centre of its shield a stepped geometric tower, a heraldic abstraction of the structure of the Millennium Bridge, flanked by a pair of herons.

Foster's parents paid fourteen shillings a week to rent the tiny house in Crescent Grove. His paternal grandparents, his uncle and his two aunts, as well as his cousins, all lived within a few streets of each other. His mother's family had come from Ardwick, regarded as a cut below Levenshulme in the carefully graduated hierarchy of Manchester's gritty urban hinterland. Despite the aspirational and suburban tone of its name, in the days when Foster lived there Crescent Grove was the kind of place where doorsteps were washed down daily, and debt collectors called, L.S. Lowry style, once a week. His mother would trade old clothes with the rag-and-bone man for a branded cleaning product known as Donkey Stone. It was made from pulverised stone mixed with bleaching powder and cement. Every week she used it to whiten her doorstep, as much in a conspicuous display of respectability as for any ostensibly hygienic purpose. On her hands and knees she would scrub the stone threshold clean. Foster got into trouble if he scuffed or marked it. Throughout his early childhood, bathing for Foster meant a once-a-week immersion in the kitchen in a galvanised zinc tub.

The floral wallpaper in the front parlour at No. 4 was permanently damp. There was a gas meter in the corner that needed to be constantly fed with shillings to keep the cooker in the kitchen alight. In the living room, where the only source of heat was the fireplace, a radiogram stood next to a damp patch on the wall, poised to pick up the Light Programme of the BBC as well as Radio Hilversum and Luxembourg. It was Foster's job to move the radiogram away from the wall when it stopped working, and to twist a loose valve, a procedure that left him vulnerable to the occasional electric shock.

There was no telephone in the Foster house, the nearest was

in a cast-iron box just outside the Methodist church on the Stockport Road, five minutes' walk away. There were no books bar his textbooks and, apart from the *Manchester Evening News* and Foster's weekly copy of the *Eagle*, not much in the way of newspapers. Almost everybody in the neighbourhood left school as soon as they could, which in those days was at the age of fourteen. When he finally got to university, Foster would find himself buttonholed in the street by neighbours who, for the most part, regarded him as some kind of idler, still sponging off his parents in his twenties.

> The next-door neighbours had a son, Sam Bradley. He chased after me one day, stopped me and said, 'Look at my hands, they are so different from yours. I am working, you aren't, so why don't you get a proper job?'
>
> I had been severely bullied by other boys in the area. But Sam didn't touch me. He just couldn't understand what I was doing at the university.

In Foster's memory, his was not a close-knit family, even if there were grandparents, uncles, aunts and cousins living just a few yards away from his Donkey-Stoned front doorstep. There were resentments and divisions among the Fosters. Some things were left unsaid within the family. His aunt Nettie's husband, for one, was seldom spoken of. 'I think he may have been a deserter in World War Two, but it was never spelled out,' says Foster. Foster feels he never knew enough about his mother. 'I was always curious about her. I am almost certain that she had been adopted as a baby. Her name was Smith, but the man I knew as her brother was called Beckett. She was very beautiful, and in her looks she had a Mediterranean quality.'

Grandmother Rosa Foster had a house a short walk away on Prince Albert Avenue, which she and Foster's grandfather William shared with his uncle. One of his father's sisters, Kate, lived a few doors down, on the same road. The lamplighters would knock on the door every morning to wake her, as they put out the gas streetlights. She had a daughter, Edna. His father's other sister, Ethel, lived on the far side of the Stockport Road. After Foster's parents died, his aunt Ethel wrote to him, asking for his help. Her own house was threatened with demolition to make way for a slum-clearance scheme, so could Norman perhaps find a way to help her stay in the neighbourhood? He responded quickly and bought the house at 6 Crescent Grove, next to the one that his parents had lived in, for her.

He remembers his grandparents' house as always being dark. It was still lit by gas, even after the war. The two old people used to sit in the gloom, in matching chairs on either side of the fireplace. In Foster's eyes, his grandmother did not treat his mother well. When Foster's father was rushed into hospital, desperately ill, one Christmas towards the end of the war, Lillian was left to fend for herself. Her sister-in-law pointedly took Norman's cousins into Manchester to see Father Christmas in a department store, but left him at home.

In fact, life was not always so bleak. There were shared family holidays, sometimes taken in North Wales, sometimes in Blackpool, with his uncles and aunts and his cousins. One summer they all went to Norbreck, just outside Blackpool, to stay in a bed and breakfast. Foster remembers asking his mother about the two black lines on the shirt that his uncle wore at breakfast. She told him, 'When he washes, he turns his shirt inside out, and the water leaves a mark.' In the Levenshulme of his childhood Foster remembers that most people could not afford more than a few items of clothing. 'Those that they had would be slept in.' It's a significant memory, given the close relationship between hygiene and modern architecture's missionary impulses. In Levenshulme's Free Library, Foster had discovered Le Corbusier. Imagine the impact on the fastidious boy from Crescent Grove, after coming back from Blackpool and the sight of his uncle's shirt, of *Vers une architecture*'s messianic prescriptions for the life hygienic.

> Demand a bathroom looking south. One of the largest rooms in the house, the old drawing room, for instance. One wall to be entirely glazed, opening if possible on to a balcony for sun baths, the most up-to-date fittings with a shower bath and gymnastic appliances. An adjoining room to be a dressing room, in which you can dress and undress. Never undress in your bedroom. It is not a clean thing to do and makes the room horribly untidy. Teach your children that a house is only habitable when it is full of light and air and when the floors and walls are clear.

Foster may have felt that he was an isolated only child. But he remembers Levenshulme as a close community. It was a place in which he knew all that there was to know about his neighbours. Stockport Road offered the consolations of relatively prosperous Northern working-class life. There were fish suppers seasoned with salt and vinegar, wrapped in newspaper with mushy peas to be had from the local chip shop; regular customers would be treated to free scraps of batter. Further along the road, in Longsight, was the pool hall in which Foster occasionally played billiards with his father. Then there was Robinson's Café in Levenshulme, where his mother worked much later as a waitress. The UCP shop – the initials stood for Universal Cow Products – sold tripe from a marble-topped slab in an interior gilded with brass and embellished with mahogany. And in Poplar Villas, just round the corner from the Fosters, there was a school of ballroom dancing.

The people who lived in Levenshulme ranged from relatively prosperous small businessmen to men who, like the father of Norman's schoolfriend Ronnie Deakin, could only find menial work after the war. Deakin's father was a dustman; 'My mother was very disparaging about him,' Foster remembers. The Liptrotts, at the end of Crescent Grove, had a garage business. In his student days, Foster worked there as a part-time mechanic in its oil-stained inspection pit, getting filthy in the process. Alan Liptrott would go home from the garage to listen to Schubert. The Streets across the way owned a removals firm that had a yard next to the house. On the other side of Crescent Grove in Poplar Villas lived Mrs Flood; although bedridden and known to be of a nervous disposition, she was nevertheless an accomplished watercolourist.

Foster's parents were certainly not well off. After the war, his father worked as a labourer at Metropolitan Vickers in Trafford Park to keep his family together. He put in long hours, and had to rely on a succession of buses to get across Manchester. But when Norman was born his father was managing a pawnshop in Eccles, driving to work from the first family home in Reddish in a Jowett van, a distinction that suggests a certain level of entrepreneurial ambition, even if the exorbitant rates of interest that his shop charged would not have endeared him to some of his customers. In his retirement, Robert Foster cut an elegant figure, stylishly dressed in a single-breasted suit, with a slim knot in his tie, and mirror-finished shoes. Foster's mother was a fine-featured, elegant woman. His parents made a striking couple.

Robert and Lillian were constantly struggling to make something of themselves, but as time went on they were slipping down the ladder of social status rather than making their way up it. Foster calls his family working class. In fact, in the infinite gradations of class with which the British delineate themselves, the Fosters were more aspirational that that. They belonged to that nebulous territory at the point where the upper working class starts to shade into the lower middle class. Even if they were less successful than some of their neighbours, they had accepted the challenge of living life measured by a set of expectations framed by others. They worked hard. They saved because they wanted to provide for Foster's education, and because they dreamed of being able to run a small business. It would have allowed them to achieve the same step up that some of the family had already taken. One of Foster's uncles ran a bakery, and another, Sid Beckett, had a butcher's shop. Sid and his wife, Bertha, lived in a semi-detached house in Chorlton-cum-Hardy in what seemed to the Fosters unimaginable affluence. Sid had a piano which his daughter played cautiously, and paid for violin lessons for Norman's reluctant cousin Lionel.

Foster remembers his parents taking him to see a small shop that they were thinking of buying, accompanied by an estate agent. But none of their plans to start their own business came to anything. As a teenager he became acutely aware of their frustrated ambitions and their limited horizons. Later it was what drove him to escape the world of Crescent Grove. They had failed in what they had wanted to do with their lives. He was not going to do the same.

*

The Levenshulme Free Library where the young Foster would retreat from his damp living room, and from the school bullies, to escape from the claustrophobia of his parents' home still exists. Turn right out of Crescent Grove, and right again on to Stockport Road, go one hundred yards south, past the Farmers Arms, the United Reformed Church, and the Union Inn, *Erected AD 1923*, and turn right on to Cromwell Grove. The red-brick gables of the library and its hammer-beam roof suggest a manor house trapped in the bleak streets of south Manchester, which can be seen spreading endlessly to the horizon. It is a kind of civic oasis, next to the Chapel Street Primary School, and opposite the prim municipal baths and public washhouse built in a chilly neo-Georgian style, like the Levenshulme post office on the other side of Stockport Road. The twin entrance doors to the baths, raised up on flights of steps, are both topped by a keystone incised with a single, brutally impersonal word. 'Males' on the left and 'Females', under polite sash windows, on the right.

If the young Foster had looked up at the moulded clay garland over the library door as he went in, he would have seen a representation of a set square and a protractor incised within it. It was here, in a building paid for by Victorian philanthropist Andrew Carnegie, that Foster began to discover the meaning of architecture in Le Corbusier's *Vers une architecture*. In the early part of 2008, the many hours that he had spent in Levenshulme's library were put to good use when Foster + Partners won a highly visible commission for remodelling the New York Public Library's historic main building on Fifth Avenue. The same Andrew Carnegie who had established the Free Library of Foster's youth had set up the foundation that financed the construction and fitting out of thirty-seven local libraries in New

York, in the hope that the poor but gifted and ambitious might do something to redress the disadvantages of birth, upbringing and lack of education. Foster told the Americans, perfectly correctly, that he himself had once been exactly the kind of person that the libraries in New York were setting out to reach.

Today, Levenshulme library is struggling to dissipate the musty air that comes from housing thousands of books wrapped in yellowing clear plastic, worn thin by the pressure of countless fingers. In its efforts to modernise itself, the library seems intent on ruthlessly limiting the intellectual challenge of the books on its shelves. On his return in 2009, Foster was left saddened and depressed by the lack of books of real substance.

Foster's most vivid memories of his childhood are of his mother, rather than his father. When the war came, his father, who had been rendered unfit for active service by his injuries in the war of 1914–18, left the pawnshop he had been managing in Eccles to become a guard at Fairey Aviation, an aircraft factory at Heaton Chapel, outside Stockport, that was building Fulmar fighters for the aircraft carriers of the Royal Navy's Fleet Air Arm. For a while, Lilly Foster took over her husband's old job at the pawnshop. It involved her taking an eight-mile journey, first by tram to the centre of Manchester, and then on by bus to Eccles. In her absence, five-year-old Norman was looked after by family and neighbours in Crescent Grove. As he once said, 'My parents worked and worked and worked ... they worked so hard that I wasn't really able to get to know them.'

The war as it was fought in the skies over Manchester was the source of both fascination and terror for Foster. Except for a short period when he was evacuated to rural Alderly Edge in

Cheshire with his mother, Foster spent World War Two in Crescent Grove. He experienced a curious mix of fear provoked by the random violence of the air war and a spellbound wonder at its glamorous-looking artefacts. Aircraft, weaponry and uniforms intrigued him. Night after night in 1940 and 1941 Manchester's sky was crowded with hostile aircraft. The sound of their grinding propeller engines punctuated by explosions was all-pervasive as Germany did its utmost to destroy Britain's industrial base. Lit up by searchlights and shell-bursts, the images of his wartime childhood have merged in Foster's imagination with what he saw later in the art that dramatised and even aestheticised the technology of modern war. He has a vivid memory of walking past the park next to the library, holding his mother's hand and looking through the railings at the wreck of a crashed fighter, its nose buried in the ground, the huge identifying roundels painted on its hull clearly visible. As he describes it, the wreckage was like a sculptural installation. It was a fragment of something alien that had hurtled out of the sky and wedged itself into the landscape. But though the image of this battered and twisted object is burned so vividly in Foster's consciousness that he cannot get it out of his mind, he confesses that he is unsure whether it is a memory that is real or imagined. 'I still don't know if there is an element of fantasy, or whether I actually saw it,' he says. 'I believe that I did really see it, but it seems such an improbable image. It could be the result of a memory of seeing one of those wartime paintings of Paul Nash much later. Or it could really have been something that I saw one morning on the way to school.' In fact, Levenshulme did experience at least one wartime plane crash. For Foster it was the unexpected close-up of a flying machine brought to earth, the functional beauty of a shattered propeller blade and the stark contemporary heraldry of the roundel that identified friend from foe, that imprinted itself on his mind, not the lacerated and broken remains of a machine in which a young pilot was burned to death.

The horror of warfare and the helplessness of its civilian victims is as vivid in Foster's memory as his fascination with its technology:

> I remember waking up during an air raid once in my mother's arms in the communal shelter and hearing bombers go over in the middle of the night. I remember talking rationally about what kind of bomber it might be and then just breaking down into a flood of tears. I remember being absolutely and abjectly terrified.
>
> I was very protected. I didn't suffer, I wasn't on the front line. I wasn't in central Europe, which was invaded, so in that sense the fact that I could be so terror-stricken in a relatively protected environment was a measure of how relatively well off we were. The next day, we would see the wreckage, though you wouldn't know at that early age the real terror that it represented. I remember picking up bits of metal the day after a raid and not really making the connection about what shrapnel was, just of finding these pieces that seemed so interesting.

This was a world before television. Foster saw the concentration camps, and the entry of Allied troops into Auschwitz, as a ten-year-old schoolboy, watching the Pathé newsreel at the Palace Cinema before the main feature.

The terror of the night raids aside, for Foster the privations of war mostly took a mundane form in Manchester. He was with his mother in the grocer's shop when dried eggs became available for the first time. Lilly Foster struggled to make sense of the concept, and had to ask several times, 'How do you prepare it? How do you cook it?' before going home to put the powder to the test. His own memories are of a distinctly tactile, material kind; to this day he can recall that the box the egg powder came in was made of brown cardboard, and that it had been oiled in some way, which made it slightly moist to the touch. He can also recall helping his mother with routine housework. When she did the weekly wash Foster would be with her, turning the handle of the mangle to squeeze water out from the blankets.

Unusually for the time and place, his parents were able to send him to a private school. In 1941 he was enrolled at Dymsdale School, housed in a double-fronted detached Victorian villa on the other side of the tracks from Crescent Grove. In peacetime a girls-only private school, during the war Dymsdale took in boys as well. It may have been private, but it was not ambitious enough to give its pupils the chance to sit the newly introduced eleven-plus examination – the great class barrier of the British educational system – on its own premises. Instead, Foster had to catch the bus into the city centre. He secured a pass, thanks to the vividness of the essay he wrote as part of the exam. With nothing more than the images on the cigarette cards he was collecting to inspire him, he described the duel between silver Auto Unions and white Mercedes Benz racing cars on the Nürburgring during the late 1930s. The images of those cars have remained with him ever since.

His success in the eleven-plus won him a place at Burnage High School. After Foster left, the high school became a grammar, and then, much later, it was turned into a comprehensive. In this latter incarnation, in the early 1990s, the school was the scene of a fatal stabbing; Foster was shocked to learn that an Asian pupil had been knifed to death in the playground. Today Burnage is once more in the process of being rebuilt, this time as a college specialising in media and the arts.

In Foster's day, there were prefects to ensure that boys wore the school cap, with its silver-and-black badge, on their way in through the school gates. Among the successful graduates was Roland Smith, who went on to become the head of British Aerospace.

Academically, Foster was good at mathematics, but his favourite subject was art, which, in addition to drawing and painting, involved learning a basic history of architecture. It focused chiefly on castles and cathedrals. Modernism did not figure much, however Foster does still have the copy of Frederick Gibberd's *The Architecture of England: from Norman times to the present day* that he took home from his classroom. His art master, Mr Beetham, was the only teacher in his grammar school to take any interest in Foster.

There is a photograph, taken in Foster's last year, of the thirty-two pupils who made up the school's fifth form. Foster sits in the front row, looking acutely uncomfortable in his grey flannels. While the rest of the schoolboys in that row sit with their hands clasped in their laps, Foster alone has his hands pressed anxiously down on his knees, as if he is poised to leap up and try to escape. Throughout his time at Burnage, Foster suffered from a sense that he was an outsider. At his first school, Foster had been the only boy from a working-class background. At Burnage he found himself doubly out of place: he was the only boy who had been to a private school, and yet he was the son of a manual labourer (his father was by this time working as a painter in a factory). Though the school was situated in a modern part of Manchester, surrounded by solid, comfortable-looking houses that made Crescent Grove look like a throwback to a grim nineteenth-century past, it proved to be an environment in which Foster did not feel comfortable or happy.

To make matters worse, Foster did not enjoy physical education or participation in any of the sports on offer at Burnage. His previous school had provided no opportunity for boys to learn how to play team sports. He remembers the acute embarrassment that he suffered at Burnage the first and only time that he was asked to hold a cricket bat: 'I had it the wrong way around, with the sharp pointed side toward the front. I never recovered from the mirth around me that provoked.' The misery of team games helped him to become highly skilled at forging his father's handwriting to produce the letters to his form master that were required to get him excused from games. These letters took the form of an infinite number of variations on the same basic message: *Please accept my genuine apologies ... please excuse my son ... yours faithfully R. Foster.*

Later in life, Foster became a serial marathon runner and a cross-country skier, two essentially solitary sports that wiped out those memories of school. He is also a committed cyclist, covering the most gruelling rides every year, hurling himself fearlessly, even recklessly downhill in the Alps and the Pyrenees. The passion for cycling began at an early age: there is a photograph of him on a tricycle as a toddler. From the time he learned to ride a two-wheel bike, at fourteen, bicycles were very important him. Foster has vivid memories of customising a high-performance racing bike, taking care to choose the best components that he could afford, to get the colour of the tubular steel frame exactly right, and to take off visually intrusive brand-name stickers. A committed member of the Thame Valley Road Racing Cycle Club, he often took part in its seventy-five-mile weekend rides.

When he wasn't on his bicycle, Foster retreated into the self-sufficient solitude of books, model aircraft, drawing and watching the trains go by at Crescent Grove. If the wind was in the right direction, it would briefly envelope Foster's house in smoke and steam.

> I used to stand for hours, next to the line, waiting to see the names on the engines. Every locomotive, from the humble Thomas the Tank Engine-style goods engines to the sleek express locomotives, was listed in the train spotters' guides published by Ian Allan on shiny cream paper. I remember waiting for ages, getting more and more despondent as countless goods trains came and went but never a 'namer'. Then in an almighty flash one of these express trains would explode into view. I had only a split second to grasp the name, and then I would leave in high spirits.

Foster enjoyed making models, and was fascinated by model aircraft and trains. He spent his pocket money on Trix construction kits and Meccano sets, building up models by painstakingly bolting together complex structures assembled from the girders and plates of the system. He recalls pushing the limits of what the manufacturer envisaged was possible by bolting an entire crane to the winding shank of the blue clockwork motor so that, as it unwound, the boom slowly traversed a complete circle. And he was continually drawn by the magic of the Bassett-Lowke shop in Cross Street, with its displays of precision-made miniature locomotives. Foster would make special expeditions by tram to the centre of Manchester to gaze at its window display for a glimpse of brass connecting rods and tiny lathe-turned smoke stacks.

Foster was no more than seven when he made his first seriously considered design. It was a drawing for an imaginary single-seater aircraft, based on the only technology for a flying craft of which Foster had first-hand knowledge: a model powered by a twisted rubber band. When adapted to the task of carrying a human pilot it took on a Herculean scale. It had high wings, and a ribbed structure. Foster drew himself in the cockpit, a remote-looking figure, isolated high above the ground with the joystick gripped in his right hand, and the lever ready to unleash several kilometres of the tightly wound rubber needed to power his huge craft to reach take-off speed. He quickly progressed from rubber bands to the unimaginable luxury of a carbon dioxide engine. It cost him a guinea, a sum that took him months to accumulate. The experience taught him a number of lessons, not least that the fuel for this particular engine came in the shape of a gas cartridge that was not only extremely expensive, at half a crown a time, but was also so heavy that it defeated every aircraft that he designed to use it. Eventually he was able to afford tiny diesel engines with exotic names – the Frog 100 and the EDBee – which powered more successful designs.

Foster was regarded as a bright pupil. He was in the A stream, the elite who would normally have been expected to stay at school until they were eighteen, and even go on to university. But though he got seven O-levels he unexpectedly failed both his French and Divinity papers. In a more affluent home, this would not have put an end to the idea of staying on at school, or higher education. But for Foster's parents, the failure was seen as a signal that it was time he started work. He was sixteen by this time; two years older than the vast majority of school leavers of his generation, but two years younger than the middle-class teenagers who stayed at school to take the advanced or A-level general certificate of education examinations.

While he was doing his O-levels, Foster's father got him to take the entrance exam for Manchester Town Hall's trainee scheme. He passed and his parents were delighted when he started work there in 1951 in the Treasurer's Department, but it was a job he had taken to please them, rather than from choice. From the beginning he approached the work with a sense of disappointment, and a determination to do better as soon as he could.

The Town Hall, a model of Northern civic splendour, was designed by Alfred Waterhouse, who, until Foster eclipsed him, was perhaps the most prolific and commercially successful architect that Britain had ever produced. It sits in Albert Square on a triangular site, its three street façades concealing a courtyard that accommodates a great hall behind a picturesque skyline of serrated gables, topped by an imposing clock tower. A sequence of grand interiors are connected by endless corridors, which Waterhouse pierced with intricate staircases. Inside the great hall, Ford Madox Brown's series of epic murals tells the story of Manchester, from its origins as a Roman fort, to the arrival of the first Flemish weavers, culminating in the building of the Bridgewater Canal.

After moving to London, Waterhouse built the masterly Natural History Museum in South Kensington, then came several Oxford and Cambridge colleges, and more than fifty private houses, including the Duke of Westminster's seat at

Eaton Hall. He was knighted, and was painted by Alma Tadema, the most fashionable portrait artist of his day. He died in 1905, leaving £250,000 – a fortune worth many millions by today's standards.

Foster spent two years working at the Town Hall, and didn't build anything in Manchester before establishing himself in London. But in its scale and material success, his career would one day parallel that of Waterhouse. The two men share a number of traits, being fashionable, renowned businesslike and noted for jealously maintaining a reputation for practical planning and budgeting. Even if Foster had much humbler origins, and lacked a brother who was a founder of the accountancy giant that still carries the Waterhouse name to provide the connections that bring work in the early stages of an architectural career, he has built a firm that has worked throughout the world, on an unprecedented scale.

As soon as you mention Waterhouse's name, Foster starts sketching the aspect of the Town Hall that has left the most lasting impact on him: the astonishing spectacle of the cascading fountains of the cisterns above the urinals in the men's lavatories.

> I remember that the urinals were beautifully crafted with every cistern enclosed in glass. Each stall was delineated by a great sculpted separating fin in vitreous porcelain, while the wash basins were strung out along the wall in serried ranks. If you stepped up on to one of these banks of urinals, you felt really elevated; they were like great islands.

In 1951 a sixteen-year-old with Foster's background would have been unlikely to appreciate the wilder shores of Victorian taste that the Town Hall represented. John Betjeman had only just begun to push back the prejudices against the kind of Victorian eclecticism that was then seen at best as a joke, at worst a hideous and impractical embarrassment. It is perhaps not surprising that it should have been the Town Hall's celebration of the technology of water cisterns that left the deepest impression on Foster. But there was much more for him to look at.

Every day on his way to his desk, Foster would take a different route through the building to find another staircase to explore. The three principal staircases were named for the English, Welsh and Scottish stone of which they were built. Foster was able to pick his way through a riot of polished marble, and chiselled representations of thirteenth-century English gothic. Every aspect of the decorative detail had a narrative to tell. The bees depicted in the tiled ceilings are a version of the symbol of the city. The stone ridges between the vaults are cut to look like ropes spun out of cotton, so as to remind Mancunians what it was that their city's prosperity had been built on. The front entrance is guarded by a representation of Agricola, the Roman general and governor of Britain, claimed by Manchester as the city's original founder. In the entrance vestibule, you find the incongruous spectacle of Early English groin vaults, electrically lit by polished brass candelabra dangling above statues of two of the greatest of Manchester's scientists, John Dalton and his brilliant student James Joule, rendered in white marble. In Joule's case, Alfred Gilbert's florid style borders on Art Nouveau.

During his two years at the Town Hall, Foster spent his days doodling at his desk and looking for a way out of the claustrophobic future that his parents had, with the best of intentions, planned for him. While mired in the purgatory of the cashier's office, he produced one of the most complex of his youthful drawings when he should have been working. Every time a manager went by, Foster tried to hide the drawing, choking at their approach.

But there were also people to talk to about life beyond the Town Hall.

> I remember Mr Cobb, who was a clerk in the treasurer's department. He noticed that I was always sketching, and wandering off to look at buildings in my lunch hour. He told me about his son who was studying to be an architect, and I think it was the first time I began to think about it as something that I might do.
>
> I remember taking a very long walk one lunch hour to see the Daily Express buildings in Ancoats designed by Owen Williams. It was quite a distance, and even though I walked very quickly, there was no time for lunch.

The newspaper has long since abandoned the building but even today, there remains a whiff of the Art Deco glamour of the era of Evelyn Waugh's *Daily Beast* about the old Express Building. Designed in 1938, it still conjures up images of sub editors working in green eye-shades, their gartered sleeves rolled up, surrounded by typewriters and stacks of paper. It would have been a place to find copy boys running from desk to desk, and reporters barking into Bakelite telephones.

Owen Williams was essentially an engineer rather than an architect, but he offered his clients both services. He gave the building a sleek, instantly recognisable skin that made a big impression on Foster. The Express Building was unmistakably modern, which is exactly what the Town Hall was not. 'I knew it was there, and I went looking for it. It was not in a part of town that you could just stumble across it. I remember the chromed strips and the Vitrolite that the black façade was made of. There was no way to get inside.'

Designed twenty years after that visit, the undulating black glass façade of Foster's design for the Willis Faber Dumas insurance company's offices in Ipswich pays an inventive tribute to the Express and Foster's own youthful hunger for ideas and images. Certainly Willis Faber is rooted in a more sophisticated idea of what architecture can be than the Express, which is all surface rather than substance. The Ipswich building is more than the slick skin, which Williams used as a means of establishing the Express as progressive and forward-looking. Williams used the same black glass in Manchester as he did for its headquarters in Fleet Street and its outpost in Glasgow. He was branding them all as parts of the same empire.

Willis Faber is a sequence of spaces. Go through the entrance airlock, and you find yourself in a dazzling atrium with escalators to move you silently up towards the roof garden. On the ground floor, colour saturated with sharp yellow paint and acid green tiles, was a swimming pool. Corporate amenities of this nature may be commonplace now, but they were almost unheard of when Foster found a way to deliver them within the client's budget, on the verge of the three-day week and the 25 per cent annual inflation rate of the 1970s. Technically they are worlds apart, too. The Express was a chrome-trimmed Austin 7, while Willis Faber is more like a minimal and businesslike BMW. The glass skin in Ipswich has no frame, and hangs from the concrete floor slabs on invisible steel pins. The Express was at heart a glamorous but unsubtle piece of Art Deco packaging devised for the purpose of concealing a print hall and a set of utilitarian offices. Willis Faber works on many more levels. It may be rooted in memories of the tradition represented by the Express Building, but it also embodies an echo of the glass skyscraper split into crystalline fragments that Mies van der Rohe speculated about for a site in Berlin on Friedrichstrasse, in the years immediately after World War One.

Foster was becoming an acute observer of his surroundings, understanding the city around him in terms of urban fabric as much as of individual buildings. 'I remember walking around one of the Manchester arcades that has since been destroyed. It was the Lancaster Arcade, and built on a curve so that you could not see the ends when you were in the middle of it.' He also explored the Barton Arcade. These were architectural innovations that he was to put to good use in his own career. He got to know the Kendal Milne department store, the gothic Rylands Library, and the Central Library built in imperial Roman style next to the Town Hall.

Manchester was the embodiment of a great city for Foster, but its character was being eroded brutally as he grew up, and in his student days there was serious damage being done to its fabric. 'James Stirling told me once that he made a point of not going back to Liverpool, where he was born, when he was asked to give lectures there, because of what the planners had done to the city. I felt much the same about Manchester,' says Foster.

The city is no longer a place that he recognises. But as a teenager, it opened his eyes to a wider culture far beyond the limits of Crescent Grove. He discovered Manchester's Art Gallery, where he visited an exhibition of the entries for a competition to design an Oxbridge college. He still recalls Howell, Killick, Partridge & Amis's project. Ian Murray, his friend from the Town Hall, introduced Foster to the music that Manchester had to offer, and he listened to the Hallé Orchestra conducted by George Weldon performing Tchaikovsky and Rachmaninoff at the Free Trade Hall. Later, a performance of Sibelius conducted by John Barbirolli in the Free Trade Hall reduced Foster to silence. He remembers listening to the premiere of Vaughan Williams' *Sinfonia Antarctica* on the BBC Third Programme in the living room at home, with one hand holding the valve in the back of the radiogram. In Levenshulme's Regal Cinema he went to see *Gone with the Wind*, though he preferred Orson Welles in *The Third Man*. He recalls Piccadilly before the building of the Ramada Hotel and Albert Square, which was then the dignified urban setting for the Town Hall. His time there left him with a set of memories and city experiences that would form the raw material for his consuming interest in urbanism, and the echoes resurface again and again as ideas in Foster's work.

During the first of his two years at Manchester Town Hall, keen to make his way in the local government hierarchy, Foster took night school classes at Manchester College of Commerce, studying commercial law, commercial general knowledge and accountancy. He hated it. In a desperate attempt to get a university place and escape from the Town Hall, he switched to A-levels in English Literature and Geography. However, trying to compress two years' worth of grammar school sixth-form studies into three evenings a week for less than a year was an impossible task that defeated him.

With no deferment on educational grounds, when Foster turned eighteen in 1953 he became eligible for national service.

Because of his fascination for aeroplanes, he chose to join the Royal Air Force, though he had little expectation of getting the chance to fly. His scepticism was fully justified. After basic training at RAF Hednesford, the air force's induction camp for national servicemen at Cannock Chase, he was assigned to an engineering unit maintaining a radar installation and was never posted overseas. Most of his military career was spent in a grass-roofed aircraft hangar on the edge of an airbase in the East Midlands. He remembers the sense of futility that came from the knowledge that the Rebecca III radar equipment he and his team were maintaining had been designed for use in an obsolete generation of propeller-engined aircraft. Its slow response time would have been of little use deployed in the new jets.

Aircraftsman Foster 2709757 came home from his national service in 1955, feeling fortunate not to have been shipped straight out to Egypt in time for the abortive invasion of the Suez Canal by Britain, France and Israel. He had enjoyed his time in uniform and emerged from the RAF more assertive and more independent than he had been at the time of his call-up. Though he remained uncertain what exactly it was that he wanted to do, he was adamant that a return to the Town Hall was not an option. The prospect of going back there seemed to him more like the dispiriting threat of a jail sentence than a career. 'My parents really did not understand why I wanted to give up a safe job at the Town Hall, although they were in every other sense very supportive. I had to discover for myself, in my own way, my ambitions and interests. That took quite a long time.' In a last-ditch attempt to make him see reason, his father and uncle took him to one of the pubs on the Stockport Road to discuss things over a pint of beer, but he wasn't having his mind changed, and he told them so.

National Service gave me a break from home, and a taste of independence. There was parental pressure to go back to the Town Hall, but I wasn't in a mood to do that. It was a job that offered respectability and a pension, which, at the age of twenty-one, I could not get excited about. I came from a background where the only honourable kind of work was manual labour. At the Town Hall, I had moved up into the sort of middle-class world with all the security that my parents never had for themselves, and they yearned for me to have. For all the people around me, and for my parents, that position was an incredible achievement, but I found the Town Hall totally depressing.

For a gifted child growing up in a family that was loving but distant, with no experience of any kind of higher education, working out what he wanted to do did not come easily. He put off making irrevocable decisions about his future by taking on a series of stop-gap jobs while looking for something that would take him out of Levenshulme and the world that his parents knew. During this period Foster wrote to a number of companies that interested him, offering his services. With no qualifications beyond the seven O-level passes out of the nine exams that he had taken at Burnage High School when he was sixteen, he got nowhere.

It took him a long time to find the escape route. At one fruitless interview for a job selling office duplicating machines, he was asked why he had applied. 'Mainly because it offered the prospect of a company car, and for the £1,000 salary,' he replied. The gap between Foster's submerged abilities and his already manifest ambitions disturbed his interviewer enough for him to suggest that what Foster really needed was not a job as a salesman, but professional help in understanding what to do with his life. As a result of that conversation, he began to look for a way out from a year spent drifting aimlessly.

Foster went to see a government-funded unit set up to help ex-servicemen back into civilian life by matching their skills with employers. He filled in the forms, and did the tests. 'They said, "You have to find something creative," and they gave me two addresses.' The first was for a company making rubber flooring that had a vacancy in the design office. It did not long detain him. The other lead was a contact with John Beardshaw, a local architect.

> His office was in a row of Georgian houses, next to the university. I went to the interview and was able to make myself sound like a pretty good prospect. I was able to say that I had worked in the city treasurer's office, in the audit department, and that I had studied commercial law. It was all true, but it was also pretty blown up. But anyway, I got a job as an assistant to the contract manager.

This was not work calculated to make the most of Foster's creative potential. 'We were out of the office most of the time, lifting manhole covers on building sites to test if the contractors really had dug manholes underneath them.'

Foster had begun drawing seriously when he was six years old, and he started to think hard about architecture during his school days. But it was never inevitable that he would become an architect. What pushed him towards the subject were the books that he had started to read as a youth: *In the Nature of Materials*, Henry-Russell Hitchcock's sprawling 400-page eulogy to Frank Lloyd Wright; *Vers une architecture*, Le Corbusier's description of architecture as the masterly play of light – and the accompanying and apparently surreal pictures of aircraft and cars and grain silos juxtaposed with the Parthenon.

But even when he came home from national service, Foster still had no real understanding of what it meant to be an architect, or of how to become one. 'I was hypnotised by design,' Foster remembers. In particular he was enthralled by the design-conscious furniture of the period, a rosewood and teak universe bounded by the Gomme company's G-Plan range at one end and, at the other, by Hille's production of the modern move-ment's classics that seemed to promise drip-dry Dacron-lined modernity with every afrormosia table top and leg. It was a vision of a world that was everything his own home was not. And he wanted to be part of it, and so, manifestly, to leave the Crescent Grove of his childhood, and less explicitly perhaps, to leave behind his parents and their view of the world and their values.

Foster, at his attic desk in his tweed sports jacket and his grey flannels, was still in awe of the old-seeming men in smocks in the drawing office in the front room on the first floor of the house. He assumed that these people were consumed with the same passion he had developed in the reading room of the Levenshulme Library for the wild-eyed architecture of Frank Lloyd Wright and Le Corbusier. And thrillingly, they were actually building, not just dreaming of architecture. To Foster their exotic work clothes were a badge of belonging to a Masonic sect that he could never join as much as a practical way of keeping their clothes clean at a time when ink and rubber were flying across the drawing boards. 'I lived in wonder of the guys who wore the white smocks,' he said. But in London, the smock was passing into oblivion. By then it was an already slightly archaic means of establishing a hierarchy between the assistants who did the working drawings in an architect's office and the partners in suits who led the design work and were trusted to talk to the clients.

The Beardshaw office was an unlikely place for Foster to make up his mind to become an architect. There was nothing memorable about the office's designs, which can best be described as workmanlike and commercial. The only project for which Beardshaw was responsible that got even a cursory mention in the contemporary architectural press was Television House, built for Associated TV in Manchester at a time when it was struggling to compete with Granada. And there is little to mark it out from its contemporaries: a simple slab with a banal curtain wall, set in a masonry-skinned steel frame. Occasionally, Beardshaw would try something a little more daring, like the time that he hired a Polish assistant to work with him on designing a petrol filling station with a free plan. Architecture as practised by Beardshaw was a traditional sort of profession. It was like being a country doctor, or running a small solicitor's office. Foster might have learned how to work with reinforced concrete, and plate glass, but the practice was run on lines that had otherwise changed very little since the early nineteenth century. Beardshaw took on apprentices, who paid to go through a training process with him. But working there was the best chance that Foster was offered to get close to the practice of architecture, and he took it eagerly.

It was not long before Foster discovered for himself the

distance between the narrow pragmatism of provincial architecture in the Manchester of the 1950s and the pursuit of
architecture as personified by Howard Roark, hero of Ayn
Rand's *The Fountainhead*, with his burning passion for building
at any cost in truly Nietzschean fashion. One morning he
happened to be talking to an assistant in the drawing office who
was a part-time student at the college of art. 'I asked him what
he thought about Frank Lloyd Wright. He looked at me, puzzled,
and asked: "Is he at the art school too?"'

Shocked, but also reassured that he was not in fact dealing with
demigods, Foster started to engage with the other architectural
assistants, usually at lunch over sandwiches. 'How do you
become an architect?' he finally asked the least intimidating of
them.

'You find a school of architecture, you apply and, if you are
accepted, you go,' was the reply.

'It's that simple then?'

'You have to do a portfolio first.'

'What is a portfolio?'

'It has to have some drawings, and some paintings to show
what you can do.'

'Let me see one,' asked Foster.

It was all patiently explained to him: 'This is a shop drawing,
and this is a perspective, the client sees this one.'

Which is how, one Saturday morning in the spring of 1955,
Norman Foster came to be painting the view from his bedroom
at Crescent Grove, looking over the rooftops and the chimneys.
It was the finishing touch to a portfolio that was stocked mainly
with copies of other people's work from the drawing office at
Beardshaw's. Every evening he was careful to be the last out of
the building, so that he could borrow drawings without being

disturbed. He took them home, copied them in his bedroom on the table by the window, and was the first back into the office in the morning to return them to the wooden plan chest before they were missed.

When Foster had completed his portfolio, he showed it to Beardshaw, who was impressed enough by this unexpected metamorphosis from contract administrator to would-be architect, in his most junior employee, to transfer him to the drawing office.

> When I had assembled enough of a wodge of drawings, I thought I should tell Mr Beardshaw. I knocked on his door.
>
> 'I have decided I want to study to be an architect and I thought I should let you know. I've got a portfolio.'
>
> 'How did you manage that?'
>
> 'I borrowed the drawings, I have done some paintings.'
>
> 'Show me,' he said. 'Its amazing, you are a square peg in a round hole.'

Foster was issued with a tee square, a spiral-bound copy of Burnet, Tate & Lorne's book of graphic standards and set to work in the drawing office.

'I drew on linen and worked with ruling pens. They were very hard to use, and the effect of discharging a blob of ink over a drawing would be disastrous. You had to prepare surfaces with talcum powder before starting.'

Beardshaw tried to encourage Foster to stay in his office, suggesting that he could easily study part-time, and continue working to pay his way through the years that it would take to qualify as an architect. He began to push more challenging projects Foster's way to persuade him that it was worth staying.

'He gave me what he called a problem job. There was a client who wanted a new house, but his wife wanted to keep her old curtains, which meant that the windows had been defined before I could start.' But even with this kind of sweetener, it was already too late to persuade Foster to stay.

Beardshaw was later to prove very helpful to Foster when he set up his first practice, Team Four, with Richard Rogers. When Team Four got into trouble with the Architects Registration Council for practising without having any fully qualified partners, Beardshaw gave them a professional umbrella and allowed Foster and Rogers time to get themselves registered.

They have been merged into a single school now, but in the 1950s there were two places to study architecture in Manchester. One was the university, and the other was the municipal art school. Displaying the shrewd chess-playing skill – that ability to see beyond the immediate and take a long-term view – that has characterised his approach to making decisions at every stage in his career, Foster talked to people in the Beardshaw office about which school was better and was advised that the university school definitely offered the best prospects.

Foster was interviewed by Professor Reginald Annandale Cordingley, Manchester University School of Architecture's gentlemanly head. He had been running the school since 1933, and was best known as a serious architectural scholar. He was responsible for a well-regarded monograph on the Mausoleum of Augustus in Rome, as well as for editing a massive edition of the *Banister Fletcher History of Architecture on the Comparative Method*, to which Foster was later asked to contribute. On being shown Foster's painting of the view from the window at Crescent

Grove, Cordingley suggested that it would make a fine Christmas card.

Foster was offered a place on the architecture course to start in the autumn term of 1956. In order for this to happen, some flexibility with the interpretation of the academic regulations was required on Cordingley's part. He waived the two A-level passes that were normally a condition of entry, and assigned Foster to a dormant architecture diploma course that ultimately offered the same qualification as the mainstream degree in architecture.

But there was one obstacle Cordingley could not finesse. In the 1950s most British art schools were still funded directly by the local authority in whose area they were based. Manchester's education department told Foster that he would get a grant only if he agreed to study at the municipal art school.

When Foster got the letter from the council spelling out its refusal to support him at university, he was furious. If he was going to spend five years somewhere, he wanted it to be the best possible place. He insisted on getting a personal interview with the official in the education department who was responsible for the decision. It was a heated conversation, one that left Foster more determined to go to the university than ever.

'Why can't I get a grant?' Foster asked.

'He said to me, "We fund the art school, and you can qualify as an architect there."

'"But it's not as good," I said, and told him what he could do with his grant.'

If Foster couldn't get a grant, he would work his way through his studies to support himself.

In the days of universal grants for students of modest means, and for all mature students, he felt hard done by, as well as humiliated that he was going to have to live with his parents for the next five years. Staying on at Crescent Grove, with its voraciously hungry gas meter, was not the way to live the bohemian student life that he had begun to dream of. 'At the time I went to university I really was angry. I am sure that I had a chip on my shoulder. I was the only guy not getting a grant. I was the only student living at home.'

Foster was excited, and not a little anxious, about starting his university career but, back at home after his first day, he was crushed and disappointed by his parents' lack of curiosity about all that he had been doing.

'I don't remember my mother asking me about how things had gone. I think that she assumed it would end badly, so she didn't want to ask too many questions, but she never said anything, which upset me a little.'

Over the years, Foster has tried to smooth away the hurt. 'I have come to realise that it wasn't that she was indifferent to what I had managed to do. She was always anxious, and expecting that things were not going to turn out well, and so did not want to raise her hopes.'

As soon as he started at university, Foster's ambition took over, pushed by a determination to prove himself. 'I was so highly motivated that, when I got into architecture school, nobody was going to stop me. The opportunity to study architecture was the most incredible privilege. I would have paid to do it, which is effectively what I was doing.'

In fact, once Foster got to Manchester he found the staff sympathetic about his financial problems. Thomas Howarth, author of an early study of Charles Rennie Mackintosh's work, did all that he could to get Foster a grant. Eventually, just before

Howarth left Manchester for Canada, he found a way to get Foster a bursary after his third year.

In Foster's day, Manchester University's school of architecture had a reputation for teaching traditional drafting and technical design, but it was not noted for its ideological conviction or for the rigour of the intellectual content of its courses. Students still followed the approach that Professor Cordingley had first laid down twenty-four years earlier when he had got the job of running the school. He expected students to acquire the skills needed to do watercolour washes, and to make a measured drawing; a process that sent Foster to a variety of buildings with a tape measure and a sketchbook. The idea was to size up a building, and thus be able to analyse its essential physical and spatial characteristics – a distant echo of Piranesi's surveys of the ruins of Rome. It was down to the individual student to select the buildings that they would explore and draw, but there was a tacit understanding that they should be focusing on Georgian buildings, since their classical proportions and details were thought to offer the most telling lessons.

Foster, however, showed an independent streak. While the other students in his year were sketching Georgian houses, most of his time was spent clambering over much humbler, industrial buildings. He surveyed a Victorian gin palace, as well as making measured drawings of several barns, and then of a windmill. In the summer of 1959, he cycled into North Wales, measuring and drawing a handsome stone barn at Cochwillan, Llanllechid.

Foster has kept those survey drawings, just as he has kept every single notebook and student brief that he has ever possessed. The set of drawings featuring the barn at Cochwillan are impressive, going far beyond atmospheric sketches, or a representation of a flat elevation in their scope. There are notes all over the sheet of paper that record Foster's thoughts as he clambered over the building, registering details about the condition of the barn and its construction. His notes are in a style that looks very different from the characteristic handwriting that he has developed over the years, and which his whole office now tries to reproduce. But it wasn't the handwriting of an immature schoolboy either. Foster in the late 1950s was faithfully reproducing the architectural handwriting of a previous generation. With an elaborate flourish for the looped tail of the 'y', and semi-gothic forms for the letters 'a' and 'e', it is the carefully artistic but clear hand of a bow-tied professional from the 1940s.

That same summer, Foster spent three days at Rufford Hall in Cheshire. He explored the medieval house and drew the elevations with spirit, but what really intrigued him was the oak-pegged timber roof structure inside the stone walls. He devoted no less than thirty sketches to exploring exactly what it was that all those timber joints were doing and how the beams fitted together. It's the sense of clarity of Foster's fluid drawings that impresses most. He drew an eighteenth-century barn, built from clunch – the local chalk stone at Burwell Priory – and patiently analysed how every beam was put together, and how they supported the thatched roof.

Later, Foster's elegant study of a windmill at Bourne in Cambridgeshire would win him the silver award in a national student competition. His prize was £100: a substantial sum in 1959. On this occasion, Foster knew that he was drawing to impress and not just to record information. He drew front, back and side views of the mill, but carefully composed them to form a single drawing. He used an Egyptian Bold Extended letter face, drawing it freehand for the title, and peopled the drawing with figures to provide a sense of scale. But they also have the effect of making you wonder how exactly Foster managed to measure all the complex elements that made up the top of the windmill's sails, 60 feet above the ground.

By looking at buildings like these, Foster was demonstrating that even as a student he had a mind of his own when it came to understanding architecture. 'It wasn't that I rejected the Georgian tradition – I enjoyed it; but the obsession with drawing up decorative details year after year, almost by rote, seemed questionable at best.'

Foster's latent interest in vernacular buildings was triggered by the *Architectural Review*, the professional magazine that during this period was documenting the impressive utilitarian English tradition of mills and barns and docks, which its editors saw as an antecedent for the modern movement. It devoted entire issues to the kind of industrial buildings and cotton mills that Foster saw around him in Manchester at the time.

In the design projects that Foster worked on there are also traces of the themes that were going to become important preoccupations for him in his professional career.

My very first design project was a boathouse and retreat in the Lake District. The expectation was that you would design a shed for the boat and put a little cottage alongside it to stay in at the weekend. But my design was different. I integrated the boathouse and the retreat to form a single building on the waterfront. The boat went directly inside the building and the living accommodation was located alongside it, behind a glass screen facing out on to the river. I was the only student who integrated the project in that way.

This idea of combining functionally disparate elements and building types into a single envelope was to shape many of his early projects once he had set up in practice. It reflected an unwillingness to accept the limits of conventional building types, and the belief that he could find a way to achieve more with limited resources by going back to the fundamentals of a design problem, rather than accepting preconceptions.

In his architectural history classes, Foster was sketching the Pantheon from photographs, and producing imaginative three-dimensional representations of the forum in Rome that reflected Professor Cordingley's expertise.

The course progressed by setting design projects of increasing complexity until, at the end of the third year, students were put to the test by being asked to synthesise everything that they had learned so far. To move into the final two-year phase of the course, they had to get through an intensive three-day charette that involved the design of a complex building, and the resolution of its technical and construction details. In Foster's year, the brief was for the design of a theatre, and it involved not just a formal plan, but also all the acoustic drawings necessary to demonstrate that their design was a realistic proposition. Foster passed without difficulty. Alongside this, Foster was set projects that tested his drafting and his imaginative skills. He was asked to portray the end of the world, and to evoke the period detail of a Roman amphitheatre. He carefully kept the cyclostyled hand-out notes that provided him with a brief history of the English House. His own notes and sketches record the history of architecture on the Banister Fletcher model from the Parthenon to the Pantheon. He designed a Skiffle Dive, but the surviving photographs from his time at Manchester show Foster wearing a bow tie and tweed rather than teddy-boy draped jacket.

In his last two years at Manchester, Foster embarked on a parallel town planning course, alongside his architectural studies. With the encouragement of Professor Thornley, Foster began to think about the idea of building architecture at the scale of infrastructure. From the earliest days in his career, he had been as interested in how a city might be designed as he was in the individual building.

Foster became fascinated by the work of Gordon Cullen and Kenneth Browne, who were using the pages of the *Architectural Review* at that time to put forward their ideas about Townscape, a picturesque contemporary Anglo Saxon offshoot of Camillo Sitte's ideas about city planning. They explored the way that we experience our urban surroundings as a sequence of self-contained but interrelated spaces as we move in and around them. They looked at how one part of a city after another is gradually revealed as we move through them. They analysed how the elements of an urban composition are built up. And they recorded their observations through a series of drawings that attempted to interpret the elements of the urban landscape and their interaction with each other. Foster's graphic technique, in particular his trick of annotating his sketches with stylised hearts and eyes, owes a conscious debt to Cullen and Browne, who were using these devices in the *Architectural Review* in the 1950s.

In his final year Foster worked on a new museum for the Faculty of Anthropology at Cambridge. A three-storey glass-walled gallery would have housed the collection's largest pieces. Foster and Partners built the Law Faculty for the university forty years later.

His accomplished drafting skills helped Foster work his way through the course. He remembers, one weekend in 1958, being brought in to work in the office of George Grenfell-Baines on an unsuccessful entry for the competition to design Toronto's new City Hall. Grenfell-Baines, who went on to establish the Building Design Partnership that grew to be one of Britain's largest architectural practices, had a career that has striking parallels with Foster's. Born in Lancashire, the son of a railwayman, Grenfell-Baines left school at fourteen, then worked in the city surveyor's office, before finally getting a place at Manchester University's architecture school.

Foster moonlighted for the big Manchester architectural offices when they needed a deft perspective artist to seduce a client, or to win over a planning committee. He fitted in jobs as a labourer, and even for a while as a bouncer, while studying.

He was also beginning to travel. Every vacation, after intensive bouts of well-paid manual work and the occasional financial bonus of a scholarship or travel prize, he would go somewhere new, touring Europe to look at buildings. He started to haunt the classic urban landscapes from Shepherd Market to Greenwich in London and abroad from Helsinki to Florence, coming back with notebooks full of annotated sketches. He paced out the Piazza del Campo in Siena, helped by the fact that his feet measured exactly twelve inches in length. He toured Palladio's houses in the Veneto and saw BBPR's Torre Velasca in Milan. He went to see what little Utzon had built in Denmark before he entered the Sydney Opera House competition. He saw the early work of Arne Jacobsen, as well as buildings designed by lesser-known architects such as Kay Fisker. He sketched the interior of Ronchamp, although without much sympathy. These were conventional architectural tastes at a time when more adventurous schools were already beginning to point their students towards early Viennese proto-modernists, or Italian rationalists.

Foster was rapidly outgrowing Manchester. He spent the summer of 1960 in Hugh Casson's office in London. Casson presided over a practice that was well regarded at the time. The Casson Conder Partnership was designing Cambridge University's new arts faculty buildings on Sidgwick Avenue, in the form of a series of updated cloisters, built from brick, and hoisted up on columns to leave the ground open. Foster worked on the project, and the experience suggested the brief for his final student scheme when he got back to Manchester.

Foster told Casson's biographer, Jose Manser: 'I looked at what they were doing, and thought that this would be an office where I could learn something. I was right, it was an extremely civilised and enjoyable experience. Unlike many of the offices that I'd had experience of in Manchester, they had a real passion for architecture, wanting to talk of it, and live it all the time.'

It is hard to imagine two personalities more different than Casson and Foster. Boarding school and Cambridge-educated, the product of nannies and a home of comfortable upper-middle-class ease, the quintessential gentleman amateur, Casson's languid patrician air was in the sharpest contrast to the driven, dedicated, and endlessly professional Foster. They barely spoke in the office, though Foster acknowledges a debt to Casson's facility with the pencil. 'I think I still do characters that bear a close resemblance to his when I'm putting people in a drawing.' A quarter-century later the two architects were at the Prince of Wales' table for dinner at Hampton Court on the night that Charles launched his first and most violent attack on the architectural profession. Even though Casson, in his role as a judge in the National Gallery competition, was in some measure responsible for provoking the attack, he claimed to be sympathetic with the Prince's views. Foster was ready for a blunter response.

The university may have boasted the best school of architecture in Manchester, but it was not, as Foster knew by the time that he had finished there, the best school in Britain. The Architectural Association in London was a lot bigger, and much more adventurous. Mainstream modernism had already come to be seen as old hat there, and its students were sceptical about the sentimentality of the kind of Scandinavian-inspired sweetness and light of the Festival of Britain, for which Hugh Casson had been responsible. Manchester was only just getting around to discovering it.

Manchester was very good for me; it was good because it was demanding on draughtsmanship, and technique, and under-standing buildings. But Manchester was not what I would call a good school of architecture in the sense that I would judge one now. There was never any discussion about architecture. You were given the grade and that was that. There was no debate about the work.

Manchester University was very traditional. It was nothing like, say, the Architectural Association, or what was then the Regent Street Polytechnic. I remember visiting the studios there and finding an unbelievably creative environment. Manchester, on the other hand, was very conventional, and very disciplined. It was frustrating because you never had the opportunity to debate. You would know what was expected, you would produce the work, it would be assessed, and maybe a week or two weeks later you would get it back with a mark. You would never have a chance to present your work. There was no dialogue. We were still studying the Classical orders and drawing them in ink on linen. It was very tough in a traditional academic sense, but stylistically it was very limiting.

This was a faithful reflection of a period when, as the architectural historian, Foster's friend Reyner Banham, whose criticism he started reading in 1959, put it, architecture in Britain was still 'the staid Queen Mother of the arts'. There was something quite different going on in architecture which entirely passed Manchester by.

In London, Peter Cook and David Greene at the Architectural Association were about to start work on *Archigram*, the student magazine that was to become famous by attempting to drag architecture into a world in which Yuri Gagarin had just become the first man in space, the first weather satellite had been launched from Cape Canaveral, photocopiers, holograms and the contraceptive pill had just been invented.

Archigram declared that:

A new generation of architecture must arise with forms and spaces which seem to reject the precepts of the modern, yet in fact retains those precepts. We have chosen to bypass the decrepit Bauhaus image which is an insult to functionalism. You can roll out steel any length, you can blow up a balloon any size. You can mould plastics any shape. The blokes that built the Forth Bridge, they didn't worry.

In comparison with the Archigram group at the Architectural Association, whose student projects included designs for living pods and gasket-jointed houses, Foster's boathouse and even his university museum seemed pretty tame. Subconsciously, Foster knew it too, but he didn't know where to look for something more challenging.

As his studies were coming to an end, Foster realised that he needed more from his education. He wanted to carry on his studies in America, in pursuit of all the things that Manchester hadn't been able to give him and which he was just becoming aware of. In the monochrome climate of post-war Britain, and before the disasters of Vietnam, the political assassinations and the burning ghettoes, America still seemed like the source of plenty, and of freedom. Foster had done well enough to stand a good chance of getting accepted to take a master's degree anywhere in America. What he needed, as well as a place to study, was the financial help to pay his way.

Foster looked at his options. He could apply for a Fulbright scholarship, as Richard Rogers did; that would get him to America. In fact, the two first met at a reception in London for Fulbright students heading for Yale. But the Fulbright had at least one drawback for a student who was continually thinking about the next step but three. In principle, students on Fulbright scholarships could not legally stay on after graduating to work in America, although it was a handicap that didn't get in Richard Rogers' way when he got a job in San Francisco after leaving Yale. There was an alternative, the Henry Fellowship, tenable at either Harvard or Yale, which would allow him to hold a green card, and to work in America.

Foster successfully applied for both scholarships. 'I turned down the Fulbright because I wanted the flexibility to work. I could not imagine going and just studying.' He had seen the Henry Fellowship advertised on a university noticeboard, applied, and was asked to go to London for the interview.

'I found myself walking in to be faced by a room full of people asking questions at a table that seemed to stretch into infinity, like a *New Yorker* cartoon.'

The Henry was aimed at encouraging a link between Oxbridge students and the Ivy League. Foster was unusual in applying, and subsequently securing the grant, from Manchester. 'I don't think anybody from a provincial university had ever got one before. I really bust through the Oxbridge thing.'

Foster spent the summer after finishing his degree working for John Beardshaw at his office in London. Then he set off for America, leaving home without much reflection on how his parents would view his departure.

'Perhaps I was insensitive, they had provided everything they could for me. The least important thing of all, funding my education, was the only thing they couldn't provide.'

Two

I could have stayed in America

America, from the viewpoint of the young Norman Foster sitting in the cheap seats at Levenshulme's Palace Cinema, looked like the only place to be. It was not just the distant promise of James Dean, or the music of the Inkspots and the Andrews Sisters, which in those days appealed to him much more than Elvis or John Coltrane, or even the cars with the high-rise tail fins. More important for an ambitious architect, it was obvious in 1960 that America had taken on the leadership role in design that Europe had once had. The continuing prestige enjoyed by the Bauhaus exiles who abandoned Germany for America in the 1930s made that inevitable. They had invented modernism, and everywhere that they went, they took the definitive version with them.

The alternatives were not promising. Le Corbusier was certainly enormously influential. But he had stayed in France during World War Two and conducted an ill-advised flirtation with Mussolini and the Vichy government. By the time he lost the leadership of the design team working on the United Nations building in New York, he was looking very much like the face of Old Europe. For younger architects such as James Stirling,

Le Corbusier's sculptural manner of the 1950s looked like a betrayal of his radical past. Italy and its rationalist architects had been discredited by their association with fascism, even if their work interested more adventurous members of the younger generation. And Britain had all but ignored the modern movement.

Walter Gropius and Marcel Breuer, pausing only briefly in London on their way westward across the Atlantic, had, with the mellifluous assistance of the young Philip Johnson, captured America's intellectual heartland. Having taken over the direction of Harvard's architecture school, Gropius had appointed Breuer to the faculty. After the war, they moved from the avant garde to the corporate world, and began building on an expansive scale fuelled by America's apparently unstoppable economic boom. Another European subject of Johnson's attention, Mies van der Rohe, had moved to Chicago from Berlin just before the outbreak of the Second World War, and taken on the directorship of the Illinois Institute of Technology's architecture school. He built the IIT campus, and finally realised his first skyscraper, the Seagram Tower, in New York. Its bronze mullions and glass curtain wall composed with infinite care set the pattern for every sophisticated office building around the world for the next thirty years.

All this imported talent – the 'Silver Princes' as Tom Wolfe acidly called them in his book *From Bauhaus to Our House*, the superior architectural beings from the far side of the universe, greeted by what he sharply characterised as rows of awestruck natives prostrating themselves as soon their saviours had crash-landed – certainly had an immediate impact on an influential generation of American architects. I.M. Pei and Paul Rudolph were taught directly by the refugees. Louis Kahn, Eero Saarinen and Rudolph tried to build a specifically American form of modernism in architecture and they in turn were attracting their own followers.

Foster was well aware of the striking direction that their work had taken. He was especially interested in Louis Kahn, who managed to be both monumental and fascinated by the thinking of Buckminster Fuller.

For any young architect who wanted to get close to the centre of energy for their subject, America was an essential destination in a way that England was not. What attracted Foster to Yale rather than to Harvard or Princeton were the people that he hoped would be teaching him. In spite of a moment of doubt when he discovered that Kahn had just left New Haven for Philadelphia, Foster had decided that only Yale would do. Just as in Manchester it had to be the university and not the art school, in America, it had to be Yale because it was the best.

And there were many who agreed with him. Yale in the 1960s was developing a reputation for attracting bright, ambitious students. Sometimes they were too ambitious. With a raised eyebrow, Thomas Beeby the Chicago architect, who went through Yale a year behind Foster, sardonically suggested of his student days, that:

It was the era of the great hero and everyone wanted to be a master architect. They had master classes and you could study with Lou Kahn at Penn or you could go study with Paul Rudolph at Yale or you could go and study with Sert at Harvard. Yale was the most energized place. It attracted an amazing group of people who came to study with Paul Rudolph. They were an extremely diverse group. Charlie Gwathmey was there, David Childs [the man who went on to dominate America's leading corporate architectural practice, SOM, and to wrest control of the Ground Zero site from Daniel Libeskind] was there. It was pretty heavy stuff. It was all about becoming a genius, you knew where you were going to hone your skills and become one of the great architects of your period.

But architecture was not the only thing on Foster's mind. America looked like the kind of classless yet glamorous society in which he could not just thrive professionally, but also enjoy himself. He still had wartime memories of the stylishly dressed and seemingly affluent GIs at the dance hall off Stockport Road, under the shelter of the barrage balloons tethered on Crowcroft Park. The America of Foster's imagination was a place that would allow him to escape from the lingering sense of anger and frustration that he still felt about life in Britain.

At home, he saw himself as an awkward, provincial outsider, held back by his accent, his lack of social ease, and a background that would do little for his chances of succeeding as an architect. In America he could wipe out all that uncomfortable personal history and start again. Success in America would come on the basis of nothing other than his own talent. The street that he grew up in, the school that he had gone to, and his lack of family connections would not hold him back. By moving to America, he was reinventing himself and starting again.

Armed with his fellowship and his place on the master's programme at Yale, he was being allowed to join the ranks of the privileged. And with a green card, he had the means to stay permanently. Foster came very close to doing just that. If he hadn't met Richard Rogers and the chance to start a practice with him in London had not come up, Foster would very likely have made his life in America.

Foster set out to make as much as he could from his admission to what he clearly saw as his own personal new world. Most scholarship students making their way to America from Britain in the early 1960s were content to spend three long days at sea playing deck quoits on the crossing from Southampton to New York. Richard Rogers took the *Queen Elizabeth* and was met by a reporter from the Yale daily newspaper who wanted his first thoughts about coming to America, in the manner of so many architects from Le Corbusier down. They published his picture in the paper too.

To Foster the sea crossing seemed like a hopelessly old-fashioned waste of time. Why would he want to sail all the way to New York when he could fly? Starting in the way that he meant to go on, he took the plane. He justified the price of the ticket in what was to become a very Foster-like way. In Foster's mind, the flight could not be regarded as an extravagance if it was understood as the most efficient answer to a problem, a high-tech solution that would allow him to make a better job of things. It's the way that he explained himself to his cautious and financially careful mother. Just as twenty years later he would, taking his lead from Buckminster Fuller, compare the high-tech solution of launching a communications satellite to the apparently cheaper but actually much more profligate strategy of laying 2,000 miles of undersea transatlantic cable. Of course, the fact that Foster loved to fly also played its part in the equation.

Foster spent the summer of 1961 working in London for John Beardshaw, living above the office next to the *Economist* building in St James's. He stayed on until the last possible minute to earn as much money as he could, planning to arrive in America in September just as the Yale term started. The cheapest fare that he could find involved stopping off in Iceland on the way, but at £100 for a one-way ticket, it still cost almost as much as he earned in a month. And for once technology let him down. The silver-skinned Icelandair DC 6 Super Cloudmaster, powered by four piston-driven propeller engines had a technical problem at 20,000 feet over Scotland. While the mechanics waited for the spare parts they needed to fix it, Foster was frustratingly stuck for two days in a hotel outside Prestwick Airport in a town with no pubs. Even so, he managed to arrive in time for the start of term. The immaculate and stylishly dressed Eldred Evans, third of the three British students on the course, got into trouble for turning up five days late.

Foster landed in New York, at what was still called Idlewild Airport: John F. Kennedy had little more than two years left to live. Eero Saarinen, however, had died just a few days previously; his masterpiece at the airport, the TWA terminal with its complex soaring concrete shells representing a bird in flight, was almost complete.

When he finally got to New Haven, Foster stepped off the Greyhound bus and found himself being welcomed into the Ivy League by the master of Jonathan Edwards College in which, as a Henry fellow, he had been allocated a handsome set of rooms. It was a Sunday evening, and the master and his wife were hosting a cocktail party in their garden overlooking the college's quadrangle. The master's wife, it seemed, was related to the mayor of Liverpool. Foster was dismayed to be asked if he happened to know him.

Yale is an enclave of privilege, filled with the scent of that very particular variety of well-heeled American philanthropy. It sits at the centre of what is now the battered little city of New Haven, where very few home-grown twenty-year-olds share the opportunities that are open to a typical Yale undergraduate of the same age.

New Haven was originally laid out on a grid plan of nine square blocks in 1640, an ancient beginning by American standards. George Washington mustered the local militia on the green during the War of Independence. Led by Benedict Arnold, before he went over to the redcoats, they marched on the British, three days' away in Massachusetts.

New Haven is where Sam Colt made the first of the revolvers that bear his name in Eli Whitney's factory. The university was founded in 1701. But Yale adopted the Oxbridge model of residential colleges for its students only comparatively recently in its history. It picked English gothic as the most appropriate architectural language to use for building them at a moment when the gothic revival had already come and long gone.

Look at Yale's most conspicuous architectural landmark, the Harkness Tower – completed in 1921, and modelled on the tower of the fifteenth-century parish church of St Botolph in Lincolnshire – through half-closed eyes and you could for a moment feel that you were back in a dreamlike version of the later Middle Ages. But the regularity of the blocks on which the university is planned somehow denies the essence of the scholarly gothic on which the architecture is based. Jonathan Edwards College opened for students in 1932, by which time its stone-faced buildings seemed completely out of their time, more like a curious blend of archaeology and stage set than a reflection of a living cultural tradition. The master's lodge sits on the corner of High Street, above the main entrance. There is another gate named Wheelock, a dining room, a common room, and an elaborate collection of chimneys and oriel windows supplied apparently by the metre.

Admission to Yale brings, along with much else, access to the leisured ease of the Jacobean-themed reading room of the university's Sterling Library. Completed in 1930, its battered green leather sofas look like something from the House of Commons and combine with its Latin inscriptions over the fireplace and its inglenooks facing the cloistered garden outside to suggest a place desperate to look older than its years. Even Yale's gymnasium is built in exuberant gothic style, and it comes equipped with a tower not much less imposing than that of Durham Cathedral. It is, in short, a university that might have been imagined by Ralph Lauren.

But beyond its gothic zone, New Haven in Foster's day was suffering from the early symptoms of the urban decay that Jane Jacobs identified in her book, *The Death and Life of Great American Cities*: a rotting centre and spreading affluent suburbs.

Away from the security of the city lights and the campus police it would become a troubled place to live after the race riot of 1967. There were whole streets in New Haven in which the only functioning buildings were adult cinemas. Everything else for blocks at a stretch had been shuttered and abandoned, burnt out or flattened. The blight and the squalor outside the university precinct was made all the more poignant by the fragments of Early Americana in the form of colonial church steeples, marooned in the midst of it. In the 1970s, New Haven's Union Station, designed by Cass Gilbert with imperial swagger, was boarded up, and passengers caught the train to New York from a prefabricated hut tethered beside it along the tracks. The impact of empty factories, white flight and dereliction was not helped by brutal planning policies that rammed freeways through residential neighbourhoods. In Foster's time in New Haven, these disastrous strategies were directed with what were no doubt the best intentions by an ambitious mayor, Richard Lee, who saw himself as the Robert Moses of the Kennedy era, and was determined to make New Haven into an international model for urban renewal. He was remarkably successful at lobbying Washington to divert federal funds to New Haven ahead of other cities. The money allowed him to turn the place into a laboratory for wholesale urban redevelopment.

Lee justified calling in the bulldozers to demolish large swathes of his city by talking melodramatically about what he called the 'shame' brought upon New Haven by the 10,000 disease-carrying rats that he claimed his rat catchers had exterminated while cleaning up a single city block. His was a form of urban renewal that reflected what was soon to become American strategy in Vietnam. He was ready to destroy the city in order to save it. But before the real impact of what he was doing became apparent, he got himself on the cover of *Saturday Evening Post* looking young and statesmanlike. And he shipped in all the famous architects that he could find in vain attempts to help fix his ruined city. Lee eventually became the longest-serving American mayor of his time. To help keep himself in office, he persuaded both President Kennedy and Rocky Marciano to campaign for him.

Yale's president at the time, Alfred Griswold, was moving in very much the same direction as Lee, and investing in all the most conspicuous twentieth-century architecture that he could squeeze on to the campus.

Foster's graduate class had its studio in the most impressive example of this new policy of architectural patronage. Foster's drawing board was situated on the top floor of Louis Kahn's first significant building, his extension to the Yale Art Museum. Kahn's wing is a suave and lucid design, deftly inserted into the gothic edge of the campus in 1952. His design defers to the Ruskinian taste for Venetian gothic of the rest of the arts buildings, but exhibits a firm sense of conviction of its own. On the outside, Kahn's caramel-coloured brickwork is disciplined by three stone bands, with most of the glazing confined to the sophisticated proportions of the north wall overlooking what in Foster's day was the construction site of the new Art and Architecture Building. Inside the door, just by the gallery's bank of lifts, are the van Gogh sunflowers that Foster remembers passing every day on the way up to his studio. The ceiling is a tetrahedron grid of polished cast concrete. The floors are black slate, a combination that comes close to the palette of materials that Foster and Rogers would use for the house they built together in Cornwall.

As he wandered around New Haven, sampled his first deli sandwich and discovered the cavernous pizzeria in Little Italy, tended by an elderly man in a white apron and surgical shoes who shuffled back and forth between table and oven, Foster found himself coming face to face with some of the most inventive new architecture in the world. There was little to match it in Britain at the time, least of all in Manchester, where most new building work in the 1950s and 1960s took the form of provincial paraphrases of metropolitan originals. Yale wasn't like that, it had the real thing. It was a place that was working with those architects who, through sheer self-belief, were establishing themselves as the creative leaders of their profession, devising a new version of contemporary architecture, one that had moved on from the machine age aesthetic of the early modernists.

Louis Kahn has become the most highly regarded of the generation of architects that worked in Yale. But Eero Saarinen, who designed the Morse and Ezra Stiles colleges, also had a major impact, even if Reyner Banham was particularly rude about his attempts to be simultaneously picturesque and modern. Until his untimely death at fifty, Saarinen was one of America's most promising architects. In his brief career he explored a range of very different forms of architectural expression. At Yale, he built not just student halls of residence, but also a stadium with a roof like a whale for the university hockey team.

Other architects active in New Haven in the early 1960s included Philip Johnson, who was responsible for a group of research laboratories, and Gordon Bunshaft. At the time that Foster arrived, Bunshaft was about to start building the Beinecke Rare Books Library. The prominent Yale architectural historian Vincent Scully was even ruder about it than Banham had been in his onslaught on Saarinen.

Living in his parents' house in Manchester, and working to support himself, Foster had been a social oddity. Working your way through college in America was entirely normal and Foster felt comfortable there immediately, though as a graduate student he found that work left little time for socialising with the undergraduates living all around him. But as Scully would have told him had he asked, Yale was far from the classless society Foster imagined. As an Irish Catholic art history student at Yale in the 1930s, Scully had worked just as Foster had done in Manchester. Waiting at table on his more affluent, white Anglo-Saxon Protestant fellow students, had left him in no doubt as to the nature of the social hierarchy at Yale. Foster was certainly never invited inside the sinisterly windowless red sandstone Greek revival home of the Skull and Bones society, the fraternity that counts both Bush the Younger and Bush the Elder as members, though he passed by it daily on his way to the architecture studio.

In the winter of 1961, Yale meant Paul Rudolph, the dapper chairman of the Department of Architecture, a man with a crew cut and a button-down shirt that made him look like an off-duty astronaut. Rudolph's reputation as a home-grown American modernist had never been higher. Born in Kentucky, Rudolph got his first degree in Alabama. But like Foster he had shown enough promise to be able to quickly make the transition to a larger stage. He moved to Harvard to complete his education and became a student of Walter Gropius at the same time as I.M. Pei and Philip Johnson. It was like being anointed into the church of modernism by its high priest, if not its John the Baptist.

Rudolph joined the US Navy during the Second World War and was stationed at the Navy Yards in Brooklyn. He used the combination of his wartime experience and his relationship with Gropius to develop his own vigorous and inventive approach to architecture, demonstrated by a string of houses that he built in Florida when he was newly qualified. Adapting the navy's technique for weather-proofing mothballed ships, he had the Cocoon House that he designed on Siesta Key sprayed with plastic roofing film. It was exactly the kind of creative free association that was to shape Foster's own work. And there are traces of some of Rudolph's other ideas in Creak Vean, the house that Rogers and Foster designed together when they set up Team Four. Like Rudolph's School of Forestry at Yale, Creak

Vean deals with a vertiginously sloping site by bridging it, creating a main entrance at high level and then stepping down towards the main floor. Its grassy cascade of steps, however, is derived from Foster's memory of Alvar Aalto's work at Saynatsalo in Finland.

Appointed to run Yale's architecture programme in 1958 – on the basis of his buildings rather than his track record as a teacher – Rudolph moved his practice to New Haven. By the time that Foster arrived, Rudolph had given the school the sense of direction it had previously lacked. He was attracting every famous architectural name that he could persuade to stop by to deliver a lecture or pass judgement on the work of his students. He invited the most formidable practitioners to sit on the juries that were a feature of teaching at Yale, and he argued furiously with them in front of the students. There wasn't any other school in America that had the ambition and the cash to do things the way that Yale did.

Rudolph was a homosexual, and charismatic enough to attract attention beyond the architectural compound. In 1962, *Vogue* sent Elliot Erwitt to Yale to photograph him for a lengthy profile. Erwitt documented Rudolph's classes, portraying him at work as a teacher and a designer, and as the host of glamorous cocktail parties. *Vogue* opened the feature with an unforgettable double-page image of Rudolph taken with a lens long enough to bring down a helicopter gunship. Erwitt shows Rudolph standing entirely alone on the roof of one of the most extraordinary of his creations, New Haven's Temple Street car park, which was built to evoke the melancholy splendour of a ruined Roman aqueduct in massive cast concrete. He is a tiny figure, almost lost in the background of the photograph, until you focus on him, caught standing proudly four-square, arms folded, next to his cherished Jaguar XK 150 coupé, with its white-wall tyres and its wire wheel hubs, looking like a Roman general preparing for a triumph beside his chariot. Framed by his own monumental work, and with the city crowding in around him, it is the personification of the architect as a solitary hero in the Ayn Rand tradition: an individual with a vision, standing alone against the world, ready to follow the dictates of his own genius.

Erwitt's photographs, and the coverage that *Vogue* gave them, convey the lustrous glow that Yale bestowed on its students at that time. Foster was to learn from Rudolph not just how to be an architect, but also how to look and behave like one. He dressed like Rudolph, he started to draw like him too, and one day he was going to design a house and a studio for himself, just as Rudolph had done. In the meantime he combined his studies with work as a draughtsman, earning $1.50 an hour in Rudolph's studio in the attic of his house on High Street, five minutes walk away from Jonathan Edwards College. From the street, you could not tell that there was anything out of the ordinary going on behind the nineteenth-century façade of Rudolph's house, with its Corinthian porch and pedimented windows. Foster describes its interior, planned with a set of complex interlocking stepped levels, as a miniature version of the Art and Architecture Building that Rudolph was working on for Yale at the time. Rudolph wrapped a double-height glass extension around the sides and back of the house, behind a brick wall that defined a courtyard. The interior was studded with salvaged architectural fragments that were used to embellish its rooms. A fragment of a gothic carving of a medieval bishop stood by the window, a Roman senator's head stared out from the chimney breast, impaled on the end of a stainless steel rod. There were lessons to be learned here on ways of working with historic buildings that may have helped shape Foster's remodelling of the Royal Academy in London, twenty-five years later, his first exercise in dealing with a significant existing piece of architecture. Like Rudolph in his house, at the Royal Academy Foster could create space out of nowhere by co-opting the gaps around the edge of a building. And also like Rudolph, he was ready to exploit the visual tension between old and new to impressive effect. Rudolph had goatskin rugs slung across the floor, and 'daring' furniture made from perspex and foam. The young student from Levenshulme was dazzled.

In the studio itself, there were just six stools and a cushion-strewn conversation pit, in which Rudolph would from time to time gather his assistants for a moment of reflection on whatever project they were working on. These were young men who all dressed exactly like him in narrow ties, button-down shirts and crew cuts.

William Grindereng, one of Rudolph's former employees who worked in the studio in New Haven, remembers that getting into the office involved negotiating a stairwell that came ver-tiginously up through the floor in the middle of the room.

> There was an element of danger in most of what Rudolph did, both for himself and sometimes for other people. The stairwell came up through the floor. It was just a hole in the floor with no railing around it. The building inspector insisted that he put a railing around it. He said, 'I'll move out of this building before I do that.' He could be very stubborn. He never put a railing around that stairwell.

Potentially even more dangerous than the hole in the floor was the staircase that climbed up one wall of Rudolph's living room.

It took the form of a row of stone blades, cantilevered from the wall and rising a sheer eighteen feet without a handrail of any kind. Henry-Russell Hitchcock, the distinguished architectural historian was seen to come close to disaster on at least one occasion when he attempted to negotiate the steps while somewhat the worse for wear after rather too much bourbon. At another party, James Stirling behaved even worse, relieving himself in full view in the yard beyond the glass wall.

Rudolph's drawings were remarkably intricate and full of energy, precisely delineated in decisive, scalpel-sharp, hard ink lines that were as dry as a steel engraving. Foster learned the style, and spent hour after hour working on Rudolph's renderings in the master's manner. The drawings were very large and, according to Foster, Rudolph used them to test alternative possibilities in his designs, very much in the way that architects use computers today. Various versions of sections of the building under consideration would be drawn up, then tested superimposed in position on the larger drawing, and deleted if appropriate.

Foster learned a lot from Rudolph's furiously determined energy. 'He was capable of doing all the design drawings and the details for a project all by himself in the course of a single weekend. In that sense he led by example,' Foster remembers. Much of Foster's work consisted of straining his eyes to the point of snow blindness, applying layer upon layer upon layer of ink cross-hatching to build up a patina of shadow and light on Rudolph's presentation drawings. He went on to work on some of the design drawings for the Art and Architecture Building itself.

In the spare, fluid lines of the pencil sketches that fill Rudolph's notebooks, you see the inspiration for Foster's own compulsive drawing. Foster simply can't stop drawing. He makes drawing part of his conversational technique. Talk to him at lunch, and he picks up scraps of paper and starts drawing to illustrate a point. He draws to help him think and to make notes to himself; in the car that ferries him around London, there is permanently a pad of drawing paper and a row of freshly sharpened pencils, ready and waiting to pin down his fleeting thoughts. He has to write letters, of course, but prefers using drawing as his chosen method of communication. He draws for pleasure, and – as much later, facing cancer surgery, he meticulously recorded every detail he could see from his hospital bed – he draws to achieve peace of mind.

Foster clearly cared a great deal about making a good impression on Rudolph. He pushed himself beyond all limits, working through the night at the drawing board. Rudolph knew this, but he was also ready to exploit weakness in others to get even more out of the disciples in his studio. Foster remembers being reduced almost to tears after one marathon session when Rudolph rejected his efforts with the cutting words, 'You don't care enough.' But beyond the anguish, Foster was capable of filing the incident away for use on the day when he would be on the other side of the drawing board.

The level of debate at Yale provided Foster with a startling insight into an approach to architecture entirely different from what he had known in Manchester. Students at Yale were expected to defend their work in front of a demanding panel of critics. Foster took to it at once. He could put in the hours, and then enjoy having somebody ready to talk about what he had done. For the first time in his education he was really getting to explore the meanings of architecture, beyond the practical, measurable issues. 'Architecture', Rudolph told his students, 'is a process of finding out what you need to know.'

Rudolph was Foster's first serious teacher, and he gave his student a series of clues about the future. 'He was a restless explorer of form, and a great critic. His early works were very fresh and inspired,' says Foster, who has always loyally defended his mentor's fluctuating reputation. In 2008 he went back to Yale to pay tribute to Rudolph at the rededication of his Art and Architecture Building. Foster and his wife donated over three million dollars to endow a chair at the school, acknowledging his debt to Yale and the United States.

Rudolph was endlessly demanding. 'If there wasn't something to look at, a model, or a set of drawings, there was no conversation,' says Foster. Thomas Beeby, who was at Yale just after Foster, remembers Rudolph as an extraordinary teacher:

> Paul could just look at a drawing and read it – read it plus read all of the details, the way it's structured. He would ask you questions like, what would you think about this building? Imagine walking down this hall and when you get to here, you look at the end and what do you see? This is all about perceptual grasp of what the spaces were like. He had an amazing grasp of three-dimensional space. He was a great teacher and he had an absolute standard; nothing was good enough, because there were always things wrong. The structure didn't work, the circulation didn't work, you couldn't get the trash in, it looked bad, the windows were too high.
>
> A lot of people took it very personally. Rudolph never picked on me. But he could be very cynical and cruel if he wanted to. He would pick on people and he would jump up at the end of the critique. There was a great shuffling at the end not to be the last person because somewhere in the last three persons in

the class he would just jump up, yell at you and leave. The last two guys would have no chance. We were always trying to figure out how not to be one of the last three guys.

In fact, there was more to architecture at Yale than posturing and raw ego. It demanded unconditional effort from its students. 'Yale forced you to concentrate on your own work: to be critically astute about your own work, to look at your own work and to be able to criticise it,' remembers Beeby. 'You were on your own, it was just you and the piece of paper. You're not part of a movement, the guy next door can't tell you what to do because he's not going to have a similar project. Yale was all about self-realisation.'

Of the eleven students in the master's class in Foster's year, three were British. There was Eldred Evans, a young woman who had been at the Architectural Association and was acknowledged as one of the most gifted of its graduates. Later she would design the Tate Gallery's Cornish outpost in St Ives. There was Richard Rogers, two years older than Foster, born in Florence in 1933, the eldest son of a doctor with a British passport and an Italian mother. His parents bought a house in Surrey and moved to England just before the Second World War. He didn't much enjoy his days at boarding school, where he developed a rebellious streak. Subsequently, he studied at the Architectural Association, a school that was everything Manchester was not. And then there was Foster, who quickly, and perhaps surprisingly, developed the ability to act as a spokesman for the others. Rogers, who was dyslexic and could hardly draw beyond a scribble, still recalls Foster, in his commanding manner, presenting the projects that they had worked on together.

Both Rogers and Foster were close to Carl Abbott, one of the American students on the course. Abbott was the owner of a Volkswagen Beetle in which they were able to tour the country, looking at the key modern buildings of America.

A photograph taken of the three of them in the winter of 1961 by Su Rogers shows her husband in the centre, wearing a Russian-style astrakhan hat; Richard is smiling, but looking a little awkward, one hand is curled into a fist, the other hangs at his side. Abbott is on his left, bareheaded, as if he were the fifth Beatle. Foster is on the right, wearing a dark snap-brimmed fedora that doesn't make him look very much like Frank Sinatra at all. The collar of his hound's-tooth check coat is turned up against the wind, and he is holding his camera in one hand, level with his waist, its leather case dangling down on a strap. He is unsmiling, and wears a tie: the image of an intense, anxious young professional. Foster looks much happier in the photographs that show him at work on the top floor of the Art and Architecture Building.

There was something of a divide between the British and the Americans in their shared studio. The British were a little older, and preferred to debate and to argue rather than to draw. They saw themselves as more mature, and more like professionals than their US counterparts – a pretension which, not surprisingly, was the cause of some irritation. After one episode of more than usually provocative Anglo-Saxon prevarication, a placard appeared over their drafting tables. 'Stop talking, start drawing,' it demanded. The British struck back with a slogan of their own on the other side of the studio that urged the Americans to 'Start Thinking'.

In fact, as M.J. Long recalls, there were other times when American patience with the anglophilia of Rudolph's Yale wore thin. When Jane Drew, the British architect working alongside Le Corbusier on the job of designing the less inspired parts of Chandigarh, came to lecture, she was greeted by a banner hanging from one of the windows of the Kahn building bearing the words *Et Tu Jane Drew?* in exasperation at the arrival of what they assumed to be yet another condescending Brit.

Abbott, however, stayed close to the British. He saw Foster when he was working in San Francisco, and when Team Four started he came over to London and worked in the office for a while. Abbott remembers sitting in Hampstead listening to the radio, and having to come to terms with the news that Kennedy had just been shot dead.

There were several other British faces at Yale. Su Rogers was at the School of Planning, on the way to converting herself into an architect after her sociology degree at the London School of Economics. Colin St John Wilson, who would one day build the British Library – and marry M.J. Long – was teaching there. And James Stirling, Eldred Evans' lover at the time, was a visiting critic.

Yale turned out to be the place that shaped all three of the men, Foster, Rogers and Stirling, who were to dominate Britain's architectural landscape in the 1970s and 1980s. For all their differences in style and background, Rogers and Foster became close friends immediately. They worked together, sharing studio space and collaborating on projects. Each offered the other a skill that they did not themselves possess, and they began to talk about establishing an architectural practice together when their student days were over. Even though it has diverged over the years, their architecture has retained an essential range of common interests. It was Stirling who recommended Team Four to Peter Parker, the client for their most important commission, the Reliance Controls factory in Swindon. And it was Stirling who was the most outspoken judge in the competition for the Newport School in South Wales, won by Eldred Evans, that Foster entered and lost. Later, Stirling wrote Foster an uncharacteristically enthusiastic letter complimenting him on the new Sackler Galleries at the Royal Academy.

The first brief Rudolph set Foster was for a school. Rudolph, who three years earlier had designed just such a school in Sarasota, was impressed by what Foster produced. Foster, he said, was 'thinking like an architect, even if he did draw trees that looked like cauliflowers'. The school was followed by a design for an office tower, which was again a brief based on a project that Rudolph himself had worked on in 1960: the Blue Cross, Blue Shield offices in Boston. Foster, in response to Louis Kahn's famous dictum about buildings being divided between served and servant spaces, conceived of making the useable office floors free of structural columns, intrusive stairwells and washrooms. Instead, the 'served' floors spanned between pairs of 'servant' towers to which stairs, lifts and washrooms were confined. It set a precedent that Foster was later to apply to the Hong Kong and Shanghai Banking Corporation (HSBC) headquarters.

Foster and Rogers collaborated on the next project set by Rudolph: the design for a group of research laboratories for the Yale campus. 'This is an urban problem. It is also the problem of the architect, as planners and developers have failed to rebuild our cities. They are obsessed with numbers (people, money, acreage, units, cars, roads, etc) and forget life itself and the spirit of man,' Rudolph wrote in his unusually discursive brief for the students. Their proposal took the form of a megastructure, stepping towards the existing campus buildings. A continuous series of buildings, running one into another, was organised around a spine of lower structures that housed car parks, and cafés, with the laboratories radiating off it.

What is most striking about Yale in Rudolph's time is that he produced students with wildly divergent outlooks on architecture. Some, like Foster, came away more convinced than ever about the essential rightness of modernism. But others who were there at almost the same time reacted violently against it. Alan Greenberg, who graduated a year after Foster, taught himself how to design in a grand country house classical manner reminiscent of Edwin Lutyens. Stanley Tigerman, and Bob Stern, who went on to orchestrate Disney's extensive architectural patronage for Michael Eisner in a hubristic collision of low- and highbrow, started looking for stronger architectural flavours than the followers of Walter Gropius could conceivably offer. Stern, who eventually became Yale's dean of architecture, has presided over an equally diverse school, attracting the Prince of Wales' favourite, Leon Krier, as well as Zaha Hadid, to teach and lecture.

Rudolph was not just running the school, he was preoccupied first with the design of Yale's new Art and Architecture Building, and then with realising the commission that should have been his first masterwork. Planned from 1958 onwards, the project was in essence an essay in the baroque version of modernism, characterised by deep hollowed-out voids carved into a big concrete mass, marked by the corduroy concrete ribbing that in Rudolph's declining years was to become his overworked signature. But as Foster later came to realise, it was a building that at heart was a paraphrase of Frank Lloyd Wright's Larkin Guaranty offices in Buffalo. For purists, this was moving by quite some distance too far away from the refined simplicity of the pioneering modernists. For those who were not fond of concrete, there was no respite from the harshness of the material. In summer it was too hot, in winter it was too cold. The orange carpet grew an alarming coat of mould. And some painters complained that the ceilings were too low and their studios too dark for their canvases.

As soon as Rudolph left, his successor Charles Moore announced that he disapproved of the building wholeheartedly because it was such a personal manifestation for a non-personal use. Six faculty members and sixty-two students went a lot further, and signed a petition demanding that the university move them out of the building immediately. Dean Keller, the professor of painting and drawing, wrote to the *Yale Daily News* supporting them. He called the building 'a total failure', and produced a withering critique of Rudolph's work, and indeed of his approach to architecture and his personality.

> When I asked innocently why sculptors were put in low-ceilinged rooms underground, and why rabbit warrens with thin strips of windows next to the ceiling were to be the studios of the painters, I was looked on with, let us say, polite contempt.
>
> The architect could have arranged his studios on the north side, and made adequate space. He never had the slightest interest in the painters' problem. And as for the sculptors, it would seem that he'd never heard of them. The architects as usual came off best, but even they had problems ... it's a dangerous building, ill conditioned for air, which is fetid.

Moore weighed into Rudolph with almost as much ferocity. 'Mr Rudolph is an important architect, who works as an individual, and ran the school that way. He did things by himself, and seemed to make people like it.' Certainly Rudolph was not a man to share responsibility for anything with anybody. He told *Architectural Forum* in April 1958 that 'Gropius may be wrong in believing that architecture is a cooperative art. Architects were never meant to design together. It's either your work, or it's his.'

There was something about Rudolph's personality that came close to self-sabotage. Foster describes him as supremely self-confident but at the same time shy to the point of catatonia. 'I remember that he asked a group of us back to his house one night. He got us there, sat us down, and then couldn't find anything to say to us. And as the silence dragged on, it got harder and harder for anybody to break it. He was trying to be nice, but outside work, he felt lost, and it made him even more difficult.' Rudolph was regarded as brusque, quick to take offence and emotionally needy.

As soon as the Art and Architecture Building was finally finished in 1964, Rudolph left Yale. According to Vincent Scully, Rudolph was heartbroken when the distinguished architectural historian Nikolaus Pevsner made it clear in his speech at the inauguration what he thought of the building.

At the height of the campus unrest of 1967, the Art and Architecture Building was badly damaged by a fire started by what Rudolph's obituary in the *New York Times* described as group of student arsonists, and subsequently unsympathetically altered. In fact, the New Haven Fire Department never found conclusive evidence of the fire having been started deliberately. What began the arson theory was a student-published leaflet circulating on campus shortly before the fire gutted two floors of the building, asking 'Why Has Yale Not Gone Up in Smoke? See the Art and Architecture See Every Building See them Soon,' it urged, in a way that many understood as a threat that was soon to be substantiated. Of course, if the Art and Architecture Building was not deliberately torched by its occupants it suggests that Rudolph's building immolated itself through some undiagnosed electrical fault, not really a prospect that could be seen as much more comforting.

After the fire Rudolph's reputation tipped into a steep decline, which accelerated as he completed a series of increasingly formulaic brutalist concrete buildings, and some unlikely high-rise neo-orientalist work in Jakarta in which he seemed to be suggesting that the appropriate way to make office towers in the tropics was by stacking vernacular-style huts thirty or forty at a time in a form that could be interpreted as referring to a pagoda. He died in 1997. Only now, forty years after the fire, has the Art and Architecture Building been properly restored, and a real attempt been made to make a case for Rudolph as a pivotal figure in post-war American architecture. It's the kind of trajectory that can lie in wait for any architect whose work achieves a certain prominence, Foster included, as history starts to evaluate their late work against the background of an earlier career. What happened to Rudolph had already happened to Wright.

Nearly three decades later, after Foster had established his international reputation with the completion of the HSBC's tower, Rudolph found himself being cruelly overshadowed by his former student. While he was building a pair of boldly modelled mirror glass office towers for the disgraced Australian businessman, Alan Bond, in Hong Kong he was asked if he had been influenced by Foster. His answer is as equivocal, and as prickly as you would expect:

> Not really, no. How should I put that? It simply was not on the
> cards. The Norman Foster building is hung, first of all, as you

know, although you don't sense that it is hung. That is one of its great disappointments, mainly because everything comes down to the ground. How can you have a hung building if everything comes down to the ground? The thing happens to be on a sloping piece of land and Norman Foster never figured out how to relate his modules, which are so demanding, to come down to the diagonal. How can you have a hung building if everything comes down to the ground, for God's sake? It is open at the bottom, in the middle. On either side there are cores and all these little goddam cores come down to the ground.

Rudolph went on to question the approach of two of his most famous students:

Mechanical systems and structural systems are exact opposites. The structural system can be very regular, as we all know. As to the mechanical system, anybody who has looked inside a Ford knows that it's a very irregular thing, and so it is with a building. I am interested in the play between the two. That's one reason why Norman Foster's work, and also Rogers' buildings are so fascinating for me. I am writing an article on Foster's building in Hong Kong because he has juxtaposed the mechanical system to the structural system. He controls it very very well. On many levels it's a marvellous building.

The celebration of the mechanical system, illustrated at the Beaubourg with Rogers' building, now that is a different matter. Nobody can say that buildings are better or worse because of their articulation of the parts. Nobody can say that a building that shows all of its mechanical systems is better than a building that doesn't show any of it. You simply cannot do that. It's not just mechanical systems, you can't say that a building that shows its structure is better than one that doesn't. It seems to me that it has to be implied and that forces have to be resolved. The literal showing of the structure isn't necessarily better.

Norman Foster's building is finally an impossible building in Hong Kong in spite of the fact that I love it. There is nothing for you really, because it's so insistent about one way of looking at something. This damn module going on and on is so tense, you have to leave it. I'm trying to figure out why the module was taken to the degree that he did, vertically, horizontally and so forth, it's just impossible.

If Rudolph taught architecture as a practical, not to say physical art, a matter of heroic wrestling with form, there were other influential figures that Foster came into contact with at Yale who offered different, more cerebral insights into understanding architecture. After Rudolph, Yale's biggest draw, and not just for architecture students, was the showman historian and critic Vincent Scully, a scholar whose bravura lectures could include as many as seven slide projectors operated simultaneously by a dexterous assistant. More than once Scully was so distracted by his performance that he lost track of where he was and fell off the lecture-theatre stage in mid-flow of an exegesis of the greatness of Frank Lloyd Wright. M.J. Long once saw him pick himself off the floor and go back to his theme without missing a beat, despite sustaining a minor flesh wound to the forehead. And it was certainly Scully that set Foster off on his journey across America to see every Wright building that he could. That journey was what tilted Foster towards Wright, and distanced him a little from his previous regard for Le Corbusier. Scully is the man who once went head to head in an argument with

Norman Mailer in the pages of the professional magazine *Architectural Forum* in defence of modernism, accusing the novelist of 'lazy potboiling paragraphs'. Later he confessed to feeling defeated by Mailer's depiction of the heroes of modern architecture leaving man 'isolated in a landscape of empty psychosis', a proposition which he felt unable to challenge.

During Foster's time at Yale, Scully was fighting to save New York's glorious Pennsylvania Station from demolition. When, despite his efforts and those of many other protestors, it had gone, Scully memorably suggested, 'Once you entered the city like a god. Now we scuttle in like rats.' Scully provided a hugely entertaining revisionist commentary on the history of modernism. Foster remembers him as an insightful critic, as interested in talking about the comparisons between the *Magnificent Seven* and the *Seven Samurai*, showing at the local movie theatre, as he was discussing Frank Lloyd Wright.

When Foster arrived, Scully had just delivered his famous attack on the rebuilding of Manhattan's Park Avenue and the impact of SOM's Lever House, Walter Gropius's Pan Am tower and Mies van der Rohe's Seagram building on it. He called it 'the Death of the Street', and the phrase was to resonate around the world of architecture. Scully was mounting a frontal assault on contemporary architecture. It did not matter how distinguished an individual work of architecture might be as an isolated object, for Scully, it still had to respect the urban landscape and its essential character. A street overwhelmed by high-rise towers that turn it into a ravine, or disrupt it by opening up empty plazas, is no longer a street. And a city without streets is not a city.

Also in evidence at Yale in Foster's period was Philip Johnson, the sardonic ringmaster of American architecture, wealthy enough to build his thesis project at Harvard for his house at New Canaan, to which Foster and the others were invited more than once. Johnson always had an ability to find new talent, and he went out of his way to connect with the British contingent at Yale. Later, Foster flew Johnson and his companion, David Whitney, in his Jet Ranger helicopter to see the newly finished Sainsbury Centre. Johnson was working on the Crystal Cathedral in California at the time, and was fascinated by the Sainsbury's steel tracery and the way it filtered daylight.

The third of the key intellectual influences on Foster in his student days, Serge Chermayeff, arrived at Yale at the start of his second semester to start teaching the master's course alongside Rudolph. Chermayeff, a Russian born in Grozny, in what is now Chechnya, had a career that can only be called colourful. His oil-rich millionaire father sent him to public school in England. The Russian Revolution left him penniless, and he spent five years after leaving Harrow working variously as a professional ballroom dancer and a journalist. After a period in Latin America, he became a designer for Waring and Gillow; then, having married his employer's daughter, he turned himself into an architect through sheer force of will, eventually going into partnership with the German refugee Erich Mendelsohn. While Mendelsohn and Chermayeff were working in London, they built one of the few authentic pieces of International Style architecture in Britain, a house in Chelsea. Many decades later Foster was to remodel it for Paul and Helen Hamlyn.

Chermayeff, who was in his sixties by the time that he got to Yale, was more interested in the social and theoretical underpinning to design than in building architectural sculpture for its own sake. Foster was dazzled by his ideas. 'Chermayeff was an intellectual. You could have all the visuals you wanted, but he wanted to know why you were doing your projects. Dialogue and discussion were more important to him than the drawings.'

In Foster, Chermayeff saw a potential disciple, and he tried to encourage him to stay on at Yale as a research fellow after he completed his master's degree. He gave him an early draft of *Community and Privacy* to read. This was the book that he was going to publish with Christopher Alexander, exploring settlement patterns, and their relevance to contemporary planning.

Community and Privacy, strikingly designed by Chermayeff's graphic designer son Ivan, is less an academic thesis, and more of a call to arms along the lines of Rachel Carson's onslaught against pesticides in her book, *Silent Spring*, that was first published in the same year. After its perhaps surprising dedication to Walter Gropius 'with affection, admiration and gratitude', *Community and Privacy* begins by quoting the ringing words of President Kennedy delivered in a message to Congress in the spring before Foster arrived in New Haven:

Within 15 years our population will rise to 235 million. And by the year 2000 to 300 million. Most of this increase will occur in and around suburban areas. We must begin now to lay the foundations for livable, efficient and attractive communities of the future.

Land adjoining urban centers has been engulfed by urban development at the astounding rate of about one million acres a year. But the result has been haphazard and inefficient suburban expansion, and continued setbacks in the central cities' desperate struggle against blight and decay. Their social and economic base has been eroded by the movement of middle and upper income families to the suburbs, by the attendant loss of retail sales, and by the preference of many industrial firms for outlying locations.

Our policy for housing and community development must be directed toward the accomplishment of three basic national objectives.

First, to renew our cities, second to provide decent housing for all our people, third to encourage a prosperous and efficient construction industry as an essential component of general economic prosperity and growth.

This is the kind of discussion that prefigures the way Foster subsequently engaged with the future development of the city. For Chermayeff, the real problem was with mass culture, or what he called 'the glitter and debilitating chaos of Henry Miller's air-conditioned nightmare'.

In Chermayeff's apocalyptic vision:

in almost every city the pleasure of participation in city life through leisurely pedestrian movement is lost in the turmoil of cars. There may indeed come a time when travel and communication if left unchecked will make the city environment so diffuse that active urban life, as it once was, will disappear. It is even possible that unused leisure and purposeless mobility will be so abundant that they will kill all but museum experience of the city-born arts. The comprehension of events and the delight in beauty that humanity rich and poor alike may derive from its physical environment cannot be achieved in a condition of anarchy.

So dire was the situation that 'Even housewives are protesting about what is happening to the city,' claimed Chermayeff, clearly no new man.

Bicycles have fascinated Foster since he was an adolescent: for their mechanical precision, as well as their performance.

Norman Foster, born 1935, in Reddish, moved to a house on Crescent Grove in Levenshulme, on the outskirts of Manchester (top right), before his first birthday. His grandparents, uncle and aunts all lived in nearby streets. Norman was the only child of Lilly and Robert Foster. He remembers them as loving but distant parents who worked too hard for him to have the time to get to know them as well as he would have wanted. Foster's tricycle gave way to a long line of bicycles on which he spent his later adolescence exploring Manchester and its surroundings.

barge boards

attic

purlin

②

①

pine rafter

oriel

Jetty

carved corner posts

foundation for wattle & daub | SILL | Stone foundations

① Thin strips of willow or hazel held in position by bent willow pegs.

② Thatch of reed or straw.

16TH CENTURY

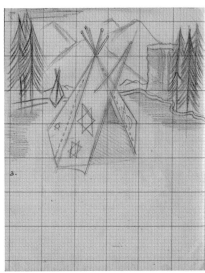

3.

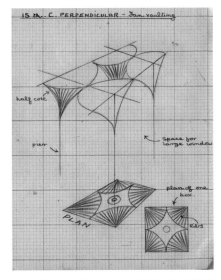

15th & C. PERPENDICULAR – Fan vaulting

half core

plan

space for large window

plan of one box

PLAN

ribs

In 1946 Foster passed the eleven-plus exam, the great class barrier of the post-war British educational system, and secured a place at Burnage High School. As these pages from his childhood sketchbooks show, he had already begun to draw. He found his art master the most sympathetic of his teachers, and for his Art O-level took a course in architectural history, which, alongside his discovery of Frank Lloyd Wright and Le Corbusier on the shelves of the local library, was his first introduction to architecture. But after failing two out of his nine O-level exams, he left school to work at Manchester Town Hall.

As a student, Foster began to win prizes for his elegantly analytical drawings such as this one of Bourne Mill in Cambridgeshire (right). Paul Rudolph, the dean of the architecture school at Yale, where Foster won a scholarship to spend a postgraduate year, was an inspired teacher who pushed Foster hard with a demanding series of design exercises, starting with a school (below). Foster also worked with Richard Rogers, whom he met at Yale, on a master plan for a university campus (bottom).

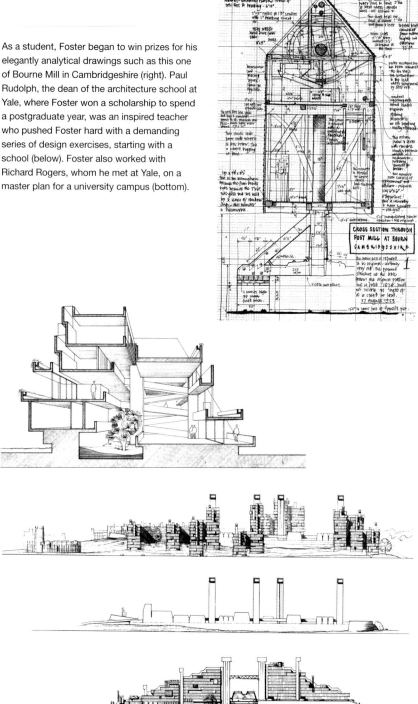

As an undergraduate at Manchester University, Foster (top picture, in bow tie; above, in sunglasses), unlike many less well-off students in the 1950s, couldn't get a grant, and had to fund his studies with a range of jobs. At Yale he met Richard Rogers (above right, centre) and the American Carl Abbot (above right, right).

Foster returned from America to join Rogers in setting up Team Four, a shortlived architectural practice. In three years they built Reliance Controls (above), a factory outside Swindon that has now been demolished, and was perhaps the first example of High Tech in Britain; and a number of houses, the most impressive of which, Creak Vean, in Cornwall (right and below), was for Richard Rogers' father-in-law, Marcus Brumwell. Foster's seductive drawings helped secure planning permission.

WEST ELEVATION

EAST ELEVATION

CH 32A

TEAM 4
ARCHITECTS

Before Creak Vean was completed, Foster and Rogers designed a simple glass-canopied shelter for Marcus and Rene Brumwell, on a headland overlooking the Fal estuary close to the site of the house, where they could sit out of the wind, enjoy a spectacular view, make tea and listen to the wireless.

After Team Four was dissolved, Foster started a new practice, Foster Associates, with his late wife, the architect Wendy Foster. Initially they worked on a series of simple, domestic projects, then designed a series of industrial buildings. The breakthrough projects were the offices for Willis Faber in Ipswich, and the Sainsbury Centre at the University of East Anglia, of which Buckminster Fuller (top) memorably asked, 'How much does your building weigh, Norman?'

Chermayeff offered a number of remedies to this wide-ranging series of crises facing the city. In his view, it is 'only through the restored opportunity for first-hand experience that privacy gives, that health and sanity can be brought back to the world of the mass culture ... Privacy is most urgently needed and most critical in the place where people live ... Traffic and noise must be treated as invaders. Man will have to design and build his own ecology.'

Chermayeff's answer to the problem of planning: 'It is urban hierarchy, demonstrated through an apparently endless series of diagrams exploring nodes and networks.'

It was a powerful manifesto, arguing in essence for an understanding of design at the level of the city rather than the individual building, and one which left an important mark on Foster. Initially, it was in his academic work. With Chermayeff's encouragement, he worked alongside a group of his fellow students on the City of Tomorrow competition, sponsored by the Ruberoid Company, that set out to shape the future of urbanism. This, his last project of the year at Yale, was based on many of the ideas contained in *Community and Privacy*, but it also provided a direction for his later career. In Chermayeff's writings, Foster found a distillation of the thoughts that he had begun to form in his speculations about urbanism. According to Chermayeff:

Maybe the day is not far off when planners, designers, development promoters, and other professionals recognize the mere fact that the space between buildings is just as important for the life of the urbanite as the buildings and that they act consequently. If the total land use is planned scrupulously to achieve an optimum use at any level, the inner city could hold just as many vertical, multi-purpose buildings of short term occupation as it could homes on ground level for families with children. Working as active parts in the technological urban context, these ground floor homes could be successful where suburbs have failed.

Foster and the rest of his group of students worked together on a sophisticated and highly accomplished master plan for a city that was based on Chermayeff's ideas of how a level of density that offered the vitality and intensity of a genuine metropolitan culture could still sustain the essentials of civilised life. As well as embodying a set of planning principles, it resulted in a very professional-looking large-scale model that could almost have emerged from the Foster + Partners office of today. The design was fleshed out by specific architectural proposals. In a knowing gesture, Foster inserted a version of the office tower that he had designed earlier at Yale, in his first semester, as the model for workplaces in the new city. Alongside them, the project included residential areas in the form of a high-density, anti-suburban model that was a realisation of some of the diagrams that were later to be published in *Community and Privacy* as a book.

Some of the other students were less impressed by Chermayeff's doctrinaire austerity than Foster. Thomas Beeby remembers of Chermayeff:

He was this arch-functionalist, right? So you had to justify everything you did functionally. He would stop and snort and carry on endlessly about how stupid people were. You had to sort of listen to all this. You were not allowed to do design, we constructed diagrams for 85 per cent of his studio and in the end he would let you design something that was supposedly a functional building. We had this sort of subversive thing going where he would get all his diagrams. Then the last part, which would be this enormous model, which was a stadium complex. It had to be a group project, it was part of the approach. Men don't work alone anymore, because that is what geniuses do, and architects are not geniuses.

Yale, as Foster remembers it, was a pressure cooker. The hours that trainee hospital doctors put in when they are on call have nothing on the addiction to work of a class of architectural students motivated by a teacher as demanding as Paul Rudolph. There was a sofa in the graduate studio, and students took turns to catch some sleep on it as they worked into the night, occasionally interrupted by Rudolph's habit of coming in unannounced for impromptu midnight tutorials. It was a pattern that was to set the pace for the twenty-four-hour working day at the Foster studio in Battersea, which never closes.

Every chance they got between the punishing schedule of design projects, round-the-clock work and presentations, Abbott and the British contingent would set off to see America, and all the key pieces of architecture that they had heard about on the way. They tracked down every Frank Lloyd Wright building within reach of New Haven that they could find, and talked their way inside most of them.

Money was short, so Abbott found himself having to pay for most of the petrol for the Volkswagen. Sometimes they stayed four to a room in cheap motels. When they got to Falling Water, Wright's most spectacular tour de force of domestic architecture, Abbott had to show Foster the gap in the fence, so that they could break in and save the price of buying tickets. They were stopped by the docents on the way out, but by this time they had already seen what they wanted and it was too late to make them pay.

They drove down to New York for bruisingly dry Martinis with James Stirling at the bar of the Four Seasons, the restaurant in the base of the Seagram Building designed by Philip Johnson. The maître d' spotted Stirling as he was slipping an ashtray into his overcoat pocket, and equally discreetly put it on the bill. They looked at Frank Lloyd Wright's recently opened Guggenheim Museum. They went to Greenwich Village to listen to jazz in smoke-filled rooms. In Chicago, they pored over the work of Louis Sullivan, Frank Lloyd Wright's mentor, and looked closely at the retractable sliding fire escapes in back alleys. They also looked at the Monadnock Building, designed at the end of the nineteenth century by Burnham and Root, as a forerunner of the modern skyscraper, and went to genuflect at the office of Mies van der Rohe.

Foster was looking not just at the acknowledged masterpieces. Using film as sparingly as possible to save money, he was photographing gas stations and Airstream caravans and crop-spraying equipment, and all the aspects of the American industrial vernacular that inspired so many British architects with its anonymous and effortless confidence.

They drove down to Philadelphia to hear Louis Kahn speak at the University of Pennsylvania in his semi-mystical way about allowing a brick to be what a brick wanted to be. Foster certainly learned lessons from Kahn, who had begun to explore what the impact of Buckminster Fuller's approach to geometry might be on high-rise architecture.

Foster and Rogers made the first halting steps towards starting an architectural practice together while they were still at Yale. Rogers had a friend in London, a landscape architect called Michael Branch, who had a modest plot of land and wanted to build on it. Foster and Rogers began to work on the design in a house on New Haven's outskirts, borrowed from the sculptor Naum Gabo, a friend of Su's parents.

Foster has a surviving drawing from that period on a fragment of yellow drafting paper. It shows a house strongly influenced by Louis Kahn, anchored by a massive chimney, and divided into distinct blocks. But Branch had trouble getting the money to build and the project seemed to peter out.

Foster graduated from Yale in the summer of 1962, in a marquee on the lawn at the centre of the university. It was a ceremony overshadowed by the glamorous lustre of the President of the United States, just ahead of the Cuban missile crisis. John F. Kennedy came to Yale to collect an honorary degree, and to deliver a speech that spoke of America's obligations to the world.

Foster stayed on the East Coast for a few more months. His town-planning qualification from Manchester got him a job with Pedersen and Tilney, a local firm working on urban renewal schemes in New Haven, that was his first practical experience of working beyond the scale of the individual building. Foster helped to find a way to secure Federal funding for a Pedersen and Tilney project in Massachusetts, arguing that the area had been blighted by a nearby airbase.

Then he drove to San Francisco by way of Cape Canaveral in a little sports car, an MGA, to work for Anshen and Allen. In those days they were regionalists, trying to find a contemporary architectural language to express the essential character of the Bay Area. In their hands it came to be associated with big roofs with swooping overhangs that seemed to owe a debt to Japanese construction. Foster worked for them on a competition to design the University of Southern California Santa Cruz campus.

He'd been there six months when a letter arrived from Rogers, who was by this time back in Britain. The house that they had started to design together for Michael Branch seemed to have finally come to life; Branch had decided to go ahead. And there was the prospect of more work for Su Rogers' father. Marcus Brumwell, who ran an advertising agency, had also been instrumental in setting up the Design Research Unit with Misha Black and Milner Grey, the first substantial design consultancy in Britain. The time was right for them to get on with their plans for starting an architectural practice together. Would Foster come back to Britain as soon as possible to get things started?

'I assumed that Su had written it. She wrote all the letters,' remembers Foster, who, despite his fondness for America, quickly decided that he had nothing to lose by giving the partnership a try. 'I could always go back to America,' he says.

And so he set off for Britain, this time taking the long way round. It was a journey that involved him making his first jet flight in a Comet 4B on Mexicana's Golden Aztec route from Los Angeles to Mexico City. 'It was such a beautiful aircraft to look at. It was so beautiful on the outside that even inside the cabin, it transformed the whole experience of flying.' Foster went from Mexico to the West Indies, and from there flew by way of Brussels, back to Manchester to spend a few days with his parents. He had kept in touch through sporadic letter writing over the last eighteen months, but they were surprised to see him back so soon after he had got a job in San Francisco, and even more concerned to see him almost immediately disappearing again, off to London to start his own architectural practice. 'Perhaps I had not been very clear about how I explained what I was doing. They had imagined I would be staying longer in Manchester.'

Team Four was a name carefully chosen to suggest an aversion to narcissistic self-publicity. It was hinting broadly at a collaborative approach, but also referred back to the distinguished theoretical group Team Ten, that had tried to rewrite the agenda for post-war architecture. It also had the not entirely uncoincidental echo of the kind of name that a pop group might use. Team Four lasted barely four years, from the day in 1963 when it was established in Wendy Cheeseman's flat in Hampstead, to its dissolution amid some bickering in 1967, just about the point when the firm ran out of work. Team Four produced only a handful of buildings, notably the house for Marcus and Rene Brumwell in Cornwall, and a now-demolished electronics factory in Swindon for Reliance Controls, along with some relatively modest houses in Camden Mews, and the so-called Skybreak House in Hertfordshire that achieved a moment of notoriety when it was used as one of the interior sets for Stanley Kubrick's *Clockwork Orange*.

But even if it was brief, the Team Four experience served to ignite the careers of two of the key figures in the architecture of the last years of the twentieth century, and the start of the twenty-first. And it was in the Team Four office that Norman Foster met his first wife, the architect Wendy Cheeseman. Rogers, who introduced them, had known both Wendy and her older sister Georgie – also an architect – for years. Both the Cheeseman and Rogers families lived in Surrey, and Rogers got to know Georgie when they were studying at the Architectural Association. Wendy had been at what was then called the

Regent Street Polytechnic in London. After graduating in 1963, she worked for a while in a small Bloomsbury office. Her economical, coolly elegant pencil drawings for her diploma project reveal an accomplished draughtswoman, with a sophisticated approach to architecture that clearly made a substantial contribution to Team Four. When Rogers came to consider setting up the practice, he invited the two sisters to join him and Norman as partners.

All of the people Rogers had lined up had practical advantages and could bring something to the practice that Rogers could not. Wendy Cheeseman had the flat in Hampstead Hill Gardens with a large front room that would make a useful office for the practice. Georgie was the only one of them who was fully qualified and registered as an architect, and so an essential member of the practice if Team Four were to be legally entitled to call themselves architects. And Foster could not only draw, he had a way of getting things done.

The office was on the first floor at 16B Hampstead Hill Gardens. Initially, Wendy lived in the room at the back, keeping the kitchen as part of her private domain. Foster remembers being less than impressed to discover that getting to the office involved walking through the kind of domestic door that normally gave access to a bedsit. But by 1964 Norman and Wendy had got married, disappearing off in their lunch hour one day for the ceremony, with no family and just a few friends present, then stopping off on the way back to Hampstead Hill Gardens from the registry office for a picnic on the Heath.

'We worked very closely together, and then quickly became close in every way,' says Foster. 'We decided to get married first, to present it as a fait accompli, and then to have the celebrations later.'

Just before Christmas in 1965, Wendy gave birth to their first child, Ti Foster. She named him for Jack Kerouac, author of *On the Road*, a book that was important to her. Kerouac's family and friends had always called him Ti-jean, and Wendy took the name for her son. It was a home birth, a reflection of Wendy's continuing antipathy towards modern medicine.

By this time, the Fosters had made a family home not far from the office in Hampstead. They moved from Lyndhurst Gardens to a house in Thurlow Road, and then again to Frognal, very close by, where the sculptor Anthony Caro was a neighbour. Caro became a close friend and, eventually, a collaborator on the design for the Millennium Footbridge across the Thames.

When Foster and Wendy started living together, they had to share their first home with an increasingly busy office and a secretary, Sophie, who happened to be the distinguished critic Herbert Read's daughter, and kept a large Afghan hound under her desk. Foster would walk in through one door from the back of the flat in the mornings, and meet people coming in from the outside door. On one occasion, the bedroom was pressed into service as a meeting room, with the bed transformed into a conference table with the addition of a hurriedly fabricated plywood cover. The sound of typing issuing from the bedroom was used to provide a reassuring suggestion of administrative competence.

There was a steady flow of students in search of work, many of whom would eventually do very well on their own after spending time in the office.

'We were camping out there, and eventually the office took over the whole space,' remembers Foster.

To subsidise the practice in its early days, Foster started teaching as a part-timer at the Regent Street Polytechnic and at the Architectural Association. The Cheeseman sisters, though outwardly financially secure – their father was an insurance broker who had been chairman of Lloyds – were fiercely independent, and determined to make their own way without relying on family money.

Foster recalls:

> We were doing buildings for people who were our guinea pigs because they happened to be friends and relations. They were small domestic projects which are the most difficult things to do because you don't really have the experience. You're learning on the project. In some ways that makes you more resourceful. You end up perhaps being more self-auditing than if you had the benefit of experience.

Some of the tics that have distinguished Foster's subsequent working methods were already present in the Team Four days. For a project to extend Wendy's mother's house in Surrey, one unfortunate student assistant remembers being asked to make models of variation after variation on a fireplace, until they reached a total of fourteen.

Georgie, who had a young family to concentrate on, did not stay long. Her rapid departure deprived the practice of its only qualified architect, which left the survivors professionally vulnerable. To Foster's fury, Team Four found themselves under investigation by the professional practice committee of the Architects Registration Council of the United Kingdom who warned them that, since they had no registered architects in their partnership, they were breaking the law by calling themselves Team Four Architects. Foster was all for refusing to deal with their tormentors except through lawyers.

In the event, however, he went back to his old employer, John Beardshaw, for help. Beardshaw agreed to give them the umbrella of professional status by offering a loose association with his London office until they managed to get their own qualifications in place. They also started looking for a replacement for Georgie, but all the prospective qualified candidates baulked at the possibility, despite the food and drink they were plied with.

The very first project Foster built is a tiny glass capsule sunk into a green Cornish headland overlooking the estuary of the Fal River. Foster and Richard Rogers worked on it together in 1964 when they were partners in Team Four. Their client, Marcus Brumwell, wanted a place in which to shelter out of the wind and to watch sailing regattas on summer weekends. It was somewhere for him to make tea in the sun, to sit and read, or listen to the Third Programme on his portable wireless while he and his wife, Rene, waited for Team Four to hurry up and finish Creak Vean, the house that they had commissioned from them. It was a house that Brumwell paid for by selling the canvas that he had bought in the 1930s from a penniless Piet Mondrian, when the artist was briefly in London on his way through Britain to America.

In other hands the shelter project would have been called a gazebo, and would no doubt have turned out looking like a garden shed. Team Four gave it a sunken profile and covered it with a glass canopy that was opened by sliding it back, like the cockpit of a Spitfire, as if it were the crashed aircraft that Foster remembered from his wartime childhood. It was modest in scale, but Team Four asked Tony Hunt, the structural engineer who was later to play a vital role in the design of the Sainsbury Centre, to have a careful look at the foundations in order to ensure that its concrete base didn't go disappearing down the hill on a mudslide. When I saw it, ten years after Brumwell's death, the glass was discoloured and stained with moss. Watched over by cows and sea gulls, the shelter had half folded into the landscape like the ruin of a neolithic barrow, translated to the twentieth century.

Team Four was too unstable a mix of personalities to last for long. Architectural partnerships that survive are the ones in which each partner brings something different to the practice, and does not feel threatened by competition from the others. With Rogers and Foster, no matter how close they had been at Yale, there was an inevitable jockeying for position. Both of them were determined to make their own way. Both of them were natural leaders. But both of them were in the slightly uncomfortable position of feeling to some extent dependent on their wives. Both wanted to design. Both wanted to shape the practice. As Paul Rudolph had once said, 'It's either your work, or it's the other guy's.'

'All the things that brought us together, had in them the seeds that would provoke us to go in our own directions in a relatively short period of time,' says Foster. The immediate cause of the rift was the ambiguous status of Richard's wife Su in the office. Never trained as an architect, she had not formally been made a partner at the time Team Four started, and neither Rogers nor Foster quite knew how to deal with the situation as her interest in architecture and the practice grew. Rather than address the question head-on, they avoided it, and took the decision to dissolve the partnership, dividing what little work there was between them.

It was inevitably a painful dissolution, though without lasting rancour. Foster and Rogers became closer again after Team Four dissolved. For many years they remained identified with a particular moment in British architecture. But both had different ideas about how to turn their shared principles into their own distinct buildings. Foster outlines their differences thus:

> Richard is much more interested in the potential for expression, of the structure and the services, and the potential for the dramatisation of that. I'd say that if I tried to make a simple generalisation I'm more interested in the potential for the ways that things can integrate. In other words, at some point someone saw that there was an engine and a chasis, and somehow if you could dissolve the two together, so that they would work together. The way in which a building similarly integrates the different aspects rather than necessarily seeking to dramatise any one of those elements is what interests me.

It's been a continuing dialogue between them that had a public hearing in a discussion at the home of the architect Robin Spence one night in the 1980s, when Foster and Rogers talked helicopters, with Rogers enthusing about the Bell 47 D1 with its exposed space frame structure, while Foster preferred the more contemporary high-performance fully enclosed skin of Bell Jet Ranger, a contrast that might be seen as encapsulating two different philosophical positions. The 47 D1 shows how every piece relates to every other piece, shows off its components and its connections. The Jet Ranger is an integrated sculptural form, shaped for high performance. Both are beautiful in very different ways. Foster, who has flown both machines, sees the Jet Ranger as the more advanced of the two, and thus the one which has had the greater longevity. That Foster feels more drawn to the perfection of the Jet Ranger, like a huge Brancusi, than to the legibility of a mechanism suggests a mind that is attracted to discipline and tight control, and a personality that looks for expression in objects that may be hard to read.

At the Reliance Controls building, Foster insisted on fixing the fluorescent lights into the corrugations of the metal ceiling, in the same way that the heating is incorporated seamlessly into the floor, doing away with separate fittings. It took a lot more effort, but it had the effect of making them disappear into the background. Rogers could not understand why Foster wanted to do it. A more sophisticated version of the idea would much later provide the starting point for a sequence of low-energy projects in Germany.

Over the next four decades, Foster's and Rogers' careers were continually to interact with each other. They would find themselves competing for the same jobs. Every so often they would meet up and discuss working together again, even con-sidering setting up a joint practice. None of these ideas came to anything. But in 1986, when an architectural profession reeling from the onslaught of the Prince of Wales on its competence fought back with a high-profile exhibition of contemporary design at the Royal Academy, it took the form of a three-man show, with equal billing for Foster, Rogers and their one-time tutor at Yale, James Stirling.

Each of them showed one completed and one unbuilt project. Foster gave one room to a spectacular multimedia representation of the newly completed Hong Kong and Shanghai Bank, and another to the BBC Radio headquarters in Portland Place, a scheme that was about to fall victim to Margaret Thatcher's vendetta against the corporation after a huge amount of work had been invested in it. It was cancelled just before the exhibition opened.

Rogers showed the Lloyds building, and a scheme for remodelling London's relationship with the Thames. There were clear parallels between Lloyds and the Bank, yet also differences. Lloyds used concrete for its structure, while HSBC was made from steel.

As the two practices continued to grow, their approaches diverged more and more. Just how far apart the two architects eventually became can be seen on Wood Street in the City of London, where the two of them each finished office buildings just after the turn of the millennium.

There is no better place to understand the history of postwar British architecture and the way in which one generation has reacted against the previous one. Wood Street was originally created by the Romans as a route to the parade ground of a fort located just outside the city wall. And it has been collecting architectural monuments ever since. In the course of just fifty yards, it boasts a tower designed by Christopher Wren, which is the last surviving relic of a church that originally started out as the royal chapel of the Saxon kings. There is a remarkable police station built in the early 1960s by McMorran & Whitby, in dignified classical style. A Terry Farrell Art Deco-inspired tower rears over the street at one end, demonstrating the high-water mark of the property boom of the 1980s. The next eruption of development came fifteen years later, and is represented by a pair of buildings, one by Rogers, the other by Foster. Richard Rogers' firm designed a headquarters on the corner of Wood Street, facing towards London Wall at number

88, and, immediately next to it is an office block at number 100 designed by Norman Foster.

Look at these two buildings and you can get a sense of exactly how much two architects who began their careers working together have diverged. Foster has pursued integration in his work. Rogers' approach, on the other hand, believed in articulation. The Wood Street building explored new territory for Foster. It has a Portland stone façade with a deliberately anonymous, chequer-board rhythm of alternating storey-height stone panels and rectangular glass windows that shift back and forth, one bay at a time, on each level. It is a mannerism calculated to show that this is a building that does not share the sensibility of its more conventional stone-clad neighbour, on the side away from the Rogers building, which plays by the old rules. To underscore the point, Foster has put a vertical black line to cut himself off from that building. He does not touch Rogers, his other neighbour, at all.

On the other side of the air gap from Foster, Rogers has stuck to what his office does best – romantic modernity. By pulling the structure, stairs and lifts out of the basic envelope, he creates a jagged, picturesque skyline. The piece closest to Foster is wall-to-wall glass, in an elegant concrete frame that is braced by gunmetal grey and stainless steel rods.

Round the corner, there is some muscular, exposed cross-bracing, beautifully rendered in stainless steel that has the delicacy of jewellery. There is even a touching little cabbage patch of sprouting red and blue funnels to remind us that this is the work of the firm that built the Pompidou Centre. This being a Rogers building, the cascades of steel stairs like streamers inside are painted bright yellow.

We talk about buildings as if they were individual works of

art, to be understood as discrete aesthetic experiences. But in a dense city like London, they can't exist in isolation. They are inevitably seen as part of a street or in the context of one street interacting with another. And the junction of Foster's and Rogers' buildings is centre stage, visible in long views as well as close up. In contrast to his stone front on Wood Street, at the back of the building Foster has scooped out a curved glass skin, hoisted up on a colonnade of raked steel legs. London is a city divided between two kinds of office building: the generic developed for the rental market, and the tailor-made for the owner-occupier. For Foster, the generic projects, like Wood Street, are contextual, the product of a negotiation between site, developer and planners. The specific, like Rogers' Lloyds building or Foster's Swiss Re, are exceptions with the potential to develop a more distinctive identity.

In the closing months of 1967, there was no discernable division between Richard Rogers and Norman Foster. Their work as Team Four was apparently indivisible, the product of both their sensibilities, even if the seeds for their divergence were already sown. There has never been, nor could there be, given the nature of their partnership, a dissection of what aspect of the buildings that the two worked on was the product of one more than the other. Team Four had outwardly been seamless. What came next for Foster had to be based on something else.

Three

How much does your building weigh?

In the wake of the dissolution of Team Four, Foster and his wife, heavily pregnant with their second son, Cal, set up Foster Associates. It was an ambitious name for a tiny architectural practice consisting of just the two of them, sitting in their Hampstead Hill Gardens studio designing kitchens and bathrooms from their drawing boards while looking out over Hampstead Heath. But at least they didn't have to sleep in their office. The Fosters had moved out of Hampstead Hill Gardens, leaving what had been Wendy's flat to the firm. It was a struggle to survive. Foster was still teaching part-time and the office needed whatever work it could get.

One early client was the editor of the *Sunday Times* magazine, Ron Hall, who lived just around the corner and got them to extend his living room and build a patio. As Hall remembers it, he picked Foster Associates simply because it was the nearest architectural practice to his house when he looked in the telephone directory. Hall suggests that Wendy Foster was the one who did most of the work on his house. There was also a job to design a clothes shop for boys, called the Orange Hand, distinguished by a singularly aggressive logo in the shape of a neon fist. But most of Foster's apparently limitless energy went into architectural competitions and speculative projects.

Working with Alan Stanton, his first new employee recruited straight after graduating from the Architectural Association, Foster poured everything that he had learned in California from the skinny metal and glass sheds that Charles Eames envisaged as the basis for a new industrial vernacular, into a competition design for a school in Newport. It was a development of the elegant structure of Reliance Controls, and had a deep roof that would later inspire the Sainsbury Centre. Foster didn't win. James Stirling, who was the most forceful member of the jury, put his considerable weight behind Foster's classmate at Yale, Eldred Evans. Nevertheless, Foster's drawings got a lot of attention. A few years later he was nonplussed for a moment when a bright young architect called Spencer de Grey came for a job interview. His portfolio included a school that he had just finished building for a local authority in London that had a very close resemblance to Foster's unbuilt design for the Newport competition. After pausing for thought, Foster hired de Grey, who has worked with him ever since.

Foster had trouble getting that first key job that every architect starting out on their own needs. He thought about going back to America with Wendy and their children. 'Everything was a closed shop to us. The universities were done by ex-local authority architects. Local authorities handled housing themselves, and developers just used developers' architects.' Despite having won the *Financial Times* Industrial Architecture Award for the Reliance building, Foster was reduced to writing letters to sympathetic senior architects begging for work, or even for any advice that might lead to getting some work.

But Foster was not giving up. And he certainly wasn't going to work for anybody else:

> It was a latent impatience, I suppose, and a feeling that unless you are doing something, you are not contributing. After spending five years at university, getting a master's degree in America and teaching, working for somebody else did not seem like the real thing. Given the degree of impatience that I had, and the absolute gut determination to build, I was going to find a way to make a breakthrough.

Stanton remembers Foster's relentless energy. 'He would drive us up to Derby in his tiny sports car to look at the Fletcher and Stewart building that we were working on there, a project left over from Team Four, and get us back the same morning in time for coffee. I had never seen anything like Norman's approach.'

Foster's experience with Reliance Controls suggested that the best strategy for getting work was to take up a position as the most accomplished and the most professional designer of factories in Britain: 'The only territory that had not been taken over was industrial architecture, perhaps because it was not posh enough, or not intellectual enough, or because architects did not want to dirty their hands.' He wasn't the only young British architect at the time to have spotted the opportunity. Nicholas Grimshaw had a similar strategy.

Through a mix of accident and calculation, Foster turned a chance contact with a client who didn't believe that he needed an architect at all into a commission that created a building nobody had envisaged, on a site that hadn't existed, but which, when it was finished, seemed astonishingly assured and startlingly unexpected in its location and its content.

'Apparently it is a well-scripted route to success. You get a start where nobody has penetrated before, and you command that domain and that allows you to make the leap to other areas,' says Foster.

One of the students in Foster's office, Barry Copeland, had a father working for Fred. Olsen Line in Millwall. Copeland casually mentioned that the Olsen organisation was thinking of doing something about installing showers for its workforce. Foster recalls: 'It was no big deal, they weren't thinking of using architects, they were talking to builders about getting something straightforward run up in a hurry to placate the dockers.' Foster had the scent of a job, and was not going to give up until he had it in his grasp. He got the name of Olsen's dock manager, Mike Thompson, and went to see him.

Foster arrived an hour before the interview and spent the time looking at the ships tied up on the wharf. He had already discovered that Fred. Olsen was a Norwegian family-owned business, whose main trade was with the Canary Islands. On the outward journey, its ships carried a mixed cargo. They came back loaded up with bananas. Olsen combined this trade with holidays and cruises. Thompson was expecting a builder rather than the young architect who came to see him in fashionably long side burns, with a portfolio that included precious little in the way of completed buildings.

'I asked him to show me what they were doing,' remembers Foster. 'I asked him about their future plans, he talked about a social revolution.' Three years earlier, Lord Devlin had chaired a Royal Commission charged with finding a way to deal with festering labour relations in the docks and modernise the system of casual labour in Britain's ports that, aside from the arrival of the fork lift, had hardly changed since Nelson's time. Gangs of dockers were still hired by the day through an intricate network of small employers to unload cargo, ship by ship, with no job security, no pensions, and squalid working conditions. 'They were treated like animals,' remembers Foster. But by striking without warning, they could leave food to rot, or cripple Britain's car industry by holding up deliveries of components. Generally the employers had no option but to settle their claims. In the days before containerisation, pilfering was endemic, and the whole process of loading and unloading became unnecessarily slow, and unjustifiably costly. Harold Wilson's Labour government believed that the country was being blackmailed by a group of dockers described by Devlin's committee as 'wreckers and economic saboteurs'.

The Millwall in which Norman Foster found himself in 1969 was an angry and confrontational place, home to a white working class that saw itself as dispossessed and on the edge of oblivion. Its hinterland was the birthplace of the skinhead cult, scarred by the recurrent street violence associated with Millwall Football Club's fearsome supporters, and fertile ground for the fascist National Front. The famous communist militant Jack Dash led his last strike there in 1969. It was the place in which Enoch Powell's wild and inflammatory assault on black immigration, predicting rivers of blood, drew its strongest support. There were marches to Parliament by dockers demanding compulsory repatriation for immigrants.

Foster was disgusted to find segregated lavatories for whites and non-whites. But he set about creating a job for himself, and then produced as coolly elegant a building as he could. With the conviction of an architect whose eyes are fixed on the distant horizon, he suggested that it would wipe away the traces of the class war and the squalor of the past.

Olsen's new approach was a response to the Devlin plan. In exchange for simplifying the fossilised structure of their working practices, dockers would get regular employment and modern working conditions. The scheme allowed for the introduction of shipping containers that speeded up the unloading and loading process, and made cargo less vulnerable to what was politely termed 'shrinkage'.

Olsen was planning to build a simple shed to give its workforce the basic amenities that they lacked. Thompson showed Foster his plans, and talked about changing work patterns. Foster looked at the layout. It gave him the chance to launch an attention-grabbing opening gambit. As things stood, he suggested, Olsen was proposing to put its new building in exactly the wrong place, one that would be a costly waste of money:

> 'You have all your people working on the quayside, yet you are talking about putting the amenities over here. When they have a tea break or go for a shower, do you realise how long it will take for them to walk there and back? Have you factored that in? Aside from convenience, time is obviously money.'

Foster pointed at another site, directly on the waterfront. 'Why not put it here?' he asked.

'Ah well, you are not to know, the Port Authority is building two huge sheds there, with a big gap between the two,' replied Thompson. 'So I asked, "What is that big gap for?"' Thompson didn't know, but he was intrigued enough to challenge Foster to find out, and in effect to give him two weeks to draw up a more considered plan to deal with the site.

Foster discovered that the Port of London Authority had

decided to build its two sheds as cheaply as it could. Instead of fireproofing the walls between them to stop fire spreading, they planned to leave a gap wide enough to stop the flames. With the right construction techniques, the gap could be a good place to build not just the dockers' locker room and showers, but also the offices that the management needed.

Foster carried the Olsen block in his mind everywhere he went for the entire twelve intense months that it took to design and build it. He made the sketches, and drew the kind of perspectives that attempt to convey an architect's ideas to his client. And he churned out the grinding stack of production drawings that the builder needed to get started. In a big architectural office, there are assistants to work out how to pack insulation into the roof, and how to fit two large pieces of glass together carefully so that they don't let in the rain, or crack in strong winds. When an office has successfully done things before, it has precedents to rely on to save time and effort. It's the way that architects develop a signature. They treat doors and windows the same way in successive projects, they develop a confidence in using certain techniques because they have seen them work before. In the early days of Foster Associates, it wasn't like that. Everything was new, everything was a risk. Everything needed to be tested and prototyped. Foster had to go out to find the components that he needed to be able to build his drawings.

It's the most truly hands-on project I have ever gone through, in terms of a totality, in terms of being the guy on site as well as doing the full-size drawings. There are some things you never forget. I can still remember the Olsen building's critical dimensions in the same way that I can remember the number they gave me when I was in the airforce. And I can still remember the critical structural dimensions in feet and inches for the Reliance factory.

The Olsen amenities block did two startling things. The first was to ignore the class-ridden nature of the standard British workplace of 1969. The most militant and difficult workforce in London was being swept into a world that would be as unfamiliar for Millwall's dockers, and as transformational for them, Foster hoped, as his own experience of arriving at Yale from Levenshulme. The Olsen restaurant, with its green fibreglass Charles Eames-designed chairs, its mint green carpet and its purple-painted steel staircase, looked more like a California beach house than a works canteen in the heart of one of the toughest working-class districts in Britain. It seemed a better fit for Mediterranean cuisine than bacon sandwiches. There was art from Fred Olsen's personal collection hanging on the office walls, table tennis and snooker, a television lounge and twenty-four-hour opening for the café. If espresso for the masses had been invented yet, Olsen would certainly have offered it. Like his student project at Manchester, in which he had proposed combining a boathouse and a cottage in the same building, Foster's idea for Olsen was to put everybody, management and dockers, in the same building. He insisted that they should share it with a sense of evangelistic conviction that came in part from his own experiences in the factories and warehouses of Manchester with their works entrances and their outside lavatories. At first, the idea was greeted with suspicion both by the union and by management. 'Mike Thompson told me that you simply could not put dockers and managers together in the same building. The site management claimed that the dockers were dirty, that they used bad language, and that it would never work.'

Foster had to go to Fred Olsen himself to get his way. Olsen's personal support allowed Foster to take on a quasi-management role, dealing directly with the dockers on the building, on behalf of the company. After the project was finished, Foster went back to Millwall and saw the docker's shop steward. He shook Foster's hand and asked him what he thought of the building now. Foster said, 'It looks good, but I am a bit disturbed about all the temporary caravans on the forecourt selling hot dogs. What has gone wrong, don't you like the canteen?'

The shop steward answered, 'You don't understand, that's not for us, it's for the truck drivers who don't work for Olsen. We couldn't possibly let them into our building.'

Fred Olsen was taken enough with what Foster had done to ask him to build a passenger terminal next to the amenities block, and to design his travel agency in Regent Street. He went on to work on a plan for Olsen's Vestby headquarters building in Norway, and on an even more ambitious master plan for Gomera, a resort island in the Canaries.

The ideas on which the Gomera scheme was based were astonishingly advanced for the time. Asked to design an airport, and a road around the entire island, Foster suggested instead that the way to stop the place from turning into another Benidorm was to provide a ferry service from the main island rather than rely on an airport to fly in visitors. He envisaged a set of dead-end feeder roads, rather than despoiling the coastline with a ring road and a runway. There was provision for solar energy and wind power, and grey water recycling. None of it happened, at least under Foster's direction, and most of the design work was done without Olsen paying much in the way of fees, just enough for it to be worthwhile opening an office in Norway. For Foster, the idea of having larger and more ambitious jobs to work on was important. He and Birkin Haward, one of the most gifted draughtsmen to work with Foster in the early days, drew and drew, in the hope that their seductive images would persuade Olsen to invest in them.

From the point of view of the architectural world, even more remarkable than the exercise in social engineering that Olsen represented was the fact that it was the first building in Britain to be wrapped in a glass skin with no visible means of support. Foster set out to create a building that went to extremes in the elegant refinement of its simplicity. By making the metal structure of the wall entirely invisible – the only trace on the outside of what held the glass in place was the black neoprene strip at the level of the first floor – Foster created something that looked quite different from anything that had been done before. The assembly drawings got on to the cover of Japanese magazines.

The Olsen building filled the gap between warehouses on either side, and its roof was designed to span all the way between them, without any supporting columns getting in the way. The difficult thing about that was how to allow for the roof to flex up and down if there was nothing propping it. Simply hanging rigid sheets of glass off a steel structure was not an option, given that it was inevitably going to bend. Foster's solution was to support the glass wall by sitting it on the ground, and to put slots in the window mullions that left space for the roof to move without doing any damage to the glass. The impact of wind on the glass was dealt with by using the first floor inside the skin to brace it.

Glass, forty years later, has become the universal architectural skin for almost every new office building in London. For better or worse, they are all Olsen's children, even if they lack its aesthetic and technical sophistication.

In 1969, however, glass on this scale was unheard of. Olsen's schedule meant that the builders had just a year to finish the project, and there wasn't anybody in Europe who was prepared to make the glass to the sizes Foster wanted in time. At 4.25 x 1.8 metres wide, the panes were huge. And they would need a sophisticated set of specially made fixing components to create the substructure needed to keep it safely in place. When he first suggested it, the contractors hired to build the structure and every specialist subcontractor in Britain said flatly that it couldn't be done. But Foster wasn't going to allow this to stop him from getting his way. He immediately set out to prove everyone wrong.

He knew of a manufacturer in America who had recently devised an off-the-peg curtain wall system that could do the job, and had the capacity to make the size of sheets of glass that he was after. 'Nobody in Britain could make a glass wall. There is the Pittco T wall system, yes, but that is from America. Britain is different. So I set out to slaughter that particular sacred cow, the one that says that we couldn't do what they could do in America, even if it meant importing it.'

But there was very little time. If the glass was going to reach Millwall and get fitted to the steel structure at the right moment, he had to get started immediately. Without stopping to think about whether his client was going to pay his expenses, he flew to Pittsburgh, home of the Pittsburgh Patent Glazing Corporation, to see what they had to offer.

Foster recalls arriving in Pittsburgh to find the company's representative waiting for him at the airport. 'The president is very keen to see you,' he said. Foster replied, 'This isn't a social visit. I have forty-eight hours to do the shop drawings, I have to go back to Britain with them.' The response was that this would not be possible: 'It's nothing to do with us here. You need to be in Kokomo, Indiana.'

Foster turned back into the airport and caught the next flight to Indiana. The company put on two extra shifts to work around the clock with him, and he left with a complete set of shop drawings, delineating everything needed to give the Olsen building its suave skin.

When he got back, Foster found the contractor, assuming that he would fail to deliver in time, had allowed for a six-week delay. So Foster succeeded in getting the glass to London, but the components sat in a shed while the builders caught up with the programme.

For Foster, one important lesson that he learned from Olsen, and also his experiences with the Willis Faber Building, was that it was possible to design special components rather than relying on what was already on the market.

If you have enough curiosity in the production process, you soon discover that you can design your own curtain wall, or your own ceiling, and have it made in the same time as ordering an existing design from a catalogue. The chances are that you will end up with a better product, and the cost will probably not be that different. If you come up with a good design, the likelihood is that your product will appear in someone else's catalogue for another architect to specify in a different context. So if you go to Jim Stirling's Staatsgalerie in Stuttgart, you will find the same studded rubber flooring that we developed for Willis Faber. Or go to shopping malls the world over and you will find escalators where you can see the insides moving. They did not exist before we did Willis Faber, but now they have become part of a universal building vocabulary.

Given the money that he spent on his flights, and on hiring Tim Street Porter, the most glamorous architectural photographer in London at the time, to record the working lives of the dockers before building started, it is hard to believe that Foster made anything out of Olsen financially. But Foster has always invested enthusiastically in doing things with a certain style.

There were underlying differences between the Foster way of working and the conventional approach to architectural practice. He had begun to understand that the best approach to take when tendering for a job was to ask lots of questions before offering any answers of his own. 'In presentations, our competitors would talk about how their building would look. We just asked questions, and listened. Then we would go away, and we would come back, and ask some more questions. We made sure we understood both the functional and the social aspects of what they wanted.'

He really did believe in opening up the design process beyond architects. He would get Tony Hunt, the engineer, John Walker, a cost consultant, and Loren Butt, a services engineer, sitting around a table, and say, 'Right, how are we going to design this building?'

At the beginning he had a close association with Martin Francis, who had trained at the Central School of Art and Design as a furniture designer, and who ended up designing yachts. Later, David Nelson joined the team. He had come from Hornsey art school and through the Royal College of Art, and had never taken a conventional architectural qualification either.

Foster was very suspicious of professional hierarchies, which, as he saw it, got in the way of getting the best out of a project.

> You are expected to design a building in isolation from any of the other professions and then you hand it over for them to make it stand up. In Manchester, as a student, if you were taught structures at all, there was no connection to the way that you might actually design a building. The assumption was that somebody backstage would take on the design, and find a way do it.

Foster's strategy had first taken shape in his mind while he was still at Yale, working on a student project for Paul Rudolph that was to become, in embryonic form, the basis for the Hong Kong bank. His idea for a tower building that turned a corner, evolved in a series of conversations with a creative engineer. 'I remember saying to Rudolph that to have an engineer understand what as an architect I might feel, somebody who would help shape that building, was vital. He recommended somebody to work with, and that gave the design a very different spirit from the more conventional way of doing things.'

Foster built Foster Associates to replicate that experience. Not many conventional architects' offices at that time would have hired Loren Butt, an environmental engineer who was working for a services contractor when Foster met him, so that he could become involved with the design of buildings from the outset, rather than being called in after the fact to come up with fixes for any flaws.

As Foster puts it, these were engineers who had always been trained to respond to architects by asking them what they wanted, and then coming up with somewhere to put the plumbing, and then provide an estimate of what it would cost. With Foster it wasn't a question of where to put the pipes – the Pavlovian response, as he put it. Instead, it was getting to an understanding of the fundamental idea of how you might make a building feel comfortable to be in, whether that involved pipes or not. That allowed for leapfrogging problems, rather than being more or less ingenious about dealing with what might actually turn out to be the right answer to the wrong question. Once, when Fred Olsen was asked to give a reference for Foster, he said of him, 'He will ask the right questions.'

There were other aspects of the Foster Associates' approach that would become more apparent as time went on. Foster has a way of treating architecture as if it were a form of industrial design, prototyping components, attempting to achieve the economies of scale that come from mass production, rather than relying on an intuitive on-site building process.

Architecture leaves precious little time for anything else. Norman Foster has filled his life beyond it with flying, and a punishing combination of marathon running, long-distance cycling and cross-country skiing.

In the early days of his practice with Wendy, Foster barely saw people out of the office. The two of them would go home to Hampstead, where she would cook with care and imagination, and over the meal they would analyse the working day, think about their next steps, and plan how to deal with their employees and their clients. Wendy Foster had the worldliness to help him direct his energies in the most effective way.

By 1970, Norman Foster was financially successful enough to be able to rediscover the idea of flying that had first surfaced in his mind in childhood. One summer weekend, on a family outing to Dunstable Downs, he looked up and saw a succession of gliders manoeuvring in the sky. 'I thought that they were the most beautiful objects I had ever seen, more beautiful than a Brancusi,' he remembers. If this apotheosis had happened earlier, he might never have become an architect. 'I would certainly have been a professional pilot, civil or military,' he says. It also introduced him to a world of flying and flyers that was very different in its language and its preoccupations from that of the architects he knew.

Foster was interested enough in what he saw to walk down the hill from his picnic into the London Gliding Club, where he was offered a demonstration flight in a two-man glider. He was hooked at once. He quickly bought himself a new high-performance German-made fibreglass sail plane, the *Libelle*, the first aircraft to be made entirely from plastic. Not content with drifting on the thermals above the countryside, Foster threw himself into competitive gliding. He bought a succession of racing gliders: a Finnish PIK, and then a string of ASWs, also from Germany. Weekend after weekend, Foster towed his craft up to Dunstable behind his Range Rover, covering up to 250 kilometres in the air in a session. He started to seek out places that he could achieve greater and greater distances. He went to Texas for one marathon, and Pennsylvania for another.

In a race you are pushing for speed and distance. You have to judge the light, you have to read clouds in the sky, or feel your way in blue conditions. If you really work a powerful thermal, you are doing what would be called aerobatics in a light aircraft.

It was a sport that developed Foster's peripheral vision, a skill needed for him to be able simultaneously to look ahead and also to keep track of the horizon line in relation to his wing tips.

But the adrenaline rush of racing gliders was not enough to keep him interested for long. Foster quickly moved on to powered flight. Within two years he had learned to fly both competitive aerobatics in a French CAP 10 and helicopters, and finally commercial jets. Each of them became, for a while, obsessive interests. It is an unusual progression; most enthusiasts stick to just one or two forms of flight. Foster mastered all of them – going as far as taking the controls in a Hawk military jet trainer and flying a Spitfire himself. 'They are totally different cultures, even if they are all apparently about the same thing. I put down a helicopter next to a glider at a meet once, and somebody made a disparaging remark. I silenced them when I turned and explained that I knew all about the effects of downwash on gliders.'

For years, flying filled all Foster's life outside architecture. He has accumulated 109 log books charting every hour spent flying every type. While so many architects are only truly comfortable with other architects, Foster is not one of them. He finds it easier to spend time with people who fly planes, or, like him, push themselves on skis or bicycles to extreme limits.

Indeed, Foster's present wife Elena, whom he met in 1994, realised that the only way that she could fully share his life was to overcome her fear of flight, to earn a pilot's licence of her own, and, like her husband, become a cross-country skier.

Foster had expected that his father would be the first of his parents to die, as he had always suffered poor health. He remembered the shock of seeing, as a nine-year-old child, his father brought home from work one night, dangerously ill, and rushed to hospital with a perforated ulcer. But despite this and other serious illnesses, Robert Foster outlived his wife.

Lilly died suddenly, after having a heart attack in her doctor's surgery. On the day that it happened, Foster was out of his office, travelling back from a site visit to the Willis Faber Building. Michael Hopkins, his partner at the time, took the call from Foster's father, and had to tell him the bad news. Five years later, in 1976, his father was dead too, of lung cancer. Neither of his parents ever saw any of their son's buildings completed, although they had been to visit their grandchildren in Hampstead where Foster was living by the time that they were born. Foster's eldest son, Ti, remembers visiting his grand-parents in Levenshulme, and seeing his father's bedroom kept exactly as it had been when he lived there; his rucksack on the bed, his drawing table by the window.

The death of his mother left a deep mark. In 1991, when both his parents had been dead for almost twenty years, Foster had a sharp urge to find out more about his mother while there were still people left alive who had known her and might be able to tell him about the circumstances of her birth. He met his cousin Lionel Beckett, at that time working for IBM, and took him to lunch at Terence Conran's Chelsea restaurant, Bibendum. He explained that there were big gaps in what he knew about his mother's life, and that the only link that he had left with her was through Beckett's father, Sid.

Lionel Beckett told Foster that his father had moved to Australia after his wife died and was now being looked after in a nursing home in Melbourne. Beckett went on to say that he thought it was very possible that his grandfather, who had been a supervisor in a cotton mill and had a well-developed sense of moral purpose, had indeed taken Lilly in as an adopted daughter.

Foster realised that if he was ever going to find out more about his mother's past, he could not wait any longer. He was too impatient to delay going to Australia, even by the day that he would have needed to wait to get a direct flight to Melbourne. He set off at once, changing planes and spending the night in Sydney, from where he called the matron at the nursing home in which his uncle was living. 'She told me that he was looking forward to seeing me. When I got there the following day, it was recognisably Sid, but there was no communication with him. It was a one-way conversation. He was smiling gently, but said nothing.'

'Don't worry,' the matron told Foster. 'I've seen him like this before. If you come back tomorrow, I am sure that he will be able to speak to you.' Foster went back to his hotel. But the next morning he got a phone call, to tell him that his uncle had died in his sleep during the night. 'I felt totally empty. I put on my running shoes, and took a run in the park. What do I do now? Life treated my parents harshly. I felt that I never had the kind of conversations with them that I would have wanted. There were so many things left unsaid.'

Both Olsen and Reliance Controls have now been destroyed. In the mildly humiliating case of Reliance, not before the metal skin had been mutilated by cutting it open to insert a timber-framed window bought off the shelf from a local builder's merchant – an indignity that Foster interprets as spite: the cladding had been designed to accommodate larger window openings as required.

Almost unnoticed, the Olsen building was demolished in 1987. It is a measure of Foster's lack of sentimentality that he made no comment in public at the time it was torn down. The last upstream dock in London had closed eight years earlier, and there was no shipping to disturb the mirror-smooth water lapping at the Olsen wharf. For a while the building had been the home of the London Dockland Development Corporation, the organisation charged with rescuing the area from dereliction. Then, after some false starts, the neighbouring Canary Wharf erupted with the skyscrapers that turned it into an instant financial behemoth, a massive development that sank the Olsen building in its wake.

Every physical trace of Olsen has vanished, just like the ships and the dockers who once worked there. It lives on only as a hyper-realist painting made by the artist Ben Johnson. In his painstaking depiction of its smoked glass façade, you see the ghostly reflection of the long-gone shipping that once tied up on the wharf in front of the building.

Foster has returned to work in the area again and again. The Jubilee line station at Canary Wharf, with its blistered oval disc glass roof, is the best of his underground stations. Close by is his second tower for HSBC. Across the river is the bus station that he built for what used to be called the Millennium Dome.

Willis Faber was to fare better than Olsen. In 1991 it became the youngest building in Britain to be awarded the protection of a Grade One listing, a rare distinction and a safeguard for works of architectural or historic importance, normally reserved for medieval cathedrals and baroque palaces. To stop the owner's plans to destroy the swimming pool on the ground floor to make more room for offices, English Heritage rushed it through the listing process. After listing, which prohibits any changes without official consent, was confirmed, Willis Corroon, as the firm had renamed itself by this time, withdrew the plan. The pool survives, and even though it has been drained and boarded over, it could yet be put back into use should any future occupier decide that they wanted to. Foster is as phlegmatic about this as he was about the destruction of the Olsen building. 'There are other public swimming pools in Ipswich now.' He had nothing to do with the decision to list the building, taking no part in the lobbying for or against.

Willis Faber is a more complex version of the same kind of thinking that shaped Olsen. Both were intended as civilised and egalitarian workplaces. But Foster was able to push his ideas much further with the Willis Faber project. The Olsen building was marooned behind high dock walls, so Foster had no way to develop a relationship with the city outside. Willis Faber's black glass skin reflects the delicate texture of the medieval streetscape of Ipswich. It fits in by not fitting in. Responding to an irregular island site, the outline of the building is a continuous perimeter made up of a series of voluptuous curves. A void at the centre of the building looks up towards a grass-covered roof, and allows space for a bank of escalators to move workers through the building and up to the canteen, accommodated in a glass box whose rectilinear form makes a tense contrast to the curved iceberg on which it rests. The rest of the roof is turfed, providing an expansive garden in which to enjoy a picnic lunch, and a very effective form of insulation. Along with the swimming pool on the ground floor and the roof garden, Willis Faber had amenities far beyond what was on offer to the dockers.

In its form and plan, Olsen is a strictly rational project. Willis Faber hints at another kind of thinking. It is a building that takes pleasure in the glossy sweeping curves of its skin, that make it look like a huge black glass grand piano. It is both an abstraction and, because of the way its reflective surfaces mirror its surroundings, an evocation of the traditional architecture all around it. On another level, it triggers memories of the Daily Express Building in the Manchester of Foster's youth, as well as of the visionary proposal for a black glass skyscraper in Berlin that Mies van der Rohe speculated about in 1919 in a series of heavy charcoal sketches and montages.

There is another architectural layer at Willis, too. Beyond the glossy black exterior is an explosion of vivid colour: acid green and searing yellow. And it could have gone even further in its sensuality. In the form that they have been built, Willis Faber's curves are two-dimensional, but Foster had already begun to explore the idea of a building with three-dimensional curves designed with Buckminster Fuller, the American disciple of the geodesic dome who was to have a profound influence on Foster. They called the project the Climatroffice. Taking the Willis Faber brief as a point of departure, the two men looked at how the contemporary workplace might become sunlit and naturally ventilated. They were also starting to think about a new kind of architectural geometry. There are sketches that show how Foster was proposing to abolish orthogonal geometry altogether. 'Willis Faber might have looked like a blancmange, a forerunner of the blob-like buildings of the first decade of the twenty-first century,' he says. In the event, there was too much uncertainty about the precise shape of the site that Willis Faber would be able to assemble for the building, with some neighbouring landowners refusing to sell, and the idea did not go much beyond a series of sketches that suggested but did not spell out exactly how the project would have fitted into the Ipswich street-line.

Willis Faber was also the first project that Helmut Jacoby was recruited to illustrate for Foster. In the 1950s Jacoby had made perspectives of remarkable precision and power for Marcel Breuer, Philip Johnson, Eero Saarinen and I.M. Pei. They were extraordinarily intense images that became almost as well known in the architectural world as the finished buildings they represented. A Jacoby rendering became a kind of endorsement, demonstrating that its subject belonged in the architectural big league. But the emotional effort involved left Jacoby exhausted. He gave up his career as a perspective artist, and returned to the provincial obscurity of architectural practice in Germany.

Foster tracked him down and persuaded him to come out of retirement to make two key drawings of Willis Faber for him. And he followed this up with a string of other projects, most of them never realised, such as his VW distribution centre in Milton Keynes. He was setting the tone for his future, spending freely, to give the aura of authority to a growing practice. It was another sign of Foster's unwavering determination, as well as his readiness to measure himself against the architectural masters.

Working with Jacoby also involved a deft bit of tactical planning:

I asked Jacoby to make one drawing of Willis Faber, to show it as I wanted it to be, and another version that was one storey higher. He finished both of them, but I took just the taller of the two versions of the building to show the planning officer in Ipswich. He was worried about the height.

'Couldn't you take one floor off?' he asked me.

'Well, I don't know, I could think about it, but you will have to give me three weeks to come back to you.'

The strategy worked, and Foster, delighted by Jacoby's vizualisations of his buildings, worked with him right up until the competition drawings for the Reichstag in Berlin in 1992.

In 1974, Robert Sainsbury, who had steered his family grocery business to prosperity as a national supermarket chain, was looking for an architect to build a gallery that would house the art he had amassed over forty years. It was an eclectic and wide-ranging collection, encompassing Degas, ethnographic material from Oceania, Inuit carvings and Bauhaus drawings. The first piece that Sainsbury had bought in the 1930s was by Jacob Epstein. He later acquired the monumental Henry Moore bronze that sits outside the gallery (it was Sainsbury who introduced Foster to Moore, a meeting which Foster put to good use by beginning to understand the ways, so different from an architect, that an artist sees form). Sainsbury got to know Francis Bacon, commissioning a portrait from him in 1957. He bought his work, he kept the letters Bacon wrote to him, and he supported him financially and emotionally. For her part, Lisa Sainsbury collected pottery by Lucie Rie, with whom she had a long friendship, as well as work by Hans Cooper.

Journalist Corin Hughes Stanton, whose mother had encouraged Sainsbury to start the collection, took him to see a range of buildings designed by architects who seemed promising.

Hughes Stanton, at that time working at the Design Council, would have been aware of Foster's growing reputation. Foster had recently guest-edited an issue of the *Architectural Review* on factory buildings; instead of being illustrated by the conventional carefully composed architectural photographs, it featured grainy 35mm black-and-white images that tried to convey the immediacy of the contemporary city.

Sainsbury was hugely taken by the Olsen building. He summoned Foster to appear at 10 a.m. on New Year's Day at his Smith Square house. 'Bob wanted to talk to me about what I had done before, and what I was thinking about for their project. The conversation went on and on. He disappeared at one point, then came back to ask me to stay for lunch, and continue the conversation. I called home to say that I would be late.' Foster got to see Sainsbury's study, exquisitely designed by the young Dutch Indonesian Kho Liang Ie, studded with tiny Inuit carvings. And he saw the portrait of Lisa Sainsbury by Francis Bacon hanging over the mantelpiece, one of three survivors from the series of eight that he painted of her. Dissatisfied with the results, Bacon had destroyed the rest.

It was the start of a relationship with Robert and Lisa Sainsbury that became increasingly close as the project took shape. At the beginning, though, Foster still remembers the burning flush of embarrassment after their first formal meeting to discuss the project. Unsure how to address the Sainsburys, he had discreetly asked Kho Liang Ie, who was to collaborate on the gallery interior, and received the answer: 'Bob and Lisa, of course.' Foster did as Ie suggested, and says that he realised only afterwards how horribly over-familiar he must have sounded.

What began as a working relationship began to develop into a strong personal bond after the death of Foster's parents. In 1988, when Wendy developed the cancer that would kill her in less than a year, it was the Sainsburys to whom the distraught Foster looked for emotional support. The Fosters had not long returned from a trip to America to adopt their third child, Jay, when the diagnosis came through. Wendy was determined to have nothing to do with conventional medicine but to rely instead on a macrobiotic diet and meditation. She had never been convinced of the omnipotence of doctors or by mainstream medicine, and their first two children were both born at home. She had at one point even persuaded Foster to try a macrobiotic diet in an attempt to deal with a painful arm. For Foster, macrobiotics were not a success; within a month he had lost so much weight that his watch was hanging loose from his wrist. He abandoned the experiment after being taken aside by a doctor and told that his diet was threatening to do lasting damage to his health. In the end it was Lisa Sainsbury who helped to find the nurses to care for Wendy.

Robert and Lisa Sainsbury had offered their collection to the University of East Anglia in 1973. One of their daughters had studied there, and in Sainsbury's eyes it had the particular merit of not being Oxbridge – he saw no reason to become a benefactor to the already well-provided-for older universities.

Sainsbury had a strong sense of social responsibility. A committed supporter of the Welfare State, he took the working conditions of his employees seriously. He also wanted to do something about the two-nations divide between the arts and the sciences identified by C.P. Snow. He was ready for a radical new approach to making a building to house art, and in Foster he found it.

The UEA campus had been created by Denys Lasdun in the five years after the university was established in 1963. Those were days in which the new universities looked like the precursors of a social revolution, smuggled into gentle rural landscapes on the outskirts of a string of historic towns. Their campuses were conceived as self-contained worlds that demonstrated new ways to live and work, reflected in an architecture that was more adventurous than would be possible on the outside. Lasdun designed a remarkably powerful, even ruthless scheme that created a continuous wall of concrete structures, like a set of linked stepped pyramids, perhaps the most ambitious attempt at that feverish, half-dystopian, biggest-of-the-big architectural idea of the 1960s – building a megastructure in Britain. Tradition had been abolished. The University of East Anglia wall, backed by an elevated walkway, contains student residences, as well as laboratories, teaching spaces, and classrooms. It has the massive presence of an aircraft carrier beached in a wheat field.

As an expression of a single, ruthless architectural will, it would have attracted attention anywhere. On the edge of the medieval cathedral city of Norwich, the impact was overwhelming. When the new universities got under way, a campus architect could still expect to be listened to with respect, and even indulged, despite the often incendiary nature of their ideas. But by the time that Foster arrived in Norwich, Lasdun's role had been reduced to that of the powerless custodian of his master plan. Some found his concrete too brutal, and the university estates department, who did not share his vision for the campus, had fallen out with him. Foster remembers the estates officer Gordon Marshall telling him the unhappy story of a battle nobody won. Lasdun lost the job, and Marshall suffered a heart attack. Even though Foster's work was from a very different tradition to Lasdun's, he was careful to go to see him to discuss the project before declaring his hand. Foster was planning not only to break with the concrete uniform worn by the rest of the campus, but also to site the building in a such a way that it could be interpreted as turning its back on Lasdun and the architectural ethos of the university. To avoid that impression, he wanted Lasdun's endorsement.

Foster conceived of the Sainsbury Centre as a gleaming silver tube, turning away from the campus to look out over the green landscape, and a lake. Foster's building seems barely to touch the ground; it is tethered to Lasdun's concrete megastructure by the most tenuous of umbilical cords, a high-level glass walkway. It penetrates the tube at an oblique angle, and then descends into the gallery by way of a sculptural spiral staircase with no visible means of support. It was typical of Foster's approach at the time. He abolished design problems – the joint between two materials, for example, or how to make a formal approach to a building – by avoiding them altogether. He made sure that two different materials never meet, and that there is always a neat gap clearly between them. There were no formal approaches to Foster's early buildings. If the Sainsbury Centre had followed the logic of its temple-like form, there would have been a grand entrance, reached by steps, into an opening in the centre of the glazed façade looking over the landscape. But formality was something that Foster found hard to take at this stage of his career. He introduces you to the Sainsbury Centre in as casual and oblique a manner as he could think of: through a door that makes no ceremony, and makes its entrance from the side at an angle, rather than head-on. It is architecture apparently without capital letters. And yet, it is a building of discipline and order. While Foster was researching architectural approaches to housing art, he went to look at Mies van der Rohe's Neue Nationalgalerie in Berlin. Mies' building really is a classical temple, with a colonnade that echoes Schinkel's Altes Museum, but it also offers a single soaring space for temporary exhibitions, and an underground gallery that reflects something of the spatial approach adopted by Foster.

Originally, Foster was to have been responsible for the shell of the gallery only. At the time of that first New Year's Day meeting it was envisaged that the interior would be left to Kho Liang Ie, who had excited the Sainsburys with the idea of displaying their collection on moveable screens rather than conventional gallery walls. In the event, Ie died before the project could get under way.

The nature of the project shifted in other ways, too. When Foster and the Sainsburys started talking, there had been an assumption that the building would get a conspicuous site next to the other arts faculty buildings on the campus, close to the main entrance of the university. It would serve as a marker, announcing the university to the world outside through its most public building.

To Foster, preconceptions of any kind are always anathema. His whole career has been based on trying to answer questions in a way that had not previously occurred to his clients. He told one company that asked him to design a temporary new building for them that a better solution would be to reorganise themselves in their existing premises and not build anything at all.

The Sainsburys and the university had assumed that their building should be at the other end of the campus from where it eventually landed. I suggested that we should have no pre-conceptions. They thought they had identified the site. I suggested that we should look at how many other possible sites could also be identified and evaluate them on a comparative basis.

We looked at the entrance to the campus. I suggested a more remote site, next to the science faculty, and away from the other arts buildings. In this position it would have more of a landscape dimension and would have allowed room for expansion in the future.

Putting his gallery next to the university's biological sciences laboratories appealed to Robert Sainsbury, who did not come from an arts background. 'If I had spent my time at university studying next to an art museum, I might have approached life very differently,' Sainsbury told Foster.

The other preconception was that the project would be made up of three distinct buildings: a faculty club, the school of fine art itself, and the Sainsbury collection. The open question was whether there should be a fourth, additional building, for temporary exhibitions. It was another of the multiple pre-conceptions that Foster successfully challenged; he put every-thing in a single building, although in retrospect concedes that he might have approached the entrance differently.

Foster's idea was to reduce the building to a simple but ineffably elegant tube, open to the landscape at both ends, thus allowing sunlight to filter in where and when needed. A single building would also, of course, be bigger, more impressive and more photogenic than four smaller ones.

The possibility that there might be an alternative to the polarity between one building, or four, did not occur to Foster.

He saw buildings as single statements. A more traditional understanding of architecture might have been to develop a plan with greater complexity and intricacy, one that could, albeit with less clarity, put each separate function into a single building.

Foster's relationship with the Sainsburys was an essential part of the design process.

> The Sainsburys joked with me that I disrupted their family life. They said they had sleepless nights after discussions of the design budgets. I had a formula for coming to a recommendation by giving them a menu of four options. With each option, I gave them a presentation on its strengths and weaknesses, and then from the beauty parade explained which proposal I recommended. Mostly that worked well, but Lisa once said, 'Norman, don't take me through the whole presentation, just tell me what you want to do.'

They trusted him enough to allow him not only to do things that they were doubtful would work, but also to try things that they were *sure* would not. It was only when the centre actually opened in 1978 that Robert Sainsbury finally understood that Foster's idea of separating the gallery from the public seating area with nothing more substantial than a chest-high glass screen could make a beautiful, and usable, space for art. Foster, however, did not have everything his own way. In one version of the design he wanted to make the main space a huge conservatory filled with full-grown ficus trees which would have put the restaurant and the gallery next to each other. 'Lisa said, "There is no discussion, and no debate. Tear it up." She was right, the reality of a restaurant is noise, clatter and smell.'

Foster had already tackled the problem of an all-glass curtain wall at Olsen. The Sainsbury Centre had curtain walls too, albeit on a scale that, by comparison with Olsen's two floors, is heroic. It also demanded something even more testing of the architect's technical skills: an aluminium skin that wrapped roof and walls in a single continuous movement. He had in mind a skin that climbed up one wall of the building, spilled out over the roof, and then went down the other side.

It was a challenge that nobody had dealt with before. Foster and Tony Pritchard devised a kit of ribbed aluminium-faced tiles formed in a vacuum with enough variations to cope with every part of the building. There were flat and curved options. Some were glazed, others were designed for use on the edges of the building. There were panels with extract and intake ducts, clear glass panels, and blank panels, panels with opening doors, and others with windows.

Jan Kaplicky, a visionary Czech architect working in Foster's office at the time, later produced a brilliantly delineated drawing that captured every element of a system that was both a catalogue of parts and an expression of the essence of what Foster was trying to achieve.

The Sainsbury Centre set a mark for the way that Foster would do things in future. It was the first time that he made extensive use of careful modelling to design out surprises. He had full-size furnished mock-ups made up in a garage in London to show the academics what their rooms would be like. Foster's inevitable willingness to change his mind about a design at the last possible moment was also evident. He had originally planned to make the centre with a simple portal frame. The engineering drawings were all but finished, the orders were almost ready to be placed for the structural steel. And then suddenly Foster understood that if he left the design as it was, it would, in his terms at least, be a failure. Instead of the overwhelming clarity that he had in mind, the interior would become a clutter of little boxes scattered across the floor. In an instant he saw how it could be done. The lavatories, the kitchens, the stores and the services had to be pushed into the sides, stacked up in two tiers. All the mechanical plant and ducts that are conventionally hidden in the ceiling were moved out and positioned either in the walls or in a basement undercroft, allowing the roof void to become an open mesh filtering sunlight down into the main space, an idea that later shaped the planning of Stansted Airport.

For the Sainsbury Centre, he needed a thick wall, wide enough to take everything that got in the way of the Olympian splendour of the main space. The outer face would be the external weather-proof wall; the inner one would hide an eight-foot-wide zone running from end to end of the centre. But to do that meant a total redesign of the structure and services, discarding almost everything that the engineers had worked on over the previous months. It would cost time, and it would eat into the fees from which Foster and the other consultants made their living.

Tony Hunt was shocked when Foster explained his change of mind. 'You can't do this, Norman!' he said. 'It's a fantastic idea, but it's your next project. This time it's just too late.' Hunt had already sized every single piece of steel in the structure and did not relish starting again. Foster remembers sitting at the circular white conference table in the practice's office in Fitzroy Street, saying, 'There may not be a next time.'

Foster persuaded Hunt, and all the other engineers, to start again. There was, of course, no reason for the Sainsburys to pay for their architect to change his mind. Foster absorbed the cost of the extra design work, as did all the engineers, who could see that Foster was an architect with a future, and one who could soon be the source of a lot more high-profile work. And it was this move that turned the Sainsbury Centre from an impressive building into a great piece of architecture.

There were problems with budget. The costs of building the basement, introduced as a late addition, had been under-estimated. And the swooping staircase, elegantly spiralling down into the gallery from the high-level route linked to the university's walkway, looked as graceful as a dancer but had a disconcerting wobble. Fixing it was expensive, and required steel flanges to be welded into place to stiffen it. Foster got the blame even though he hadn't designed it. As far as the Sainsburys were concerned, he was responsible for everything, including the engineering issues.

The mundane realities of the life-support systems of academic existence were banished into the eight-foot-wide wall. It was like a giant version of an aircraft hull, where the smooth metal skin on the outside and the moulded plastic cabin wall on the inside give no clue that there is a gap between them that is packed full of hydraulics, cables and structural spars.

This wasn't the only thing that Foster did at the Sainsbury Centre in the pursuit of visual purity. The academic offices form a glass-fronted strip near the centre of the building, protecting gallery space at one end from the café at the other. So controlling was Foster that he insisted nothing must be allowed to disturb the restrained simplicity of the interior. To this end, even the door locks in the glass walls of the offices are buried in the floor to make them invisible. 'I did not want to spoil the door details. I would be more pragmatic now, but getting the academics to scrabble on the floor with their keys seemed a small price to pay for such elegant details,' Foster says with a certain guilty pleasure. But Foster's initial idea of giving the lecturers roofless studies was vetoed by the university. Even so, there was much grumbling about inadequate sound-proofing that took months to be resolved.

As work started on site, the project became increasingly fractious. Robert Sainsbury took getting his own way for granted. He had never encountered the power that an estates officer has on a university campus. For Sainsbury, who was putting up more than half the cash, the Sainsbury Centre was 'his' building. Frank Thistlethwaite, the founding Vice Chancellor, was equally determined that this building was going to be the landmark that crowned his career. And Gordon Marshall, the estates officer, was not going to compromise. Foster put himself in the middle of all this campus strife, and developed completely separate relationships with all factions. 'If I hadn't, the project could have been sabotaged,' remembers Foster. 'The Sainsburys never realised the power certain individuals had in the university. Marshall had already had an almighty bust-up with Denys Lasdun, who he got on with even worse than he did with the Sainsburys.'

These were not the only tensions threatening the project. The city of Norwich was beginning to grow suspicious of the university. What had once been a source of civic pride, and jobs, was now looked upon as an expanding, and possibly subversive, intrusion in its midst. The fallout from the events of May 1968 in Paris was still setting students and junior academics everywhere against their university administrations. And there was agitation from some of those students over what, with a careful blend of snobbery with Marxism-Leninism, they chose to interpret as the university selling its soul to capitalist grocers by allowing Robert Sainsbury to build what was described as looking like one of his supermarkets. It was a prejudice that Foster's chosen means of transport to commute to Norwich would have done nothing to dispel.

Foster, having recently learned how to pilot a helicopter, was flying back and forth from London in an effort to smooth things over. Arriving in a helicopter was quite a gesture for a young architect. It was a sign that Foster was not entirely at home in the herbivorous and close-knit world of liberal Hampstead architects. The driving idea behind his work was egalitarian, the abolition of 'us and them' and 'posh and scruffy', as Foster always described his industrial buildings. But Foster was no socialist. He had made his own way out of Levenshulme by embracing the modern world, and he saw no reason why others could not do the same, without state intervention.

The Sainsbury Centre opened in 1978 at a particularly bleak moment for British architecture. In the aftermath of the collapse of Ronan Point, the demolition of scores of troublesome teenage tower blocks and the loss of faith in the ability of modernism to deliver its promises of utopia, the profession was in the grip of a kind of collective nervous breakdown. Against this background, the Sainsbury Centre was an unmistakable masterpiece. A masterpiece that had a public role beyond its ostensible purpose, because it could restore a sense of confidence in contemporary architects. It was understood as a success not just for Foster, but for architecture in general. While the idea of an extruded, tightly skinned metal tube with glass walls at each end is simplicity itself, Foster conceived it on a scale that gives it both drama and intimacy. The gallery, with its armchairs and tables piled up with books in the midst of the Sainsbury collection, has the kind of informal domesticity that you might expect to find in the library of a Palladian country house rather than a museum. But the towering height, and the uninterrupted view end to end, gives the interior a quality of genuine grandeur. The special character is heightened by the ceiling high above, the intricate web of bladed louvres screening a deep structure, and the array of lights that never quite define the ceiling plane but leave it shimmering and ambiguous. The precision of the metal-clad walls and the white perforated aluminium louvre blinds that descend at the end wall to screen the gallery from direct sunlight have exactly the kind of effortless beauty achieved by Foster's glider. It is an effortlessness that is achieved only with the expenditure of sustained effort.

The Sainsbury Centre is often described as an aircraft hangar of a space. It is true that in it, Foster entirely avoided the idea of architecture as a matter of spatial organisation, with a sequence of rooms developed along routes. He abolished spatial hierarchy and, as he was to do later with the first HSBC headquarters and with the Reichstag, he turned a building into a mechanism that could control light, rather than accept a more passive role. But the Sainsbury Centre is no dumb shed. It has the precision of watchmaking or jewellery. It co-opts the landscape, inside and outside. Walking through it can feel as exhilarating as flying in sunlit cloud.

There is a photograph of the Sainsbury Centre, taken when it opened, that has become the most powerful single image of a work of British architecture of its time. It stands in the twilight, reflected in a lake in front of it, like a classical temple in an Arcadian landscape. At the same time, its structure has been reduced to almost nothing; it resembles an ethereal machine, a glistening spacecraft, barely tethered to the earth.

The response was overwhelming. Unlike Willis Faber, whose

black glass walls concealed a private interior, the Sainsbury Centre was open to the public. And it offered them an undeniably moving experience. The vast scale and height of the structure provide a sense of dignified calm. This is a building that is clearly of the present, yet equally clearly offers the traditional qualities of architectural monuments. Nearly twenty years later, introducing Foster at the ceremony to present him with the Royal Gold Medal for Architecture, Robert Sainsbury declared that the Centre was itself the greatest work of art in his collection. Even Leon Krier, who was to become the most militant of architects looking to rediscover tradition, the man who planned Poundbury for the Prince of Wales, once admitted that the elegance of the Sainsbury Centre had moved him.

The Sainsbury Centre weighs 5,619 tons. Norman Foster knows that now, but on the day that Buckminster Fuller asked him the question, Foster had to go home and do some calculations.

> I wrote a letter back to him. I made some very interesting discoveries because in the course of finding out how much the building weighed, I realised the disproportionate amount of weight that was located in the least attractive part of the building, which was the service basement. And of course the smallest amount of weight was in this great hall for displaying works of art and teaching.

Foster remembers the day that he flew Fuller to the university in his helicopter, setting it down on the lawn in front of the Sainsbury Centre:

> We walked past a vitrine with a tiny Eskimo figure. He said, 'Isn't it interesting how good these tiny things look in this space.'

Then we walked through the cafeteria, out through the door into the greenery beyond. We spent forty minutes ambling around the building. Inside the special exhibition area, he picked up that the sun had moved. He noticed how the shadows were different from when we first arrived. You would not expect this high-tech guru to be sensitive to the way that the sun had moved.

What was not obvious after the triumphal opening was that the pristine beauty of the glorious sparkling aluminium skin was already doomed. It was not the aluminium itself that was the cause of the galloping sickness that threatened to destroy the entire building. The problem was at the points where the metal met the insulation layer concealed inside the skin. It started an unforeseen chemical reaction that aggressively attacked the metal. Foster calls it cancer, a striking choice of words. 'Once it has set in, it has the potential to accelerate in an insidious way. Like the human form of cancer, things can look great from the outside, but inside, it has the power to consume the building,'

Signs of the metal being attacked by an aggressive form of rust were first detected in a maintenance room where it remained invisible to outsiders. The nature of the design allowed every panel to be unbolted, and their replacements could be fixed in position with no more trouble than replacing the tyres on a car. Before there was any public awareness of anything having gone wrong, the entire skin had been stripped away and deftly replaced with white steel panels that were not prone to the same problems. It could have been the cause of disastrously bad publicity, fatally questioning the competence of a young architectural practice. Instead David Sainsbury, Robert's son, quietly funded all the repairs (later, David was to be a supporter of the Millennium Bridge) and Foster's reputation for technical competence remained intact. Though the incident passed without a major legal or emotional upheaval, it was nevertheless a traumatic shock for Foster.

Of the key people in the early days of his career, the people that he most wanted to please, the people who have shaped his life and his work, it was Paul Rudolph who showed Foster how to draw and think like an architect while he was still a student. Richard Rogers, his first professional partner, was a man with whom he could talk about architecture endlessly, and with whom he felt inspired enough to start an architectural practice for the first time. Wendy Cheeseman gave him roots, the stability of a family, and the resources and insight that were needed to start their own practice. When the difficult but necessary break with Richard Rogers and Team Four came, it was Wendy who was first to grasp the inevitable. She didn't want to wait for what had been a close friendship to sour. 'Let's do it now,' she said. And she had an eloquence and foresight unusual in architects.

Fred Olsen was the client for the first major building Foster designed under his own name. Robert and Lisa Sainsbury were not only his two most loyal clients, giving him the chance to prove himself, they played a part in his personal life as something close to surrogate parents.

But it was Buckminster Fuller – the man who spontaneously let slip the phrase 'spaceship earth' in a speech in 1951, long before there were any spaceships – who gave him the ambition to speculate about what architecture might be, beyond the pragmatic. Born in 1895, Fuller is one of the more extraordinary maverick figures of the twentieth century. He trained neither as an architect, nor a designer, but studied classics at Harvard – until he was expelled. Part visionary inventor, part quixotic self-promoter, he was an ecologist, futurist, cartographer, car designer and not very successful poet. After leaving Harvard, he tried to make a success of various businesses, including a short-lived construction company.

Left bankrupt during the Great Depression, Fuller struggled to overcome a number of serious personal difficulties, including alcoholism, the death of a daughter through meningitis, and a suicidal depression, and in the 1940s began teaching at Black Mountain College, one of the birthplaces of the American avant garde. His position at the college gave him the opportunity to work with the sculptor and designer Isamu Noguchi, and it was during this time that he began to keep a series of notebooks recording his observations of a world which he believed was rapidly running out of resources. The resulting shortages, Fuller presciently believed, would lead to political instability and warfare.

His inventions were many and varied. He devised his own projection for mapping the globe. He designed what he called the Dymaxion House, one of the most intriguing of all twentieth-century experiments in trying to build prefabricated houses in a manner that would match the low cost, efficiency and speed of a car manufacturer's production line. He designed the three-wheel Dymaxion Car, a streamlined tear-drop that could turn in its own length (Foster has since built a working replica, exact in every detail). Later, Fuller worked with the Beech Aircraft Company to manufacture the Wichita House, a circular pre-fabricated metal home designed to be made on production lines. The only surviving example, appropriately perhaps, is in the Henry Ford Museum in Detroit.

Fuller explored complex geometries to make large structures with minimal use of materials. Though he is perhaps best known for his work with the geodesic dome, Fuller was not in fact the original inventor of the geodesic idea. The concept had first been patented in Germany in the 1920s, and was used by the British aircraft designer Barnes Wallis, but Fuller managed put it to use on a larger and larger scale, realising a huge example for the US pavilion at the Montreal Expo in 1967. It eventually achieved far greater success than the Dymaxion house when the Pentagon started building domes of all sizes in substantial numbers to shelter radar arrays for its early-warning system to protect against Soviet missile launches.

Fuller believed in big ideas. He travelled from student congress to student congress, holding forth for hours on end in his curious, almost mechanical, monotone voice, with a vocabulary that relied on a range of words that he had invented for himself. Long before the idea became commonplace, Fuller dreamed of a sustainable planet, and speculated about putting Manhattan under a giant dome, two miles in diameter, to protect it from pollution.

In 1938, Fuller wrote: 'Scientific design is linked to the stars far more directly than to the earth. Star-gazing? Admittedly. But it is essential to accentuate the real source of energy and change, in contrast to the emphasis that has always been placed on keeping man "down to earth".'

Foster admired Fuller and wanted to work with him. He saw a kindred energy in the single-mindedness that kept Fuller circling the globe at eighty-seven. Fuller was damming about conventional notions of what constituted modern architecture. To him, architecture as it was practised in the 1960s was chiefly cosmetic:

The International Style brought to America by the Bauhaus innovators used standard plumbing fixtures and only ventured so far as to persuade manufacturers to modify the surface of the valve handles and spigots, and the colour, size and arrangements of the tiles. The International Bauhaus never went back of the wall surface to look at the plumbing ... they never enquired into the overall problem of sanitary fittings themselves. In short they only looked at problems of modifications of the surface of end products, which end products were inherently sub functions of a technically obsolete world.

Foster soaked up much of Fuller's millenarian spirit. And just as Fuller towards the end of his life found himself picketed by student radicals who took his embrace of unstoppable change as a form of corporate technophilia, so Foster has also found himself on the wrong side of the barricades from time to time.

Foster's relationship with Fuller was part of a triangular conversation that had Reyner Banham as its third participant.

Nigel Whiteley's critical biography of Reyner Banham describes Banham's view of Fuller in terms that could also reflect his view of the early Foster:

The architectural profession started by mistaking him for a man preoccupied with creating structures to envelop spaces. The fact is that, though his domes may enclose some very seductive-seeming spaces, the structure is simply a means towards, the space merely a by-product of, the creation of an environment, and that given other technical means, Fuller might have satisfied his quest for ever higher environmental performance in some more 'other' way.

In a world reacting against modernity, this was an increasingly unpopular position. Philip Johnson suggested, 'Let Bucky Fuller put together the Dymaxion dwellings of the people, so long as we architects can design their tombs and monuments.' But Foster at this point in his career was content to regard architecture as it was conventionally practised as a dinosaur on the edge of oblivion. In his eyes, a more realistic approach to the issues facing the physical world required something else.

It is an attitude that reflects a certain view of architecture, one that shaped Foster's thinking as a young architect when he was influenced by Reyner Banham. In sharp distinction to the idea of architecture as a matter of picturesque composition, whether in the Palladian or the Miesian manner, Banham looked for a fresh direction for architecture in the pursuit of technological development. He was fascinated by the Futurists and their worship of machines, and repelled by the cult of conservation, just gathering momentum in the England of the early 1960s.

Banham championed Foster in the early part of his career, because he saw in him, after his disappointments first with Peter and Alison Smithson, and then with James Stirling, as the British architect most likely to embody the kind of anti-monumental, technologically driven outsider architecture that he saw as the only worthwhile response to the contemporary world. Simply to go through the process of securing a commission and building it, no matter how much skill and effort might be employed in the process, is not enough. For the architect there needs to be a sense of narrative about *why* they are building, not just *how*. The rhetoric is rarely the same as the underlying psychological motivation.

Foster was influenced by conflicting impulses. He saw design as a means of transforming his world and that of others. He saw himself as a practical strategist, a man who could ask the right questions of his clients to solve the equally practical requirements of the situation facing them. But he began his career at a time when there was also an impatience with the mundane and a belief in the need for a constant openness to dealing with the results of the massive technological changes that the world seemed to be experiencing.

Banham was a fundamentalist. He questioned the very survival of architecture. As he saw it, architecture was already atrophying. In the near future it might well vanish altogether as a vital cultural activity. Life was changing faster and faster, so conventional architectural solutions were inevitably out of date by the time that they were completed. Unless architects could embrace an entirely new approach to their work, they would find themselves as redundant as swordsmiths, lithographers, and steel engravers.

This attitude induced a kind of delirium. Architects began to draw cities that could walk, and speculated about environments of infinite flexibility, and disposability, about plug-in cities, and thinkbelts and mobile universities.

There was certainly something of this view of architecture in the way that Foster set about his practice. But he was driven by a series of contradictory concerns. The picturesque townscape campaigns of the *Architectural Review* that suggested painting grey concrete in pastel shades, pedestrianisation, bollards and hanging baskets of flowers, while too saccharine sweet for some tastes, left a mark on his thinking. He was also fascinated by the aesthetics of aircraft, of mechanisms, of high-performance machinery.

Foster's work shifts imperceptibly back and forth from the

rhetoric of the supremely practical to the messianically fervent, from the off-the-peg instant office to the city-in-a-single-building skyscraper, from the methodical, purposeful, reassuring voice of Foster the pilot to Foster the dreaming visionary planning a vertical city.

Foster's character is marked by a continual restlessness, a constant sense that things could have been done differently, and a never-ending speculation about how things could be if only he had a chance to start over again.

If Foster had managed, through design, to transform his own life since he left that simple room looking at the railway line in Levenshulme, Fuller was telling him there was more to it than that. More to it than the look of a particular room. Fuller was promising to redesign the entire planet and transform everybody's lives, and challenging Foster to do the same.

The pair first met in 1971, when Fuller was in Britain looking for an architect to work with him on the design of the Samuel Beckett Theatre beneath St Peter's College in Oxford. The Beckett Theatre was a somewhat vague and ill-defined project that for a while Richard Burton was interested in backing. St Peter's, a relatively new and far from wealthy foundation, wanted to establish itself as a centre for creativity. Francis Warner, an academic in the English faculty, conceived the idea of an experimental theatre, secured Beckett's permission to use his name, and rounded up representatives of the great and the good, including Burton, Henry Moore, and Maurice Bowra, to start fund-raising. They hired Fuller to work on the design, a spectacularly radical choice, given that Fuller had never attempted anything remotely like it before, and that his first thought was to bury the theatre beneath the college. A submarine under the quadrangle, Foster called it.

The introduction was made by James Meller, a colleague of Foster's. They met for lunch at the Institute of Contemporary Arts in London.

In those days it was a very elegant series of Nash rooms, not the ICA it has since morphed into. I had got the office all organised to receive Bucky, but he didn't come that time. I was trying to impress him that I was the person to collaborate with, but I did not get much of a word in edgeways. I didn't realise then that he was subtly interviewing me. I was talking to Bucky about the ecological approach that we were taking on the project for Olsen's offices at Vestby in Norway. We planned to pull in cool air from the forest floor to condition the building, and to use sun reflectors to warm it in the morning. And we designed fluorescent lighting that would extract heat at source from the fittings. I didn't use the word green or sustainable, they just weren't in the lexicon, but it was an environmental approach that struck a chord with Bucky.

By the end of lunch Fuller had decided Foster was going to be his collaborator. Over the course of their twelve-year friendship, Fuller and Foster worked together on several experimental projects. The final phase of the design of the Willis Faber Building gave rise to Climatoffice: a study for a contemporary adaptable workplace. They designed solar-powered houses for Foster and Fuller's own use, and a dome for the Knoxville World's Fair in 1982. But these projects, like the theatre, were never realised.

The success of the Olsen building in London's docks, with its at that time sensational use of glass walls with no visible means of support, got Foster onto the cover of architectural magazines, and attracted two key clients, Willis Faber and Robert Sainsbury. It also allowed him the resources to pursue his early passion for flight, in the shape of the first of a series of gliders, which quickly gave way to powered aircraft.

Foster was the outsider in the competition to design a new skyscraper headquarters for the Hong Kong and Shanghai Bank in 1979, having never built a bank, or anything taller than three floors. He won with a brilliant analysis of a hugely complex site, and came up with a design which, after a rapid series of alternative options, redefined what office towers could be. The structure, like a bridge, was prefabricated and shipped to Hong Kong. The interior is dominated by a spectacular, cathedral-like void, topped by a sun scoop, and an array of mirrors that tracks the sun to bring daylight deep into the interior.

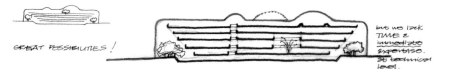

The Willis Faber building fits into an irregular site close to Ipswich's historic centre not by replicating the brick facades of its neighbours but by reflecting them in its black glass skin. The plan is a series of irregular, gentle curves, like a black glass grand piano. The interior brought glamour to the workplace, with a searing palette of yellow and green, which runs counter to Foster's reputation for careful monochrome restraint.

The late 1970s were a particularly bleak time for contemporary architecture in Britain. The soured utopias of concrete social housing triggered a crisis of confidence. The Sainsbury Centre changed all that. Confident, strikingly beautiful and radical in conception, it pointed to a new direction.

It brings what could have been several distinct buildings into one unified structure: a gallery to house the Sainsbury collection, teaching spaces, a café and a gallery. The idea of a sleek tube in the landscape came early. But it was only at the last minute, when the structure had already been designed, that Foster refined the project, switching from a portal frame cluttered with services, into the present version with a deep truss.

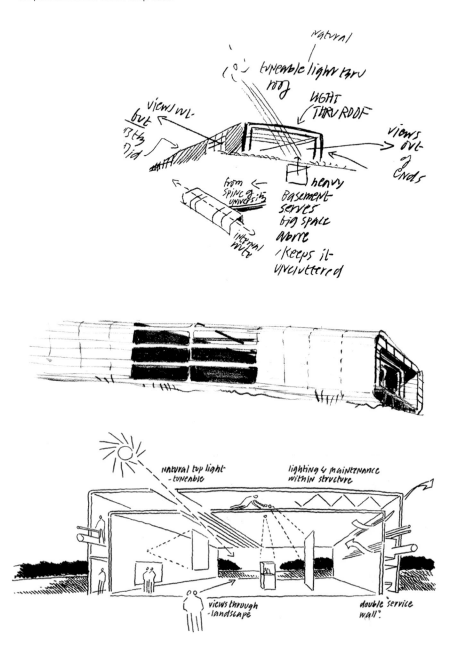

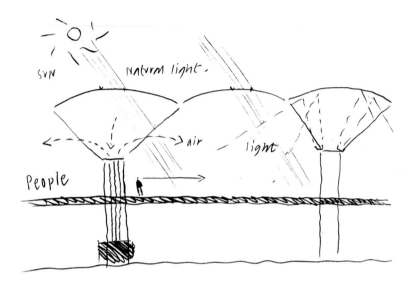

Crucial to Foster's long-term career was his decision not to move to Hong Kong with the rest of his team to build the bank, but to stay in London and ensure that there were new projects to work on when it was finished. The strategy paid off: he was appointed to design the new terminal for Stansted, London's third airport, a design that served to redefine the way in which airports are planned. Services are kept below the main circulation areas, rather than on the roof, allowing lightweight structures and plenty of daylight.

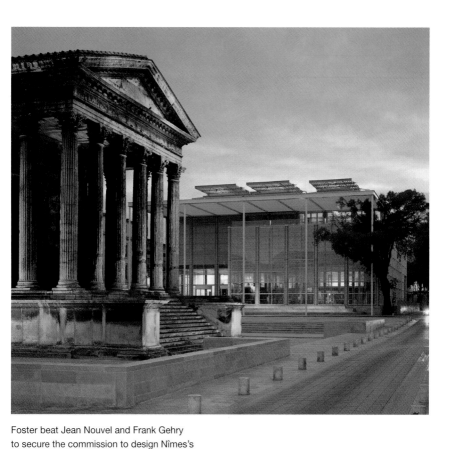

Foster beat Jean Nouvel and Frank Gehry
to secure the commission to design Nîmes's
Médiathèque, a library and art gallery just
across the street from the Maison Carrée, the
miraculously well-preserved Roman monument
at the centre of the city. In such a sensitive
context, it adopts a studiously unobtrusive
approach. Foster's interest in urbanism was
demonstrated in the way that he used the
building to develop a strategy towards clearing
the streets of parked cars and clutter.

Above: Foster's practice in London.

Foster married Elena Ochoa in 1996. She was Professor of Psychopathology at the University of Madrid for many years, and from 1997 became involved with contemporary art and photography. Her publishing house, Ivorypress, is mainly recognised for its artists' books. Norman and Elena have two children.

*

Throughout the early part of his career, Foster established connections with major historical figures in the world of design. When he needed advice on some aspect of a project, he would seek out an expert whose pioneering work in that field had inspired him. Faced with the technical demands of the cladding system for Willis Faber, he flew to Paris for lunch with Jean Prouve, the engineer, architect, designer and manufacturer who could be seen as the father of British high-tech architecture. Prouve subsequently visited London for a more detailed discussion; he came away from Foster's presentation saying that he had nothing to teach him, but that he shared his passion for gliding.

When Fuller's death left Foster without an older figure to look to, the gap was filled for a time by Otl Aicher, the charismatic German graphic designer. Asked why he wanted Aicher to work with him on a signage system for HSBC in the early 1980s, Foster replied simply, 'Because he is the greatest designer living today'.

Aicher, like Fuller, had a utopian vision of the world, and also like Fuller, he came to architecture at an oblique angle. Born in 1922, Aicher married Inge Scholl, sister of the martyred German anti-Nazi campaigners Hans and Sophie Scholl, who established the White Rose League and refused to compromise in their protests against Hitler even though they knew the inevitable outcome. Aicher was at school with Scholl's brother, and trained as a graphic designer. After the war, Aicher and Scholl established the Ulm School of Design. It was a short-lived institution that closed in factional acrimony in the 1960s, but for a while it was the focus for a principled and austere form of modernity that plausibly set itself up as the spiritual heir to the moral authority of the Bauhaus.

Ulm became a battleground between opposing ideas of what design might be. Aicher's adversaries included the critic Tomas Maldonado and the designer Max Bill. Aicher and Bill clashed over the Ulm curriculum, with Aicher winning out in his argument that fine art had no place there. While at Ulm, and later in independent practice, Aicher had a huge influence on design, creating a new image for Lufthansa, then for the Munich Olympics in 1972, and helping to shape the German Federal Republic's identity as a modern, democratic state.

Aicher made design into a kind of moral crusade, in a way that caught Foster's imagination. In Gavriel David Rosenfeld's *Munich and Memory*, there is a quote from Aicher that reveals how hard he worked to deal with the past. In the highly charged context of an Olympic games set in Munich, the city where Hitler began his rise to power, it was important to Aicher to avoid using what he called 'the preferred colours of dictators; red, and gold as well as purple, the colour of secular or religious power'. He had a life-long antipathy to the use of capital letters, suggesting that if only Germans had been less partial to their pomposity, they might have resisted fascism more readily.

Aicher was the creator of Rotis, the type font named after the village in which he had his studio for many years. Rotis became synonymous with the identity of Foster's practice and his buildings. Local sensitivities prevented Foster from working with him in Hong Kong, but Aicher's Rotis font did appear carved in the Portland stone walls of Foster's Great Court at the British Museum. It was used for the Foster letterhead, and on the directional system for the Bilbao metro system that he designed for Foster. Aicher helped to shape Foster's books and presentations. More than anything, he impressed Foster with his unshakeable conviction that design could be about big ideas.

Their relationship was more personal than professional. Foster spent all the time that he could with Aicher, learning from his intensity. The two of them worked on Foster's book; flying to Wiltshire, spending time over layouts in the studio, but also taking long walks to see the ancient white horse carved in chalk at Uffington, the neolithic sites at Silbury Hill, and the Ridgeway.

Writing of Foster's buildings, Aicher suggests that they:

> ... can be read, and understood. You discover them. What you see is what it is because it is more reasonable than the other way round. You discover ideas, logic, wit. It is not pure mood aesthetics, dull feeling. There is also no zeitgeist expressed here, no world feeling, one sees one of the best possible solutions to a set of questions.

It is another version of Buckminster Fuller's vision of architecture based on performance, not formalism.

Foster was shaken by Aicher's death in 1991. In the week before he died suddenly in a traffic accident, Foster had, on an impulse that came close to premonition, flown to Germany to have dinner with his friend. As a tribute, he helped to publish an English translation of Aicher's writings. In the foreword he wrote, 'We felt that it was important to respect Otl's passionate objection to capital letters for starting sentences or marking traditionally important words.'

But it is his description of Aicher that is the most striking. Foster writes, 'Often as he was talking, Otl would pick up a piece of paper and illustrate his point with careful strokes of a ballpoint.' Foster could have been describing himself.

Before he died, Fuller dedicated the first copy of the Dymaxion Map to Foster. He still has it, along with a so-called fly's-eye dome, twelve feet across, that Fuller produced in the 1970s and which is now kept at Foster's home in Switzerland.

> Typically a Buckminster Fuller dome is composed of rods, sometimes combined with cables. It produces something that is incredibly strong with very little mass, very little weight, and extraordinary performance. And just when you thought that you had really second-guessed Bucky on what his next dome would be like, more of the same, but with a more complex geometry, he comes up with something completely different. The fly's-eye dome is a series of moulded pieces which when they are bolted together produce a dome. Instead of it being solid it has very large holes, slightly extruded. They are like big eyes and because of the stiffening collar around the holes and the structural continuity it produces something that is recognisably a Bucky dome but different from any dome that Bucky had ever done before.

Foster was with Fuller when he was working on its design and sketched it in his notebook; Foster bought it from the Fuller family estate at the time of the Fuller retrospective at the Whitney Museum.

Fuller left Foster not just with the interest in challenging orthodox structural geometries that resulted in the Swiss Re tower in London and the Hearst tower in Manhattan, both of which can be seen as owing a debt to Fuller, but also with a readiness to think on an all-embracing scale.

> Bucky was always about taking the long view. If he were here now he'd be very eloquently and elegantly demonstrating the imperative to invest in the research for renewable forms of energy, to replace fossil fuels. He'd also link that to the scarcity of conventional fuels and the propensity of that to spark off wars and all the horrors that follow from that. Bucky had that broader perspective.

Foster has built an architectural practice on a scale that few, if any, have matched, a task that requires an entirely businesslike approach. But more than that he has always looked for ways to respond to the challenge that Fuller set him. Buckminster Fuller speculated about a dome over Manhattan. To judge by Masdar, the zero-carbon city for 100,000 people that Foster is building in Abu Dhabi where mass transit will take the form of as-yet-to-be-manufactured driverless electric vehicles, Foster could actually build that dome.

Four

Reinventing the skyscraper

We are expected to get excited about skyscrapers, mainly because they are very tall. This is an attribute that is supposed to encourage us to overlook the fact that almost everything else about so many of them, despite the residual trace of glamour in the basic idea, is uninteresting. Most towers today have painfully little charisma. With few exceptions, everything about them, bar their height, is banal to the point of catatonia. And yet in China, the Gulf, in America and in most of Asia, there is a constant urge to build the world's tallest structure, in the most simple-minded form of exhibitionism. A slick skin – if you are lucky – a marble-lined lift lobby with a flock of black-leather-and-chrome chairs, a piece of ostentatious public art, followed by a stack of identical floors piled one on top of the other, is the almost inevitable result. The architecture, if there is any, is confined to a zone one metre deep around the outer wall.

Norman Foster's first realised skyscraper, the Hong Kong and Shanghai Bank, certainly isn't like that. It was the project that took him from modest fame in Britain to visibility on an international scale. And it was his first big win in an international competition.

Negotiating the notorious final approach into the now long-gone Kai Tak Airport in August 1979, Foster flew into Hong Kong with Spencer de Grey and Wendy Foster for the competition briefing session from the bank. They were clearly the least qualified of the six contenders drawn from America, Britain, Australia and Hong Kong to design what HSBC's chairman, Michael Sandberg, claimed was going to be the best bank in the world. Foster had never built anything in Hong Kong. And unlike his rivals, who ranged from Harry Seidler from Sydney, once a student of Walter Gropius, to Hugh Stubbins from Boston, he had never designed a bank and he had built nothing taller than four storeys. What he did have was a reputation as a bright newcomer who seemed somehow to be changing the rules of the game of architecture, and who, it was already apparent, was determined to make his career on the biggest stage possible.

As a European he belonged to an architectural culture that had not yet got to grips with the skyscraper. Ever since Chicago and New York saw the arrival of the first high-speed elevators, coupled with steel-frame construction and fireproofing, which made skyscrapers possible at the end of the nineteenth century, they had been an almost entirely American speciality. The Empire State and the Chrysler building were as American as Raymond Loewy's Lucky Strike cigarette packs and the tail fins that Harley Earl put on the back of Buicks. And they did not transplant easily. The rest of the world could only look on in a kind of primitive awe. With a few exceptions, such as Gio Ponti's infinitely slender prismatic tower for Pirelli in Milan, if Europe tried to build skyscrapers, it produced faint copies of what America was doing, or else it hired Americans to design them, usually with equally disappointing results: dumpy, unconvincing, something like Eastern Europe's sticky attempts to imitate Coca-Cola. Even Stalin's wedding cakes in Moscow used specially licensed imported copies of American architectural magazines as reference material. More original European ideas about towers, such as Adolf Loos' giant Doric column for the *Chicago Tribune*, or Mies van der Rohe's glass tower for Berlin, stayed on paper.

British architects of Norman Foster's generation started their careers with little expectation of ever building skyscrapers. But Foster had at least been thinking about the high-rise as a building type ever since he was a student at Yale. In his first semester with Paul Rudolph, he worked on a tilted tower with a bridge-like structure that would one day become the point of departure for the principles on which the Hong Kong and Shanghai Bank is based. It was an elegant, and inventive design, but not one that seemed to have much chance of being of any practical use when he returned to begin to practise in a Britain which was falling out of love with modernity in general, and high-rise architecture in particular.

The first time that Foster worked on a high-rise project in earnest was in 1978. Times were hard for architects that year, with Britain in a deep recession. The first office tower in the whole of Britain to rise taller than 180 metres, the National Westminster Bank's headquarters in the City of London, designed with little finesse by Richard Seifert, was completed only in 1980. By comparison, America had the twin towers of the World Trade Center and the Sears Tower in Chicago that were almost 300 metres high and which belonged to a whole class of towers that were not much shorter.

While real jobs were few and far between, British architects struggled to find work for themselves, even if it meant taking on highly speculative projects. Foster, as part of a consortium with the engineer Frank Newby and Derek Walker, who in his previous role as chief architect for the Milton Keynes Development Corporation had employed Foster to build the ill-fated Bean Hill estate, came up with a striking scheme for an apartment tower in New York. It was commissioned by an Italian developer, pursuing a speculative option to devise a scheme for a site on Madison Avenue owned by the Whitney Museum. The base of the tower would have included an extension to the adjoining Marcel Breuer-designed Whitney building, before shooting up another forty floors above Madison Avenue. It was a challenge to a wealthy residential neighbourhood, one that saw no reason to allow itself to be taken over by towers that would put its pavements in permanent shadow. Sheer geometry dictated that it would almost inevitably have a difficult spatial relationship with the inverted and introverted ziggurat of Marcel Breuer's museum, which holds the pavement at bay and only permits access by means of a concrete drawbridge spanning its dry moat.

The project was a striking one, proposing a smooth metallic skin with rounded corners that had some relationship with the aluminium cladding that Foster had recently developed for the Sainsbury Centre, coupled with an externally expressed diagonal structural bracing. And in its mix of functions – residents' club at the top, luxury housing in the middle, and museum at the base – it was an early attempt to inject more life into the skyscraper as a building type, which, despite the attention-grabbing nature of its form and scale, has over the years mostly been monotonously mono-functional. The idea of an untested European architect building a high-rise in Manhattan on this scale was regarded as somewhat presumptuous. The Whitney clearly felt that it was being put under unwelcome pressure from Foster's developer client. The museum disowned the proposal, and the project came to nothing.

And so, a few months later, Foster Associates found itself the wild card in the competition for the HSBC headquarters, pitted against rivals such as Hugh Stubbins, who had already built two towers, both of them banks. In Manhattan's Midtown, Stubbins designed the memorable Citicorp Tower, with its distinctive ski-slope top, its silver skin, and its complex base, spanning an existing church. In Boston, he built another equally imposing landmark, the Federal Reserve tower. Palmer and Turner knew all that there was to know about building in Hong Kong. Foster was included mainly on the strength of the enthusiastic critical reaction to the Sainsbury Centre and Willis Faber, and a residual colonial link with Britain. The bank still saw its connection to London as significant, especially as it set about its long-term plan to become one of the handful of global financial institutions.

The Hong Kong and Shanghai Banking Corporation had begun life in 1865 as a transplant of nineteenth-century English and Scots banking customs to the context of Asia. Until it moved its headquarters to Britain, in another Foster-designed tower at Canary Wharf in London, it had maintained its head office on the same site on Hong Kong island since the 1870s. Queens Road, in Central, had once defined the water's edge, but successive land reclamations had left the bank building several hundred metres inland. The bank stood at the head of one of Hong Kong's very few civic spaces, Statue Square, flanked by the Hong Kong Club and the law courts, a domed Edwardian structure that is now the debating chamber of Hong Kong's legislative council, with a view out past the Star Ferry

Terminal. While everything else in Hong Kong from the Repulse Bay Hotel to the waterfront itself was considered expendable, Statue Square was a solitary fixed point of reference for Hong Kong. The statue of Sir Thomas Jackson, the most distinguished of the bank's early managers, had survived even the Japanese occupation, though Queen Victoria and King Edward VII had been temporarily dethroned to await the return of the British.

At the time of the Hong Kong competition, the bank's head office was an Art Deco tower. Designed by Palmer and Turner, a Hong Kong-based firm set up by an expatriate Englishman in the nineteenth century, the structure had, at the time of its opening in the 1930s, been the tallest and the most technically advanced office building between Cairo and San Francisco. The stepped, stone-faced tower had high-speed lifts, air conditioning, and a magnificent banking hall, full of black marble columns, with a vaulted ceiling finished in sky blue mosaics picked out in gold installed by Italian craftsmen from Murano. The main entrance was guarded by twin bronze lions, their paws rubbed smooth and shiny by the constant pressure of hands seeking financial good fortune from the contact. It was an unmistakable demonstration of prestige and the accomplishments of Western enterprise in the midst of an Asia fought over by feuding warlords, and threatened by Japanese expansionism.

But by 1979 the bank had a much more complex worldwide operation to run, more people to accommodate, and an explosion of technological change to deal with. In addition to its role as a local retail bank, with more than a million accounts in Hong Kong, HSBC had established a network of subsidiaries throughout Asia, and was in the process of expanding to the capital cities of the world beyond, positioning itself as an

investment bank with the broadest range of sophisticated financial services. To signal this new stage in its development, it was
looking to build a headquarters that would be as impressive as
the old bank had been on the day that it first opened. As the
Bank's chairman Michael Sandberg said at the time, they wanted
the best new bank building in the world.

It might have sounded like hubris coming from a colony that
had yet to fully emerge from its reputation as a sweat shop
churning out cheap and cheerful copies of Western originals.
Hong Kong was not a place that had much post-1945 architecture of any distinction. This was perhaps not surprising, given
the sometimes very sharp tensions between the colony and what
used to be called Red China, which from time to time throughout
the 1960s came close to armed conflict. For years Hong Kong
had been seen as a place to make money as quickly as possible,
while keeping one eye on the route to the exit. Major physical
investments in the future were rarely considered a priority.

Now, in the run-up to the 1997 transfer of sovereignty
to China, architectural symbolism assumed an even greater
significance. The bank was not simply a commercial under-
taking, it was also one of Hong Kong's key private institutions,
with a vital role in the smooth running of the colony. The bank
was virtually an arm of government, helping to shape economic
policy and issuing currency notes, as well as conducting a
worldwide commercial banking operation.

In the uncertainty that surrounded Beijing's plans for Hong
Kong, the bank was setting out consciously and deliberately to
make a highly visible demonstration of its continuing commitment to the future of the territory. Through conspicuous
investment in its new headquarters, HSBC would show that
capitalism had a future in the coming Chinese-administered

Hong Kong, that the bank was determined to maintain its position there after the handover, and that there was no justification for a flight of people, or of capital, at a time when the more panicky of Hong Kong's citizens were swapping their useless British overseas passports for residency papers valid in Australia and Canada.

At the same time, this blatant gesture of reassurance had to be carried out in a measured way, lest it be seen as an attempt to dictate to the Chinese government. This was, after all, 1979; well before China had conspicuously embraced a capitalist economy and opened to the world outside. Michael Sandberg had not forgotten that one of Mao Tse Tung's first acts after his victory over Chiang Kai-shek's nationalists in 1948 was to authorise the addition of an attic storey to the roof of the Bank of China building in Hong Kong, thus rendering Mao's bank fractionally taller than its capitalist neighbour, the HSBC. It amounted to a deliberate and costly assertion of China's claims to eventual sovereignty over the colony.

Thus the new HSBC building had to deal with a whole range of nuances in the kind of messages that the bank wanted to project about itself. A simple-minded glass or concrete slab, lost in the tiered cliffs of similar buildings that make up Hong Kong's waterfront, clearly would not have lived up to the bank's determination to make a clear statement about itself, about its future and about Hong Kong.

That it staged a competition at all was a measure of how seriously the bank took the project. Competitions, in the English-speaking world, were far from common in the 1970s, and the bank went to the Royal Institute of British Architects for help in organising its selection process. For clients, a competition was a chance to think hard about architecture. For architects, the competition system was understood as a means for opening the path to talented newcomers to overcome their lack of experience to secure major commissions, and tacitly, for imposing the taste of architects on sometimes uncomprehending clients. It was because of this tendency that, unlike the Sydney Opera House, where the competition was open to any qualified architect, the bank was determined to retain control of the selection process, and to screen out the possibility of unwelcome surprises. They wanted to limit the contenders to architects they were relatively confident could build them something that would work. What they did not want was a young unknown, working on his kitchen table, and with no professional indemnity cover; or a prima donna who was going to insist on following the dictates of his own genius in imposing his vision on the bank.

Roy Munden, the manager in charge of the project at the bank, built up a team of advisers that included PA management consultants, and Gordon Graham, president of the Royal Institute of British Architects at the time. Munden worked with them to draw up a shortlist of architects who would be invited to take part in the competition. Graham had also played a significant role in another architectural competition in the previous year, when he had helped to select Richard Rogers to design a new building for Lloyds of London. Foster, who had also taken part, had been unsuccessful. After his period as president ended, Graham was to become part of the Foster Associates team.

One of the key questions that the competition posed for the architects taking part was what to do with the existing building. Should its most distinctive elements be retained, essentially the banking hall, or did it make more sense to demolish everything and start again? In drawing up their brief, the bank's advisers had looked at the site carefully and suggested that competitors should explore two options. They believed that it would be possible to keep the existing banking hall and put up a slim new tower next to it, making room by demolishing the rest of the old building. Failing this strategy, competing architects were invited to propose an alternative solution which might include complete demolition, but only in such a way that allowed the bank to maintain a functioning operation of some kind on the site throughout the rebuilding procedure. It was up to the architects, but whatever approach they took, Sandberg asked that they ensure that the bank would look like a bank, whatever that was.

A bank needs a building that has the quality to suggest permanence, power and a certain degree of resources behind it, but this must be achieved without giving the impression that it is the product of an institution that is profligately spending its investors' money on vainglorious conceit.

There was also the investment opportunity to be considered. Hong Kong's financial centre occupies some of the most valuable development land in the world. The more square metres that could be fitted on to the site, the more attractive a proposition the new building would be for the bank, although there was a suggestion that quality would come before maximising the financial return.

While most competitors saw the briefing session in Hong Kong as an opportunity to explore Asia (for a British architect still an exotic location in 1979), the Fosters and Spencer de Grey cancelled their planned tour of the Far East, and opted to stay on in Hong Kong instead. They wanted to see behind the scenes at the bank and to get a fuller insight into its operations.

Over the course of three weeks the trio did not stop asking questions, sometimes to the exasperation of bank officials who could not see the relevance of a close examination of the queuing system on the existing private banking floor to an architect starting to think about how to design an entirely different building.

Foster was asking questions about Hong Kong as well as about the bank. The concept of Feng Shui, Chinese geomancy, intrigued Foster. Although Roy Munden assured competitors that the bank would take care of the Feng Shui issue, Foster decided to commission an independent geomancer. From the ensuing meeting, they took home a drawing that showed an open base, aligned between the mountains and the sea. Spencer de Grey is dismissive of those who see Feng Shui as a mystical or arcane practice: 'Mostly it is a very sensible way of thinking about alignment, ventilation and aspect.' But it was not until much later that Foster realised the connection between what he was building and that diagram.

Armed with the findings of their interrogations, they returned to the office in Fitzroy Street to consider not just how to design a bank, but also how to win the competition, and to think about how, having won, they would go about actually building it. In this, they showed an awareness that the bank were looking not so much for a finished design, but for an architect that they would feel able to work with.

Predictably, Foster was unwilling to focus on the problem constraining himself within the limits framed by the brief. He wanted to explore other options too. In fact, in the 127-page report that Foster Associates eventually submitted to the bank, a mere fourteen pages were devoted to the two options suggested in the official brief. Foster analysed both strategies, found them equally flawed and moved on. Instead, he proposed an alternative approach that he described as phased regeneration.

As he suggested in his presentation, 'designing a building without the benefit of a working relationship is rather like a game of blind man's bluff'. Foster's strategy could be understood as an attempt to get the job not so much by dazzling his clients with the image of the perfect building that he could give them, but by convincing them that he was too smart and too sophisticated to do anything so unsubtle. Foster's report was a deliberate attempt to show the bank that his team had analysed in forensic detail not just the kind of building envisaged by the brief, but every other possibility too, and that they had come to understand the issues facing the bank as well as it understood them itself.

Foster's submission wasn't all analysis and questions. He was ready to sugar the research and the findings with some seduction. The report came with a set of images of a building that Foster proposed. Despite the series of detours on the way to its completion, the image is not too dissimilar from what the new bank eventually turned out to be. The tower is shown aligned to face Statue Square, a striking structure with its façade pierced at three points by massive bridge-like beams.

On one level, Foster was offering a more intelligent solution to the questions posed by the bank than could be reasonably expected to emerge from a competition. He was offering to work with his client once he had secured the job, to make a more satisfactory building. But at the same time he was putting his cards on the table and showing what he was capable of in case they were not ready to wait for a more measured response. Phased regeneration was about keeping every option open, and allowing the bank to make critical decisions about its future shape even while the project was under way. He proposed shaping the successive incarnations of the building through a shifting balance of new and old. Initially, he would keep the Palmer and Turner tower, and the banking hall, and demolish the front of the existing bank, building a three-bay-wide bridge over it, that would then allow development to go up, or down, or both, stage by stage. In each version, the result would be a complete design in and of itself, rather than a provisional step on the route to something else.

Although Foster was keen to allow the bank to keep its options open, at the heart of his design were some fundamental principles that he intended to keep to. Most high-rise buildings have a lift core in their centre. It is an economical arrangement, combining a structure with services. But it is inflexible, and it limits the way in which the floors can be used. Foster was determined to do things differently. He moved the lift shafts to the sides of the building.

It was a brilliant analysis, and one that convinced the bank that Foster Associates were the best team for the job. There was no second round in the selection process; Foster was the only architect invited to talk to the bank's board of directors in November 1979.

Once he had been appointed, Foster went on to develop a series of proposals as the office explored their first thoughts in greater detail. As they examined the implications of their strategy, they looked for new methods of dealing with the bank's brief. Some options varied radically from the scheme that Helmut Jacoby's perspectives had shown to the bank's directors the previous November.

The first idea was to create a structure in the form of a bridge, or rather three bridges, one stacked on top of the other, aligned on Statue Square. It would have been four bays thick, with a sequence of sky lobbies, allowing circulation through a combination of escalators and lifts. In order to deal with the Hong Kong planning regulations designed to protect street-level pavements from being cast into permanent shade, the tower would have stepped back in gradual stages to taper towards its top. The bridge strategy would have allowed the new structure to span right across the old banking hall without getting in the way of operations while the tower was built above it.

There were questions raised by this strategy that could only be answered as work went on. It was ingenious, but it meant that there could be no deep basements. As the bank thought harder about its requirements, it became clear that it was going to need underground vaults. That meant that it would be impossible to keep the banking hall, and that the new building would have to be made not from concrete but steel, a material that was uncommon in Hong Kong.

The decision opened up a series of options for the architect, and to explore them Foster set a team at work to devise a range of fresh alternatives. By the beginning of 1980, they had come up with an elegant new structural solution that was known as the chevron scheme. Like the competition design, it avoided a central structural core and lift shaft; instead, the office floors were to be kept as open and as flexible as possible. The plans show a steel structure, hung from twin sets of masts by four sets of inclined steel columns.

It was a scheme that could be understood as a kind of refined structural expressionism, but also one that had some clear references to Chinese tradition. Finished in imperial red, a colour that refers deliberately to the red lacquer timber gates of the Forbidden City, in Beijing, its basic form looked back to the traditional Chinese gateway. It was a concept that had in it elements of Jan Kaplicky's inventive combination of technology and imagery. To test its impact on working conditions inside open-plan offices, Fitzroy Street was filled with cardboard columns leaning at acute angles in the early part of 1980. Roy Munden was convinced that it would work. But after the scheme was presented to the bank's board, the objections of Chinese members to the negative Feng Shui implications of downward-pointing arrows quickly led to the idea being abandoned, to the disappointment of the team that had worked on it.

The decision revealed one of the fundamental tensions at the heart of the bank's view of itself at the end of the 1970s. Was it a Hong Kong bank with global aspirations, or was it an international bank with an important Hong Kong presence? The bank's commercial success within Hong Kong depended on attracting the business of local people, 98 per cent of whom are Chinese. Thus for all the swagger with which Foster's tower is depicted on the bank's currency notes, HSBC was always keenly aware of the need to present a face that is sensitive to local traditions. When the new banking hall opened for business, a specially produced gold-wrapped chocolate coin bearing the bank's image was distributed to every member of staff as a good luck talisman.

HSBC, however, is not simply a local institution; it has become one of the largest banks in the world, strong enough to withstand even the credit crunch of 2008 that saw its British competitors forced to seek government protection.

This ambiguity partly accounts for the difficulty that Foster experienced in deciding what the most appropriate colour for the exterior was. Should the expressed steel structure, which ripples across the façade of the building like a prizefighter's pectorals, be finished in red – in China, a colour traditionally associated with the emperor, and with good fortune – or in a more neutral, 'international' colour?

There followed another scheme, one that was described as the organ pipe. This was a set of stepped slices with radiussed façades that was unpopular with everyone. The way was then open to resolve the remaining questions about the strategy outlined in the competition submission. The existing banking hall and the old north tower would all be demolished. To provide a continuous presence on the site, the six-floor extension built in the 1960s between the HSBC and the neighbouring headquarters of the Standard Chartered Bank would be converted to serve as a temporary banking centre before the old building was demolished. A schedule was drawn up which gave Foster four years from the approval of the 100,000 square metre scheme in 1981, until final completion in 1985.

The team immediately set about exploring how to build the project. Hong Kong in the 1970s had no tradition of manufacturing complex building components, or of fabricating structural steel. To make the bank would mean devising a kit of parts collected from across the world, and shipping it all to Hong Kong for final assembly. At the start of the 1980s, the British steel industry was on its last legs, but there was irresistible official pressure for that part of the contract to go to a UK supplier. The rest of the components came from Japan, America, Holland, Germany and Italy.

Once the project was under way, the financial impact of all this became evident. At times, the budget seemed to be out of control. When the project passed the £500 million mark, the bank's board of directors, who had previously been content to leave management of the new building in the hands of Roy Munden, began to express their concern. They had always called it the most expensive building in the world – and at an eventual cost of more than £1,000 million at 2009 prices, it certainly wasn't cheap. In fact it was three times the original estimate. The bank, wanting an independent verdict on whether or not to go ahead with the project, commissioned an audit from London-based engineer Jack Zunz. With the foundations already in place and the basement excavated, they asked him if they should cancel Foster's tower and start again with somebody else who could build a cheaper version. Zunz advised against it. He said that they were already too committed to back out, and that while the building was expensive, it was worth the investment. It was a conclusion justified much later when the bank was able to accommodate a dealer's trading floor, something that would not have been possible with a conventional tower with a central core.

The issue was not so much unforeseen cost over-runs as the usual pattern of over-optimistic early estimates that were prepared with site costs, fees, and fit-outs omitted in the interests of getting the project started. A similar strategy was employed, equally inadvisably, by the British civil servants who ran the Scottish parliament project in Edinburgh.

And so construction continued, with the tower beginning to take shape. With its array of cranes built on to the structure, shrouded in green netting and bamboo scaffolding, jacked up floor by floor as construction proceeded, it was a remarkable vision. The site looked as if a giant machine was engaged in assembling itself. Six huge red cranes that reared up as construction proceeded looked as if they were part of the original architectural conception. During the typhoon season they had to be positioned as much out of the wind as possible. After topping out, they were gradually dismantled and lowered back down to the ground piece by piece.

Very tall buildings have a unique capacity to create an identity for institutions, cities, and even countries. But by the end of the 1970s, perhaps because of the prevailing lack of belief in architectural ideology, skyscrapers, even in America, had become vapid, without the power to communicate or symbolise their values. Perhaps this was not surprising, when they had very little to believe in beyond a pallid species of corporate efficiency. Skyscrapers in their youth were designed by working on the analogy of a classical column. Like Cass Gilbert's Woolworth Building in Lower Manhattan, the gothic campanile that was once the tallest building in the world, they were conceived in three distinct parts: a base, a shaft and a capital. For all the efforts of Michael Graves and Philip Johnson at the height of the postmodern craze in the 1980s to revive this view, it was effectively killed off by the vision of Mies van Rohe. For Mies, his glass towers aspired to the creation of a single pure and perfect object. Despite the remarkable quality of Mies' Seagram tower, the result has been the creation of an endless procession of towers with a singular lack of content. With the rare exception of the elegantly tapered Chicago Hancock tower, they became crude and inarticulate.

Foster's HSBC tower was an attempt to address these problems.

It has allowed for a building which is not a repetitive cellular structure but a mixture of different kinds of spaces all the way up, as if it were a megastructure, complex and rewarding in its content.

When the bank appointed Foster, they gave him a unique

opportunity to redefine the skyscraper as a type and to reinvest it with architectural meaning. A curious characteristic of extreme height in buildings is the tendency that it sometimes has of diminishing its architectural power. Tall buildings can become more like very large electrical appliances than architecture with presence. The Foster bank tower is a much more complex and subtle building.

It has a very strong relationship with the public space in front of it. Only the occasional tram, a diminutive double-deck Edwardian survival, gliding back and forth against the backdrop of Foster's building interrupts a sequence of spaces that sweep under the bank at ground level across a granite plaza, across the parks and fountains of Statue Square and on down to the Star Ferry Terminal. The bank is one of the few Hong Kong buildings that captures an open view out across the harbour to Kowloon and the mainland, but also has the space for passers-by to appreciate its full height at less than dizzyingly vertiginous close quarters.

Because of the way in which the tower is hoisted up over the entrance area, it allows Hong Kong's public realm to spill out beneath it. Passers-by have the spectacle of the bank interior soaring above them as they traverse it. The tower is hollowed out to create an atrium like no other. It is topped by the array of mirrors that form its ceiling, eleven floors up, and serve to deflect the sunlight collected by the sun scoop fixed to the exterior façade down through the atrium and on to the floor of the plaza. A billowing glass curtain pierced by a pair of escalators keeps the banking hall climate controlled.

Linking Statue Square in front of the bank with the terraced gardens behind it by lifting the tower up, over a continuous civic space open to the public, was part of Foster's vision for a welcoming, urban setting for the bank. On Sundays, it becomes a gathering place for the Filipina women working in Hong Kong. But Foster had a powerful commercial argument to help him persuade his client to back the idea. Leaving the ground floor open had a massive impact on the number of floors that the bank could build above it. The plot ratio is the mechanism that planners use to regulate how much space can be built on a given site. So a plot ratio of one to fourteen – high by European or American standards, but not unusual in Asia, allows floor space up to fourteen times the area of the site. The bank had been prepared to take a less than ruthlessly commercial view of the project, in the interests of getting the best building; Roy Munden suggested that it might even be ready to give up some of the plot ratio. In fact Foster, through discreet negotiations with the planning authorities, managed to achieve a higher plot ratio, one to eighteen, as an incentive to extend the public open space under the tower. The extra space boosted the value of the tower by up to thirty per cent.

From the exterior, the most dramatic aspects of the HSBC building are the sides, with their complex stepped silhouettes and banks of glass-faced fire-escape stairs, set back in accordance with Hong Kong building codes. The main façade, looking out towards the Star Ferry Terminal and Kowloon, is more measured and balanced, and its principal impact in urban terms is the dynamic eroded composition that it presents not to the ferry but to its neighbour and rival, the Bank of China. Foster's tower briefly overwhelmed the old Bank of China tower next door – a state of affairs that China quickly reversed when it commissioned I.M. Pei to design a seventy-storey tower, at the time, taller than anything else on Hong Kong island, echoing Mao's extra storey in 1948.

On the other side, it is an eruption from the much more intricate scale of the old stone and stucco buildings of Hong Kong's business district.

Most contemporary speculative office towers are designed to be as economical to build as possible, using as many standard parts and solutions as they can, and also to make them as acceptable as possible to a wide range of users. The Hong Kong and Shanghai Bank ignores these conventions. It does not repeat itself; as you rise up the building it gradually turns into something quite different, before culminating in the helicopter landing pad, and the chairman's residential quarters in the pinnacles of the steel masts that carry the structural load. Here you feel that you are wandering through the late-twentieth-century equivalents of the gargoyles of a Manhattan apartment block from the 1920s.

This was a building designed for an owner-occupier, in a sense as traditional an idea as a hand-tailored made-to-measure suit. Even though the openness of the plan allows for rapid reconfiguration as requirements change, the bank was designed floor by floor for its departments and their specific needs, from foreign currency trading, to human resources, down to the vault in the basement for the bullion store.

And in the nature of things, over the twenty-five years since it was completed, the huge range of departments within the building has gone through continuous shifts and reorganisation. It is a level of change that has been made much more straight-forward by the basic organisational pattern of the architecture of the tower.

The Hong Kong bank is the clearest expression of the notion of architecture as an industrial process in which the ultimate objective is the creation of highly serviced, limitlessly flexible internal spaces and where formal values are eschewed in favour of exteriors that are made legible, expressing how they are made and what they do. It can be understood as the end of an evolutionary tree, the ultimate conclusion of a string of designs that includes the Pompidou and Lloyds, and beyond which it is hard to progress without retracing a certain number of steps.

For all that the construction site itself was controlled by triad gangs, swathed in bamboo scaffolding, subject to mysterious fires, and occasionally overrun by police raids aimed at stamping out illegal gambling by the migrant workforce, the Hong Kong and Shanghai Bank really is a building made on a production line in a factory. Just as a new car would be prototyped, modelled and tested with the utmost thoroughness, virtually every segment of the building has been purpose-designed and manufactured.

In the case of the elegant aluminium skin that wraps the structural steel to hide the fire protection, this included building production lines in St Louis, equipped with robot welders and computer-controlled cutting jigs. The service mains, air conditioning, electrics and lavatories, right down to the mirrors and soap dishes screwed to their walls, and door handles fixed in postion, were all packed into prefabricated modules, that were stacked up on freighters and shipped complete from Japan to Hong Kong harbour and jacked in place by crane at the rate of two a day.

It was an operation that was always on the edge of the possible. The anti-corrosion and fire-protection systems had never been used before. Even the locks were specially developed, doing without conventional keys and replacing them with special brass dowels, in which a number of notches displace the locking mechanism when turned.

No amount of modelling prepares you for the full effect of

the extruded aluminium louvres projecting from front and back at every floor level of the bank. They act as giant moiré patterns sometimes making the building seem transparent, and sometimes at other angles giving it an apparent density and solidity. The tower is divided vertically into five zones, each suspended from a double-height suspension truss by a single line of steel hangars which give thirty-three-metre clear spans, three times a conventional structural span. The trusses are supported in turn by steel masts made up of groups of four steel columns. Horizontally, the building is split into three bays, each one defined by twin mast structures that stand at either end.

The profile of the tower is shaped by the Hong Kong Building Ordinance Office regulations aimed at preventing overshadowing at street level. These have had the effect of limiting the height of the front and rear bays to thirty-five storeys on the façade overlooking Statue Square and twenty-eight at the rear, Only the central bay rises the full height of 180 metres – forty-seven floors. To complicate the silhouette still further, extra setbacks have been introduced into the east side of the tower by omitting chunks of the upper floors between the masts.

The net effect is to ensure that few floor plans are identical. Only the lower floors are conventional rectangles, and even these have an atrium void rising up to the first suspension truss. Above this the building becomes progressively more slender as it rises.

One very important priority was to end the tyranny of the central lift core, which tends to isolate each floor, setting them stacked one above the other like drawers in a filing cabinet. The suspension structure allows for lifts that stop only at the five double-height floors, which are connected by escalators. Moving around the building in this way, you pass from double-height banking halls where diagonal structural bracing stretches away in both directions, up to the senior management floors from whence the setbacks in the profile allow you to look out across blue sky and see the exterior of the building's further wings, and finally on to the remarkable helicopter pad on the roof.

Foster achieved a great deal with the bank. But he didn't get everything that he wanted. He had planned to work with Otl Aicher on giving the bank a signage system that would have been as distinctive as Aicher's work for the Munich Olympics of 1972, but he could not persuade the bank to hire him. He was also thwarted in his plan to make the floor of the plaza out of glass; that would have allowed the sun scoop at the top of the atrium full range, illuminating not just the floor of the plaza, but also filtering reflected sunshine down through the glass tiles and into the safe-deposit vaults in the basement below.

During the building of the bank, Foster was invited to compete for his second major high-rise, this time in America. In 1982, in competition with a number of American architects ranging from Cesar Pelli to Michael Graves, Foster was the only European to be asked to submit a design for new headquarters to accommodate Humana, a medical insurance company based in Louisville, Kentucky. Clearly Hong Kong was generating positive as well as negative publicity.

The contest quickly turned into a set-piece confrontation between Foster and Michael Graves, in effect between two utterly different conceptions of what architecture could be. Graves believed that modernism in architecture had run its course, and that it was time for a new form of contemporary architecture that reconnected with history, symbolism, decoration and traditional architectural techniques. Foster belonged to the camp that was still convinced of the essential rightness of modernity.

Graves came up with what was to be the first example of a fully developed post-modern skyscraper. Foster, in contrast, proposed a technically ingenious and visually striking circular tower, with a structural grid in the skin, not so far removed from Swiss Re, that did away with the need for a central lift core. It would have been topped by a soaring needle, the most slender possible form of communications mast.

The decision went against Foster, and Graves' design was built. Unlike Foster's ethereal silver and glass tower that appeared weightless, Grave's Humana tower is finished in polychromatic earth tones and pastels. It is heavy with pediments, stone and massive modelling, supposedly inspired by historic precedents.

For some years it seemed that Foster was on the wrong side in this particular fight, and that the tide of architectural development was against him. Graves dismissively suggested that he would rather practise law than be forced to build architecture like Foster's. In response, Foster remarked that post-modernism should be understood as a game to be played in private, by consenting adults only.

Graves and Foster, the two polar opposites of contemporary architecture, seemed to be continually sparring with each other, contesting the most high-profile competitions and offering alternative views of what buildings should look like. When the Whitney Museum started thinking again about how to develop its site on Madison Avenue, it was to Graves that they turned, not Foster. Tellingly, Graves – who bore even more animus towards Marcel Breuer than he did to Foster – proposed stacking up a provocative cascade of architectural fragments on top of the original museum that would have served to mock the puritanical restraint of Breuer's work.

The next high-rise that Foster designed was in Europe: the Frankfurt headquarters of Commerzbank. Standing considerably higher than the Hong Kong and Shanghai Bank, it was for almost two decades the tallest office tower in Europe. But despite its impressive height, its elegant proportions, and its high-level garden courts, it has received far less attention over the years than the Hong Kong and Shanghai Bank.

Though the Commerzbank cuts an imposing mark on Frankfurt's city skyline, it wears its effort lightly. The tower has a triangular floor plan, with no lift cores in the centre; they are positioned at the edges. And at intervals throughout the height of the tower, there are clusters of garden conservatories that give office workers a connection with the outside world beyond the bubble of the bank interior.

Like Foster's Swiss Re tower in London, it is instantly recognisable. The Hong Kong and Shanghai Bank, despite the remarkable and sustained level of innovation that went into every detail of its design and construction, does not make a mark on the skyline in the same way. Despite its flamboyant structure, its grey steel skin makes it recede into the background, dominated by brasher neighbours. Viewed from Kowloon, though it is not blocked by any structure in front of it, the fact that it is set back from the water leaves it less distinct than the newer towers that have been built since it was finished in 1985. Hong Kong has changed almost out of recognition since then. The Hong Kong Club that once stood as the bank's neighbour on Statue Square was demolished in 1982, replaced by Harry

Seidler's twenty-four-floor tower. And there is a new generation of sleek isolated ultra high-rises that dwarf Foster's building. These days, Cesar Pelli's International Finance Centre tower is the logo for Hong Kong rather than the HSBC. But Foster's tower was never a building driven by a simple-minded obsession with height. It still exudes a quiet authority that is expressed both in the impressive explosion of space overhead as you pass beneath the dangling glass undercroft, and in the impeccable precision with which every piece of the building is made.

And for the most part that is the Foster approach. In Shanghai, where you can find everything from forty-storey-high plasma advertising screens and hotels topped by what look like giant pineapples, Foster's Jiushi tower, completed in 2001, is a mere forty storeys and a model of discretion compared with what surrounds it. It is very different in London, where the Swiss Re tower has an unmistakable presence in a way that helps to define the image of London around the world. The Collserola communications mast built on the hills overlooking the city did the job for Barcelona in the way that Foster's unbuilt Rossiya tower would have done for Moscow.

In the City of London, the Swiss Re tower – built on the site of the Baltic Exchange, which was devastated by an IRA bomb in 1992 – can be seen against the sky both from the ground, and at long range. Though huge, it seems to insinuate itself into the London landscape almost by stealth. We are not even meant to call it the Swiss Re tower. That would smack too much of a cult of personality for its careful insurance company owners. In fact, after planning permission was granted Swiss Re decided only to occupy part of the tower for its own use.

According to estate agents who struggled to let the empty upper half of its thirty-four floors, the gherkin, as it has been nicknamed, is actually 30 St Mary Axe, the kind of blandly discreet name that could suggest almost anything – a Georgian rectory, perhaps, or a dignified stone-faced banking hall. Anything, in fact, except what it really is: the most conspicuous eruption on London's skyline in a quarter of a century; a single building that is as big as a small town, with 50,000 square metres of space, able to accommodate 4,000 people with ease.

Swiss Re was responsible for igniting London's post-millennial preoccupation with the skyscraper. It broke the 180-metre barrier in the Square Mile for the first time since 1979, when Tower 42 – Richard Seifert's brash NatWest Bank head-quarters – opened the field to the rush of tall buildings that have followed.

Despite its obvious phallic shape, the Swiss Re tower is much more than the one-liner you might initially expect. It is another progression in Foster's application of a green agenda to the building of high-rise towers. The structure is a muscular steel basket, sheathed in a smooth glass skin. At the pavement, it emerges from the diamond-pattern glass to create an arcade of shops at street level.

The argument against the tower during the controversy over its planning application was that it would look too dominant on the skyline. Not only would it be excessively tall, the circular plan and shape would lend it even more prominence than its size. In fact, although the gherkin is visible from long distances, it can't be seen from everywhere. As you move in and around the City, it slips in and out of view.

Clearly this is an effect that is beyond the control of the architect. But Foster has been careful to create a civilised dialogue between the tower and its nearest neighbours, which include the bronze glass Commercial Union Tower and the little-known but handsome offices for the Holland Line, a favourite of Mies van der Rohe designed shortly before the First World War by the Dutch architect Hendrik Petrus Berlage. The result is an intimate plaza, where the sun casts reflections of the diamond pattern of Foster's building over its neighbours, like tattoos or the logos on Louis Vuitton luggage.

Close up, it is impossible to see the top of the tower, which curves out of sight like a balloon. Further away, especially from the east, the tower appears to erupt over the City's fringes like a colossus.

As important as the layered exterior, with its dual skins of glass and opening windows designed to minimise the energy load, is the fact that the tower is conceived not as a single monolith but has been designed to function as a stack of grouped floors. Each group of six floors is linked by a spiralling open atrium that twists around the building, opening up the structure and offering a sense of belonging to a wider entity than merely the floor on which you happen to be sitting. The result is a disruption of the oppressive flat ceiling that is the most universal and chilling aspect of deep-plan, aircraft hangar-sized office floors.

Once, when you went up one of the few isolated towers, you were alone in the clouds. Now you find yourself up on the thirtieth floor, eye to eye with people looking back at you from the thirtieth floor on the other side of the road. The fabric of the city is being squeezed upwards, into the sky. The Swiss Re's pièce de resistance is the last two floors in the nose cone of the tower, what Peter Scott, Foster's project architect, called 'the mountain top'. The peak is a glass bubble, with 360-degree, uninterrupted views. This is, for once, an interior that justifies the word sensational. There is nothing to get in the way of an awesomely dramatic view. You have left the solid, dependable

pavements of the City of London and climbed into the strato-
sphere, to look down on the capital as if you were a mountaineer.

The view, from Windsor to the Thames estuary, is fit for a
master of the universe; the place radiates a sense of power over
the human ants below. All this was too much for a Swiss
insurance company which is so dedicated to egalitarianism that
it has not a single corporate parking place in the basement.
Even senior executives are expected to travel by public transport,
which, provided you can define a taxi as a form of public
transport, they do. There is no way that the chairman of such
an organisation could possibly have his desk up here. Unlike
Jean Nouvel's even more phallic Agbar Tower in Barcelona,
where the chief executive does indeed work in an office in the
nose cone, in London it is a communal dining room, somewhere
for tenants to take their guests for a corporate lunch, to look
down over Europe's financial heart – and get a glimpse of the
jets taking off from Heathrow, twenty miles away, or to follow
the glinting river as it wraps itself around the Tate Modern, the
Tower of London and Canary Wharf in a series of tight
serpentine coils.

It is also a place to reflect on the paradox of a structure that
seems so ordinary at street level, yet so out of the ordinary up
here in the clouds.

The *New Yorker*'s architecture critic, Paul Goldberger, not normally overawed by Foster, calls him 'the Mozart of Modernism',
and describes the Hearst Tower as the most beautiful high-rise
to be built in Manhattan since 1967. Goldberger puts Foster in
almost the same category as Mies van der Rohe and the
Seagram tower. He is even more enthusiastic about the interior.

He calls the lobby as much of a surprise as the spiral at the heart of Frank Lloyd Wright's Guggenheim Museum.

Foster has succeeded brilliantly with a commission that involved putting 100,000 square metres of offices on top of an existing Art Deco structure. It is a combination that could have looked uncomfortable and freakish. Instead, Foster has developed a convincing strategy for an office tower that is entirely distinctive but shows no sign of straining for effect. He animates the tower not just by exposing its triangulated structure – an arrangement that is strong enough to reduce the cost of the steel by 20 per cent compared with a conventional design – but by crumpling the façade, pushing each corner in and out to follow the geometry of the building, giving it a massive, craggy quality, very different from the curtain-like nature of most glass towers.

This is much more than a convincing piece of sculpture and structural logic, it is equally a piece of contextualism, and of historic preservation, that makes a strong contribution to the vitality of the city. Indeed, the Hearst Tower resembles the pair of linked towers Foster proposed in the ill-fated Ground Zero competition, albeit on a much smaller scale, which also had the diamond pattern Foster used for the Swiss Re tower in London and the Hearst Tower.

At forty-two storeys, the Hearst is modest by New York standards, yet even in a city crowded with skyscrapers it stands out. Like the Swiss Re, it tries to do things differently to overcome the sheer inevitability with which most high-rise architecture clothes a box shape, but the differences between the two are as instructive as the similarities. Swiss Re has a circular floor plan while the Hearst is rectangular. But the Hearst Tower's faceted diamond structure introduces ambiguity into the order of its structure that is lacking with Swiss Re. Its crystalline geometry is like a cubist version of the Swiss Re cylinder. The diamond panels slant in and out, touching at just five points, every eight floors. It works the magic trick of abolishing corners.

In fact the Hearst tower is symmetrical, but the diamond pattern of its façades makes it look as if it isn't. As you move around mid-town Manhattan, you keep getting glimpses of a tower whose character seems to shift with every new view. Swiss Re, on the other hand, is exactly the same from wherever you see it. And while Swiss Re is something of a non-event at the pavement, the Hearst Tower has a much stronger presence at ground level. William Randolph Hearst commissioned the original New York headquarters for his publishing empire in 1928. The Viennese exile Joseph Urban designed a six-storey Art Deco block, faced in stone, which was always intended to be the base for a tower that, even seventy years later, still hadn't been built. Urban used the language of Busby Berkeley for a design that would have looked more at home in Hollywood than within sight of Central Park on Eighth Avenue. Foster kept the stone base as a kind of skirt, allowing the tower to float above it, neither continuing the original aesthetic nor ignoring it.

Inside its skin he has carved out what he describes as a town square, but does not reveal it at once. Coming through the bronze doors of Urban's original façade, visitors are confronted with banks of escalators funnelling them through a cascading waterfall and up to an expansive vaulted space that explosively reveals itself. As they ascend, they find themselves in a light-filled cathedral, five floors high, with the elevator lobby, a staff café and other social amenities at its centre, offering an exemplary demonstration of what a high-rise can offer a city.

The two aspects of the nature of Foster's practice – the over-the-horizon visionary and the pragmatic problem solver – are given an equal amount of expression in his high-rise work. There are his efficient, smooth-skinned containers for corporations looking to project themselves as equally smooth and efficient. But there are also the projects on the outer reaches of possibility, in which he invests as much, if not more, energy. And there is something about Foster's continuing ability to push himself into a future that is going to be happening whether we want it or not that makes them compelling, if also a little disturbing at times. That is particularly true of the extreme high-rise projects that he has worked on over the years.

When the Japanese government was looking for ways to stimulate the country's economy in the post-bubble deflation years of the 1990s, one of its more imaginative strategies was to encourage its big construction corporations to explore the feasibility of radical new infrastructure projects. This led in turn to Foster being commissioned by the Obayashi Corporation to explore the idea of an ultra-high-rise tower that came to be known as the Millennium Tower. They required much more than an attention-grabbing artist's impression of how the tower would look; what they wanted to see was not just a landmark, but a detailed breakdown of all aspects of the essential technology. Among other issues, the study looked very hard at the configuration of the lift shafts. In a building planned to be 2,500 feet high, they would need to be more like a vertical mass-transit system than a conventional lift.

In the Japanese context, with vertiginous escalation in land prices in the Tokyo area, an ultra-high-rise tower would make more use of scarce land. It was also important to fit in with Foster's continuing interest in high-density living as an environmentally responsible approach.

The first idea was to site the tower on an artificial island, reclaimed from the sea in Tokyo Bay, linked to the mainland by a causeway. But there were subsequent investigations of some other sites on land that suggested other places to put the tower.

The tower would have been cone shaped, with a circular base as wide as Tokyo's Olympic Stadium and the capacity to accommodate as many as 52,000 people. At the time it seemed like a fantastic, impossible speculation: the Petronas building in Kuala Lumpur was the world's tallest tower under construction at the time, and the Japanese tower would have been a full 300 metres taller.

Since then, things have changed enormously. When the overheated boom in Dubai was cut short by the credit crunch, the Burj al Arab tower actually finished thirty metres taller than Foster had proposed for the project. What we do not know yet is whether the Burj tower will come to be seen as a freakish one-off, left beached by the tide, as anomalous as the indoor ski slopes that Dubai built in its shopping malls, or whether it will serve as a pointer to the scale of a new generation of towers.

Certainly the Japanese project would have been much more than a single building. David Nelson, who ran the project, described it as a vertical town in which the lift cores would have served as the people-mover for the main street:

We always intended to mix commercial and residential space inside the tower. The concept was to plan the tower as if it were a series of vertical railway stations, or sky centres as we called them, around a special lift system. There would have been fast lifts to serve each sky centre, around which, just like a station, there would have been a cluster of restaurants, supermarkets, cafés and cinemas. The sky centres would act as refuges in case of fire: people could shelter safely in them for up to six hours, and there would also be fire-protected lift shafts to take them back down to the ground. The tower would have been built using a weather-protected construction platform that would rise as each floor was completed, with all work being done under cover.

According to Nelson, this was not 'blue skies' speculation, but a plan with every intention of translating into reality:

We were commissioned to provide the architectural lead for the project by Obayashi, one of the biggest Japanese construction companies, and they had thirty engineers working on it. The economics had to be calculated to a sound commercial standard. We worked on two versions of the project. The first was a technical study: we had to be sure that it would be safe, and to work out what to do about steel shrinkage. At the bottom of the tower, it could be up to two metres as the full load was applied. We had to think about the cycles of the commercial market; we can count on both upturns and downturns during the building programme, so the design allowed for the mix of uses to vary as you went up. You could occupy each sector of the building as it was finished, and you could build it using a much more automated system than conventional prefabrication, using robotics on site.

Even in earthquake-prone Japan, the real problem when designing ultra-high-rise towers is the wind. A typhoon can add a load to a structure equivalent to the crowd in two fully occupied stadiums. It is this primary consideration that accounts for the tower's shape. There are major advantages to designing towers that are circular rather than square. They reduce the drag, and so the wind loading. That means less steel is needed. Circular buildings are also easier to build, because all the structural components are the same; a square building is more complex.

For very tall towers, there is another problem: under some wind loads, a vortex effect is created on the leeward side, which can start up a violent sway. To reduce it, the proportions of the tower, and the texture of the surface, are critical. 'You have to rough it up a bit,' says David Nelson. 'This, coupled with the need to concentrate most of the mass of the building at lower levels to combat earthquake stresses, quickly led us to the conical shape.'

Foster's brief was not to work on the tallest tower conceivable. 'It is perfectly possible, technically, to build a skyscraper a mile high, or more if you wanted to, but this project was about asking whether people would like to live there. In a European city, anything past eight storeys is seen as very alien, partly because it is associated with low-cost housing. In Hong Kong, I lived on the twenty-first floor, and it was a very different experience; you could live and work in the same building, and there was still a feeling of community.'

Foster used the name Millennium Tower again for a project designed at the request of Trafalgar House. It was intended for the Baltic Exchange site that was eventually occupied by the Swiss Re tower. London's Millennium Tower would have been

375 metres. This was a planning application that was not welcomed by the City of London. Envisaged as a mixed development, with homes and office space, there were suspicions at the time that it was a project intended ultimately to fail, to ease the path of the more modest, but still very tall by London standards.

But the Millennium Tower did represent the beginning of a big shift in the formal treatment of high-rise towers. It was not a box in the conventional manner of the 1960s and 1970s, nor was it adopting the historical dress of the post-modernists of the 1980s. And it moved beyond the exoskeleton that Foster had explored to its limits with Hong Kong. Rather it seemed to open the way to a more free-form, sculptural attitude to building tall.

Five

Architecture and power

Even if he is determined to present his architecture as essentially democratic in the way that European modernists of a particular kind have always tried to do, Norman Foster is not given to taking overtly political stands. Usually, he confines himself to those issues that are related directly to architecture. He did sign a letter to the *Sunday Times* in support of Richard Rogers, taking issue with the Prince of Wales's attempts to set himself up as an arbiter of public taste. He supports a charity building schools in Sierra Leone. But he has never put his name to more clearly political causes.

He was introduced to the House of Lords in the summer of 1999 by Lord Weidenfeld and Lord Sainsbury, as a politically neutral crossbench peer, and he made his politely well-intentioned but uncontroversial maiden speech on the import-ance of design four years later. He suggested that 'a debate about design is, for me, a debate about values, because I sincerely believe that there is a moral imperative for good design; to do it well and responsibly. Design is not an add-on, it is not a cosmetic, it is not window-dressing.' But Foster avoids involve-ment in the craft of everyday party politics, or of government.

Unlike Rogers, who as a working Labour peer can be found haunting Westminster's lobbies, sitting on task forces, and putting his name to policy documents, Foster is essentially an apolitical public figure who seldom attends parliament. His extensive experience of working in China, Russia and the Islamic world has left him reluctant to accept unchallenged Western claims to have a monopoly on the democratic virtues. Given the fact of the US Military Commission Act of 2006 which legitimised torture in the name of homeland security and British complicity in that policy, he cites the double standards of the Western powers when challenged about the implications of working in states with clouded records on civil rights.

But his approach to politics is more concerned with the tactics of building in a complex world. At a philosophical scale, he has the utopian streak inherited from Buckminster Fuller, complete with all the attendant inherent paradoxes. He is patently sincere about the green imperative, but he nevertheless leaves a conspicuous carbon footprint as he constantly criss-crosses the globe, underwritten by a personal carbon offset scheme. In his House of Lords speech he described design as:

> a core, primary activity because anything in any part of the world that we inhabit has to be made. But before it is made it has to be designed. There are no exceptions, whether it is on the scale of a city, the infrastructure of its buildings, the equipment in them, the infrastructure of streets and public spaces, pavements, the paving slabs, the door handles and even the invisible digital electronic world – it all has to be designed. It is a human act because design is a response to the needs of people, whether they are spiritual or material. The quality of that design affects the quality of all of our lives.

His speech continued:

Designers continually face new challenges, some caused by irresponsible past strategies, the threat of global warming and population growth. They affect the balance of an island nation as much as a mega-city on the Pacific Rim. The challenges are the same, only the scale varies. I passionately believe that we have to build more densely in urban areas and – a vital coupling – when we do that we have to improve the standard of urban living. It may mean building taller, but not always. It certainly means producing more housing of higher quality and at lower cost. I believe passionately that history is on the side of the density argument. Buildings consume half the energy produced in an industrialised society; transport and industry, the infrastructure, the remainder. Given the link between energy production, pollution and global warming, the threat to the fragile planet's eco-system, there are strong arguments for reducing the energy demands in building and infrastructure. The quest for a greener, more ecologically responsible design is not about fashion, but about survival. Designers can advocate with passion, but in the end they are only as good as those who lead; those who have the courage and the political will to set standards and raise goals.

Whatever public stances Foster does or does not take, avoiding dealing with the political aspects of architecture while running a practice with the scale and worldwide reach that his has is not an option. Architecture is an arm of statecraft, a means of representing national aspirations and a way to define power and territory. That is why architects with Foster's blend of sophistication and toughness get hired. Their architecture is used to build a sense of shared national identity, and to mark and even to shape the course of historical events. To realise architecture on a public scale demands an engagement with the powerful. It is a relationship based on mutual dependence, but it is never the architect who is in command. The successful architect is the one who is most able to use his client to realise his architectural vision, without it becoming entirely subordinated to political calculation, or worse, to the megalomania of power.

The imponderable question is, which side gets the better of the bargain? Is architecture the product of power, or is that power in fact an outcome of the exercise of architecture? As Foster has grown older and more materially successful, he has had more and more occasion to face those questions.

Within the hermetic bubble of the architectural world, a building can plausibly be read as having one, possibly harmless, set of meanings. In the wider world, beyond that bubble, it will almost certainly have an entirely different meaning.

Kazakhstan is a young state which has an unusually evenly balanced mix of the world's religious faiths, thanks to Stalin's use of the republic, with its climatic extremes, as a penal colony in which to dump his victims from all over the Soviet Union. Its president, Nursultan Nazarbayev, commissioned a glass-tipped stone-faced pyramid from Foster for his new capital Astana. Nazarbayev described it as the Palace of Peace and Reconciliation; a multi-faith monument and conference centre-cum-opera house.

Narrowly defined as a work of architecture, it can be understood as a not very successful example of Foster's purist manner. A wider understanding of its meaning would be as a more or less successful act of self-aggrandisement or nation building – take your pick – by a ruler whose administration has been plagued by allegations of nepotism, corruption and wrongdoing with even the president's own family implicated. In spite of the fact that at least two leaders of opposition political parties have died in suspicious circumstances, the West continues to support Nazarbayev, who presides over the most stable and oil-rich state in a particularly troubled region.

Nazarbayev presents the pyramid as a symbol of religious tolerance. For Foster, it is the product of building in the most challenging circumstances and timescale. In the remotest of locations, with the most extreme climate conditions, the project was completed within two years, and in the face of a last-minute addition of a full-size opera house to the brief.

Foster has an acute sense for the symbolic qualities of architecture, beyond the overt functional role that it is conventionally expected to play. Ask him which of his buildings he feels is his most successful, and unhesitatingly he will name the new Reichstag in Berlin, closely followed by the Pont Millau, the sublime road bridge in the South of France that marches in seven giant, stately steps across the River Tarn, as far above the valley floor as the tip of the Eiffel Tower is off the ground.

Foster identifies the essential qualities of both structures as being rooted in their symbolic value. 'Like the Pont Millau, which has come to define a whole region, what makes the Reichstag special is that it has transcended the boundaries of its material function and it has come to symbolise a city, and even a nation,' he says.

But it wasn't only the symbolic value of the Pont Millau that Foster had in mind when he anxiously came to inspect the impact of the decision he had made to colour the cables and the handrails white, rather than black. It was their visual impact against the sky he was assessing. Would white make them look more, or less intrusive? He had chosen white as the way to make the visually unimportant elements of the design as invisible as possible on the basis of a long-ago conversation with Henry Moore when they were positioning his reclining figure at the Sainsbury Centre. Looking at the finished bridge, it is clear that he took the right decision.

France is not Kazakhstan, but it is a state which places a strong emphasis on the political uses of architecture. Working with Michel Virlogeux, the French engineer who was responsible for the calculations on which the design depends, in the Pont Millau Foster produced a design which triumphantly demonstrates that it is still possible to make utilitarian structures look beautiful in a contemporary way. And not uncoincidentally it gave the French president, Jacques Chirac, a memorable photo opportunity when he opened the tallest bridge in the world at the end of 2004. At a time when his standing in the opinion polls was lower than any other president in the entire term of the Fifth Republic, he was able for a moment at least to look decisive, in command, and as if he were adding to his nation's prestige.

Foster's reconstruction of the burnt-out shell of the Reichstag in Berlin was loaded with symbolic meaning in a way that goes far beyond the creation of a landmark. It represents, among many other things, the reunification of the two Germanies, a new German commitment to environmental sustainability, with its biomass-fuelled air conditioning system, as well as a par-

ticularly unthreatening form of the expression of national identity. Foster + Partners is, after all, still regarded in Germany as
a British firm even as it grows steadily more cosmopolitan in
the national origins of its staff and its worldwide reach. And for
a non-German to be invited to play such a key role in shaping
an essential national landmark for Germany was clearly no
accident, but an entirely deliberate decision intended to reflect
on the character of the state. Indeed, when Foster was first
invited by the president of the German parliament, Rita
Süssmuth, to take part in the competition to design the building,
while he realised that it would be impossible to refuse, he
thought it inconceivable that a non-German would ever secure
such a highly charged commission.

During the long-drawn-out design process – the scheme went
through at least three different incarnations before it was finally
completed in 1999 – Foster found himself continually having to
deal with the political meanings of his architectural decisions.
Everything about the Reichstag, from the shape of its roof, to
the colour of its walls, to the glint in the eye of the eagle that
serves to represent the authority of the German parliament to
govern, and which dominates the debating chamber, in the end
had to be understood as political issues.

In 1991, when an almost evenly divided German parliament
voted narrowly in favour of relocating itself back to Berlin from
Bonn, where the federal government had sat out the Cold War,
the national mood was expansive. Germany was looking for a
flamboyant and monumental gesture with which to celebrate
the reunification of the state.

The Reichstag's baroque revival stone hulk had survived the
fire allegedly started by a Dutch Communist arsonist in 1933 that
gave Hitler his excuse to seize absolute power. The parliament

building had been shattered by shell and tank fire as the Red Army fought its way into Berlin in the last days of the Second World War. There followed a desultory attempt at restoring the building in a still divided city, but the Reichstag failed to find a satisfactory new role. Just a few metres away from the wall, with its death strip of mines and razor wire patrolled by dogs and watched over by machine-gun posts that the East Germans had built to slice the city in half, it was all but cut off from the rest of West Berlin, and almost unusable.

In the context of a reunited Berlin, it had be adapted to function on a practical level. The new Reichstag needed to take account of the changed circumstances of the city if it was to work as a piece of urbanism. It also had to serve as a physical representation of how the new Germany felt about itself.

Foster was one of three finalists in the competition to remodel the building. The eighty German entrants had all been eliminated, leaving him pitched against the Spanish architect Santiago Calatrava and Pi de Bruijn from the Netherlands. Calatrava had made a reputation for himself as the designer of crowd-pleasing bridges that took the form of strong architectural gestures by looking for inspiration in organic natural forms. De Bruijn had been responsible for expanding the legislature in The Hague, demonstrating a strong technical grasp of the issues involved in planning a parliament. Foster had a larger office than his two rivals, a track record that included a wider range of buildings, and a reputation for building specifically modern landmarks such as his skyscraper for the Commerzbank in Frankfurt, a project that appealed to the taste of the German political class, who preferred confident neutral modernism to overemphatic post-modernism.

In what could be understood as an act of exorcism of Berlin's recent history, as well as of Germany's troubled past, Foster proposed placing a steel-and-glass canopy soaring over the reconstructed stone shell of Paul Wallot's original building. Resembling a giant table sitting on top of the parliament, it would have entirely transformed its meaning, rendering the project a memorial to the past, while at the same time demonstrating that the new parliament building signified a departure from history. It rightly emerged as the favoured design among the three finalists. It had something new to say, in a way that its competitors did not.

But once the euphoria of German reunification had evaporated and the taxpayers of the old West Germany began to grasp the financial implications of bringing the ramshackle infrastructure of the DDR up to Western standards, all three architects involved in the competition were asked to take part in a second round. Their instructions were to find a way to make their designs cheaper.

It was an overly simple question that Foster did not feel comfortable trying to answer. 'They asked us to shrink the brief. It was as if they had asked us to design a bus, and then come back for us to turn it into a people mover,' says Foster.

Calatrava and de Bruijn set about finding ways of reducing the cost of their initial proposals, but typically Foster wanted to start again with a clean sheet. Because it was far from clear exactly how much Germany was prepared to spend on its parliament, it was not a straightforward process.

'We asked for a budget, but they wouldn't give us one,' says Foster. So he came up with what seemed like an appropriate notional building cost, based on a calculation of what an acceptable level of running costs would amount to.

There was also a need to explore exactly what elements of government would be located within the building. In the first round of the competition, Foster had envisaged locating the party caucus rooms that are an essential part of the German democratic system elsewhere, while Pi de Bruijn advocated placing the debating chamber in a detached structure.

The new Foster proposal would concentrate functional elements within one building, while reining back on ceremonial and monumental space. The result was a much simpler, and far more modest building: the soaring canopy disappeared and the new debating chamber was inserted behind the restored stone façade. It won the final phase of the competition.

There was no sign in the winning design of the rectangular based dome that had been the most conspicuous element in the original building – inspired in part by Vanbrugh's design for Blenheim Palace. Every trace of that original dome had been destroyed by a combination of war, fire, neglect, and post-war rebuilding. To make a literal reconstruction of how it had once looked went counter to all the architectural principles that Foster had come to believe in. Yet to a vocal and influential minority within Germany, it would be unthinkable to build a new parliament without a dome. In their eyes a dome is as much an essential representation of Germany as the clock tower of the Palace of Westminster is for Britain.

> As soon as we were appointed, there was a campaign led by the Right in the parliament demanding that we reconstruct the dome. I was so hostile to the idea that I said if they insisted on a dome then we should cut the contract in two. We would do our bit, and leave the rest to somebody else.

It was an uncharacteristically demonstrative gesture. Foster has built his career by making the most of an apparently imperturbable façade. He certainly does have a will that is not lightly to be challenged, but it isn't often on show to his clients.

The Christian Democratic Union was backing a proposal put forward by a German architect to add a historically faithful reconstruction of the Reichstag's original dome to Foster's proposal. Outright opposition to the idea would, in the charged climate of debate on the issue, have weakened Foster's position and compromised the design. Instead he backed down far enough, if not to produce a dome of his own, then at least to design a marker that demonstrated on the outside of the building how much had changed inside.

He describes the glass spiral that sits on the roof of the rebuilt structure as a cupola, and maintains that its shape is not a recreation of the flattened dome that topped the old Reichstag: 'As I thought more about it, I began to work on the idea of making a sign to show that something has changed at the Reichstag. The building has been transformed internally, and that is being manifested on the outside.'

While the Reichstag still looks a massive, and essentially traditional stone building from the outside, once you are inside the debating chamber the masonry is revealed as no more than a taut skin, one that barely contains the spatially explosive interior. This is no longer a building with a Beaux-Arts plan and a traditional sensibility. It has been transformed into a spectacular and entirely new single-volume space.

For Foster, the glass structure on the roof of the parliament is important because it reflects a new life on the inside. But it is more than a formal gesture. It has a functional role too. The dome is there to ventilate the debating chamber and to bring daylight into the heart of the building in an energy-efficient way. At the same time, it creates a public viewing platform, looking out over the whole of Berlin.

The first drawings for the cupola hinted that there could be a cylinder on the roof of the parliament radiating beams of light out over the city, as if it were a lighthouse, like something that might have been imagined by the German expressionists from the 1920s such as Bruno Taut and Paul Scheerbart.

Foster began the design process by envisaging all these as distinct elements, or unconnected episodes in a narrative, before coming up with a means for realising them in a workable way as part of a single coherent strategy:

> I remember agonising for a long period with David Nelson, struggling hard to understand how we could make the dome channel light inside the debating chamber and also to understand how we could bring the public up to the building at roof level. At first the ideas that we had come up with were not connected. We made huge 1:20 scale models of the dome, and also of the chamber. They were big enough for three people to stand up in at the same time. We hauled them up to the top of the Reichstag to see how things would work in situ. The only way that we could get the model and ourselves on the roof was to take them up in the bucket of a crane. We wanted to see if it would really make the interior lighter in winter and if it was possible to use the cupola to act as a screen in summer.

In the end, these initial ideas were synthesised in a glass structure with a spiralling access ramp, and an array of mirrors hanging over the chamber below to direct sunlight into the interior. This was a new version of an idea that has continually recurred in

Foster's work, ever since he proposed something like it for his scheme for Fred Olsen's offices in the Norwegian forest, and installed a sun scoop on the outside of the Hong Kong and Shanghai Bank to track the sun and direct it down into the tower's atrium. He was using a mechanism to cancel out the effects of architecture.

In Norway, Foster wanted to minimise disturbance to the woodland site that Olsen had chosen for its headquarters. The image he had of the building was of a machine that gave the impression that it had temporarily alighted in the forest, and was prepared to take off again just as gently as it had arrived, without leaving a mark. The intention had been to mount a series of mirrors on the roof, deployed at an angle that would catch the glancing rays of the sun and divert them down into the centre of the deep open-plan offices, thus making the most of the weak sunlight in that far northern latitude.

The sun-scoop concept was taken further in Hong Kong. There are twin arrays of mirrors, one located outside the building, on the south face at the level of the first double-height suspension truss, the other inside at the same level, at the top of the atrium of the banking hall. The outer array is mounted on a set of runners driven by pre-programmed electric motors that allow it to track the sun, catch its rays, and beam them on to the interior mirrors that in turn reflect them down into the atrium and on to the floor of the banking hall. Minute computer-controlled adjustments to the angle of the sequence of mirrors were calculated and preset to track the varying path of the sun during different seasons and to make the most of the available light by avoiding the internal structure. As a result, the sun's rays work their way down one side of the interior of the atrium and across the floor every day, transforming the interior with the qualities of natural light. It is perhaps the single most audacious idea that Foster has ever realised. It cancels out the effect of the plan and section, and creates architecture that is more like a responsive mechanism than a passive system.

The origins of the sun scoop can be traced all the way back to the young Foster's bicycle ride to Jodrell Bank in 1957, to see Manchester University's huge 76-metre-diameter steerable radio telescope, with its breathtaking white-painted steel dish supported on a substructure that could be made to move gently up and down in pursuit of the vapour trails left by the booster rockets falling away from the aftermath of the first Sputnik launch.

For Foster, the Reichstag roof was a means to achieve better environmental conditions, to provide public access, and to symbolise the new political order that had called the structure into being. To his embittered architectural rival Santiago Calatrava, it was a dome. And not just any dome. It was a dome that Calatrava accused Foster of having stolen from his unsuccessful competition entry. Calatrava wrote angry letters to everybody that he could think of, from Helmut Kohl downward. He threatened to take Germany to court, and wanted to sue Foster.

It was not the first time Calatrava had been moved to litigation. He took on the municipalities of both Bilbao and Barcelona for allegedly tampering with his bridges. In the end, it all came to nothing. Foster quietly pointed out that while Calatrava's design had indeed included a glass dome, it had four sides, unlike his. In any case, the idea was hardly an original one. Berlin is a city with hundreds of domes to learn from, so why would Foster have chosen to copy Calatrava's?

Calatrava remains angry about Berlin. At the time of the

opening of the Reichstag, the Spanish newspaper *El País* asked him if he had recovered from the experience. 'Yes, but everything was turning to shit. I was on the verge of closing the studio.' He refused to answer the newspaper's questions about whether or not he was on speaking terms with Foster, and went on to compare himself, with no false modesty, to Bach and to Frank Lloyd Wright: 'I am with him when he says that, with truth on his side, he is ready to take on the world. There is truth in my structures.'

The dome was not the only architectural issue with a political dimension that Foster had to deal with at the Reichstag. Towards the end of the building process, while in the course of guiding Helmut Kohl on a hard-hat tour of the construction site, he found himself subjected to a sermon from the German chancellor on youth, colour and architecture, peppered with appropriate historical references. This was not a purely rhetorical outburst. Kohl was determined that, whatever his architect believed, the parliament of the German Federal Republic would have a colour scheme considerably brighter than the intentionally sober debating chamber that Foster had proposed. White and grey, silver and black and might be fine for architects to live with, but ordinary Germans needed something more cheerful – or so Kohl believed. And in the end he got his way, even if, in the normal course of events, German building contracts give architects considerably more authority than British ones do.

Despite the fact that Foster's official client was not the chancellor but a specially designated parliamentary sub-committee, led by the president of the chamber, Rita Süssmuth, Foster thought again. He asked the Danish graphic designer Per Arnoldi to take another look at the colour palette, which accounts for a rather more vivid interior than the one that Foster had originally intended.

Foster's experiences with Kohl bring home the difference between architecture and art. Years later, Foster got to know Richard Serra, an artist who had been engaged to work on another major project in Berlin, collaborating with the architect Peter Eisenman on the Holocaust memorial next to the Brandenburg Gate. Serra resigned after a meeting with Kohl made it brutally clear to him that the Chancellor of the German Federal Republic expected to have his views on matters of artistic policy respected. Architects do not have the same room for manoeuvre.

Kohl did, however, back Foster's decision to expose the graffiti left on the Reichstag's walls by the Red Army. The Russians stormed the building twice in 1945; the first time to flush out German snipers, the second, a few days later, for the benefit of the film crews attempting to immortalise the heroism of Soviet soldiers. However unpalatable it might be to some of the chamber's more conservative politicians, who interpret the sometimes obscene Cyrillic scrawls as a desecration, they form an essential part of German history. Foster quickly had these difficult traces of the recent past carefully photographed to provide a record so that they could not casually be wiped out.

Of all the political debates about design at the Reichstag, none took more time and proved ultimately more futile than resolving the issue of the shape of the eagle that symbolises the authority of the German state and which dominates the debating chamber.

The controversy about the eagle goes back to the founding of the German Federal Republic from the ruins of the Third

Reich. It was conceived as a liberal new state, rooted in the conviction of its founders that Germany could never again allow itself to succumb to the horror of a dictatorship, or to become an international aggressor. It was a view that shaped everything, from the country's legal system and its constitution, to its foreign policy, and the nature of German architecture.

Part of the price Germany paid for its liberation from the terrible memory of its recent past was to be the abolition of monumental architecture. Assertive architecture of any kind, and in particular any reference to classicism, became impossible, for the next fifty years at least. And so the eagle in the debating chamber of the Bonn parliament was designed to look as peaceable, and as unlike the martial insignia adopted by the Nazis, as the expressionist sculptor Ludwig Gies could make it. The result was the singularly unaerodynamic form of the so-called 'fat hen', which for many Germans born during or just after the Second World War is a key part of their identity. With reunification there was a new Germany which demanded another iconography to represent it.

Foster wanted to come up with something still unthreatening, but rather more elegant than the hen. For a while he became obsessed with eagles. He drew them endlessly, collecting shelves full of reference books. He looked at heraldic precedents for Austrian eagles and German eagles. He even spent a couple of hours motionless in a Japanese mountain valley drawing eagles in flight from life.

He ended up with a futile presentation of his suggestions for a new eagle to sixty parliamentarians in a Berlin committee room. After heated and prolonged debate on the options, they insisted on sticking with the fat hen, to Foster's dismay:

I showed quite a number of eagle options, but the chances were that if anybody fell in love with one of them, there were all kinds of reasons for everybody else not to. The eagle debate was intense, and highly emotional. We finally came down to a modified version of the familiar eagle. It is a somewhat fitter version of the original but still not as lean as I would have liked.

The result is made from cast aluminium and weighs two and a half tons. 'There is a reverse side to the eagle in the chamber that nobody ever sees. If they did, some might say that it seems to be giving a sly wink and a grin.'

The design of the seating layout in the Reichstag was equally long-drawn-out. 'We looked at many different layouts, from circles and semi-circles to the British model of opposing benches. We did full-size mock-ups of the seats. In the end, it was a balance between enjoying an intimate setting and avoiding too much proximity between individuals.'

Foster succeeded in giving modern Germany a new landmark, one which, just before construction started, went through the ritual of its wrapping by Christo and Jean-Claude, to emerge after the rebuilding process in a new form that has wiped away memories of the smoke billowing from the old dome on the night in 1933 when its torching served as the signal for Hitler to seize power.

The experience of the Reichstag was an object lesson in the craft of politics for Foster. 'It was the first building that we had done that was fought and won in public by the media,' he recalls. 'Our design sessions with the politicians were supposed to be closed and confidential. Yet you could see them running out to phone the papers before we had even finished talking, and you would read about everything that had been said in print the following morning.'

It was not to be the last time that Foster found the details of the design process turned into the subject of newspaper head-lines. This is nowhere more true than in London, where his growing material success has given him a visibility that very few British architects ever achieve, and so has made him a target for often hostile press attention. It is the kind of attention that at times has overshadowed his architecture. The unveiling of the British Museum's Great Court, for example, should have been one of the defining buildings of Norman Foster's career. But in public relations terms, the museum's opening of the £97 million project just after the Millennium could not have got off to a worse start. The museum was accused of just about everything from dereliction of duty to bad faith in its attempts to make good the void torn out of its heart by the departure of the British Library for St Pancras. There were also claims that the museum was playing fast and loose with its planning permission by building the new glass roof over the courtyard a fraction too high.

Jocelyn Stevens, the excitable former head of English Heri-tage, joined the fight with relish, calling for the resignation of Graham Greene, chairman of the trustees, over what he claimed was the failure of the museum to treat its building – Sir Robert Smirke's Grade One-listed masterpiece – with sufficient respect. He claimed that the trustees knew that the stone being used was not the Portland stone specified in the contract, but was, in fact, a cheaper French substitute, which might meet the letter of the specification but wasn't what Smirke had selected when he designed the museum in 1823. What was more, this consignment of supposedly inferior stone was being offloaded at a premium price.

Stevens called for the royal opening of the museum's courtyard to be postponed until the offending work could be demolished and rebuilt using genuine Portland stone. Given that the museum's finances were already stretched beyond any acceptable limit, it was clearly an unreasonable suggestion. The controversial limestone that the museum's contractors used came from the French rather than the English end of the bed of oolitic limestone that runs under the Channel. The English variety, from Dorset, was chosen to match the original Great Court of 150 years ago. The French variety, known as Anstrude Roche Claire limestone, was a little softer, a little easier to carve, and marginally cheaper. But while the commissioners of English Heritage rebuked the museum for their handling of the affair, in the end they could not bring themselves to say that the French stone represented enough of a discernable loss of quality for them to call for the courtyard to be rebuilt.

Ten years later, the stone episode has joined the abundant lore of colourful scandal that has been a constant part of the museum's history. The magnificent main façade, for example, was built in the 1840s by Baker and Sons, a firm that hadn't submitted the lowest tender for the job, but which, according to J. Mordaunt Crook's riveting architectural history of the museum, did have the vital qualification of a managing director married to the architect's sister.

Foster's task, on which he worked closely with Spencer de Grey, was a complex one. The brief called for the creation of a new use for the centre of the museum that would integrate it with the existing galleries. What's more, they needed to find a way to do all this while remaining respectful of the original building, even in areas that had been hidden by random accretions of crude makeshift additions over many decades.

The original courtyard at the heart of the museum didn't get built in one go. It took almost twenty-five years to finish. So it would never have been entirely uniform. It had always displayed the wear and the scars of the passing of time and had only existed in its planned state for the seven years from 1847 to 1854. At almost two acres, it was bigger than Hanover Square, but according to Thomas Watts, assistant to Anthony Panizzi, the greatest of the librarians of the British Museum, it was 'a dead loss'. Another critic called it the 'finest mason's yard in Europe'. Members of the public were never allowed into what was, by one account, 'a mere well of malaria, a pestilent congregation of vapours'.

The original portico was hacked about to make way for the Reading Room, and when the museum was subjected to the dubious care of the Ministry of Public Building and Works there was constant damage from alterations carried out with all the tenderness of an army of occupation. On top of that the museum sustained damage during the Second World War from a hail of incendiaries, compounded by water penetration from the hoses of the fire brigade in an effort to put out the blaze.

When rebuilding architecture with such a complex history, what do you restore? Smirke had wanted an open courtyard, so do you demolish the Reading Room – the cuckoo planted in the nest – in the interests of authenticity? Do you plough it up and devote it to growing exotic botanical specimens, as Smirke had originally wanted? Do you restore the porticoes around the courtyard to look the way that they were actually built, or do you rebuild them in the manner that Smirke would have built them if the cash had been available to him?

To get to the north wing in the way that Smirke wanted, visitors would have to come through the triumphant colonnade at the front of the museum, negotiate the entrance hall, go out again through the south portico, cross the courtyard, and mount an imposing flight of steps before passing through another, even more impressive portico. Economy reduced this passage from the majestic to something much more modest.

Foster's portico was attacked for its materials and its work-manship. But it was not a reconstruction of something that Smirke had designed. It was a completely new design by Foster and Spencer de Grey that they had produced to deal with contemporary realities. Its deep central opening, and the square light at the upper level intended to give museum visitors a glimpse into the space, had no historical precedent.

Historical accuracy has always been a two-edged sword in architectural restoration projects. In the nineteenth century, William Morris established the Society for the Protection of Ancient Buildings to discourage the kind of over-enthusiastic restoration that in his lifetime took the form of demolishing perpendicular additions to early English gothic cathedrals in order to reconstruct them as the Victorians felt that they ought to have looked. To Morris, this was an act of vandalism that diminished the integrity of those fragments of the building that were genuine. He argued for a strategy of patching up and mending rather than pretending that the new work was anything but new.

Foster's Great Court is not what Smirke designed, but it does give visitors the kind of spatial thrills that Smirke had intended. They move from the richly painted entrance hall into a sudden explosion of light and space beyond, under a remarkable, billowing, glass-and-steel roof that deals with the challenging

No building is more symbolically charged than the Reichstag in Berlin. Its burning triggered the Nazi seizure of power; the Red Army stormed it at the end of the Second World War; and when the two Germanies reunited, the decision to move the parliament of the enlarged state back there from Bonn marked the end of the Cold War. Foster's first competition entry would have exorcised the past, placing the whole structure under an oversailing roof. Cost issues forced a rethink, and the cupola was a further development at the insistence of German politicians, who saw it as a link with the old building.

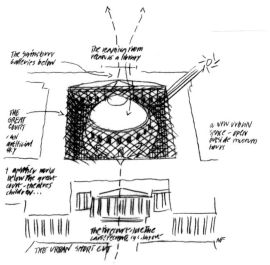

Filling the void left at the heart of the British Museum by the departure of the British Library was both a conceptual and an architectural problem. Robert Smirke had planned an open courtyard, which was soon filled up with the circular reading room. The shell of the reading room is retained at the centrepiece of what Foster conceived as a grand public space that would improve movement around the crowded museum, under a lightweight glass bubble. Most of the attention at the opening focused on exactly where the stone used to face it had come from: England, as specified in the contract, or France, as turned out to be the case.

Bridges depend on the skill of an engineer as well as the vision of an architect. In the case of the Millennium footbridge in London (right), it was a team from Arup who made it possible, and who had to come up with a solution to stabilise it once its tendency to wobble under the load of pedestrian traffic revealed itself. For the spectacular Pont Millau (below), as high off the valley floor as the Eiffel Tower, it was Michel Virlogeux.

The first presentation for the new Hearst Tower was scheduled to take place in New York on the day of the destruction of the World Trade Center. Despite the crisis, Hearst took the decision to go ahead and build a new tower to accommodate their publishing business, on a base formed by an Art Deco street frontage designed by Joseph Urban in the 1930s. The triangulated structure with eroded corners is a striking new approach to tower-building in Manhattan, which provides a strength-to-weight ratio that would have been endorsed by Buckminster Fuller, to whom it owes a debt. The interior has a remarkable art work by Richard Long (above), painstakingly placed by hand, using mud.

This photograph of the new roof of
the British Museum shows the arch at
Wembley Stadium, also designed by
Foster + Partners, in the distance, miles
to the north west. The parabola form is a
striking new landmark on the city's skyline,
and a measure of the remarkable scale of
the impact that Foster has had on London,
where he has built the most prominent
new tower, Swiss Re, City Hall and towers
at Canary Wharf.

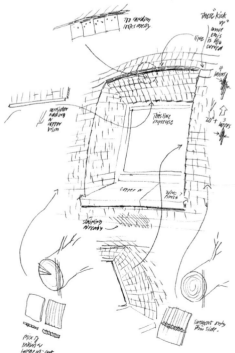

Completed in 2004, Chesa Futura is an apartment building overlooking St Moritz, in Switzerland. The free-form shape, designed to maximise views, seemed to mark a new departure for Foster + Partners in their approach to geometry. The cloud-like exterior is faced with 250,000 wooden shingles, which were cut, one by one, from 100 larch trees by a skilled craftsman.

The new Beijing airport took four years to build, less time than was needed for the rather smaller fifth terminal at Heathrow just to clear the formidable barriers represented by the planning system in Britain. The Foster team, lead by Mouzhan Majidi, Foster + Partners' chief executive, who was previously responsible for building Hong Kong's airport, started work in Beijing on Christmas Day 2003, and set up their office in the ballroom of the old airport hotel shortly afterwards.

When it is completed, Masdar will be a focus for Abu Dhabi's investment in zero-emission technologies, a mix of research facilities and offices, with homes that can accommodate up to 100,000 people. Foster + Partners plan to combine traditional methods to use wind and shade for cooling, with advanced ideas such as electric-powered, self-steering, driverless transport to achieve a carbon-neutral footprint overall.

task of accommodating a rectangular courtyard at the same time as allowing the circular Reading Room to poke through it. No two of the triangular glass panels are exactly the same; this was one of the first major Foster projects to reflect his developing interest in new geometries and much more fluid forms, made possible by new developments in digital modelling.

A mousehole entrance in the newly stone-faced Reading Room – here the stone comes from Spain rather than France – takes the visitor back a century into the most famous library in the world: the original bookstacks, desks and furniture are still intact.

The need to address an opening in a wall that has to respond simultaneously to the very different scale of the Reading Room on the inside and the courtyard on the outside is one of the classic problems of architecture. Foster had two thoughts. The first was to adopt the traditional device of applying oversized mouldings to scale up the outside of an opening determined by the smaller-scale interior. The mousehole materialised from his second thought: a plan to finesse the entrance to the Reading Room by placing an Anish Kapoor sculpture commissioned by the museum so that it both marked and concealed the opening. When the piece, a highly reflective sphere, was finally realised, the museum decided against placing it. This left the mousehole exposed, and there was no longer the option of going back to Foster's first idea.

At the north side of the drum, the Reading Room sprouts a bustle to accommodate a series of curved terraces that cascade down from the top level. There are cafés, restaurants and a shop here. Then, through the second portico, visitors move on into the old north Reading Room, put to use as a temporary exhibition space, before heading out into the street.

It is this route which creates the other new meaning that Foster attempted to give the museum. The project is not just a question of patching up the aftermath of wrenching out the British Library, nor is it only a matter of creating a new circulation route to allow the 5.4 million visitors that come each year to negotiate the museum without turning the galleries into busy corridors. The Great Court was envisaged as a project on an urban scale. It was claimed that it would provide a new pedestrian route, allowing people to move through London, from Bloomsbury down to Covent Garden, by way of the Great Court and the newly cleared forecourt to the museum. For this reason, the museum initially tried to keep the court open outside normal visiting hours for the rest of the museum. But in the event the cost of doing this proved too much for a cash-strapped museum.

A more satisfactory outcome of Foster's attempts at large-scale urbanism in London, initially at least, was the remodelling of Trafalgar Square. This involved closing the road on the north side, thus connecting the National Gallery directly with the square.

The controversy generated by the British Museum saga was, in the end, a debate about the quality of the stone selected to face the reconstructed courtyard. While there were some cultural conservatives who tried to suggest that a more traditionally trained architect would not have allowed his builders to use supposedly inferior French stone where British had been specified, the Foster team emerged unscathed from the British Museum. In the case of the Millennium Bridge, they found themselves under attack on a far more damaging issue: professional competence.

The footbridge opened in the blare of a crescendo of publicity.

The first new Thames crossing in London for almost a century, it was located on the most conspicuous possible site in Britain, linking St Paul's Cathedral with Tate Modern on the South Bank. And no sooner had it opened than it had to be closed to the public on grounds of safety.

The brief for the competition to design the bridge, organised by the *Financial Times*, was a paradoxical one. It had to be beautiful enough to be considered worthy of celebrating the millennium, but at the same time it had to be sufficiently invisible so as not to compromise the view of St Paul's. The dean of the cathedral had already voiced his concern that the Gherkin would compete with St Paul's dome, and the Prince of Wales had chimed in with his thoughts on the need to protect St Paul's setting from modern intrusions.

Working with Anthony Caro, and the engineers from Ove Arup, Foster's strategy was not to duck the challenge, but to make the bridge axial, formally aligned head on with Wren's dome. He also suggested that the structure of the bridge should dissolve into something almost invisible. Its only significant presence would be at night, when it would read as a blade of light. For the engineers, that meant a low structure which did not have the effect of creating a visual tunnel, or cage. 'We wanted people to be able to see out at every point,' says Roger Ridsdill-Smith from Arup. 'We saw it as a flying magic carpet, floating just above the river.' The resulting design beat off a submission from Frank Gehry and Richard Serra to win the competition.

The bridge has the effect of changing not only how a key part of the river looks, but also how it functions. For the first time it became possible to walk directly from the trading floors and the corporate headquarters of the north bank to the south-of-the-river world of lock-up garages, council flats and railway arches that is still at the heart of the London borough of Southwark.

Southwark's foreshore is one of the few vantage points from which it is possible to understand the pattern of London's growth and to get a sense of the city as a physical entity. You can see the mark left on London's topography by what, beneath all the reinforced concrete and plate glass, is visibly still the same marshy flood plain pockmarked with gravel banks that the invading legions of Emperor Claudius encountered in AD 43. From here you can read London's history, economic and political, inscribed in the physical form of the city like the rings of a tree.

Despite such violent intrusions from the twentieth century as the instantly recognisable saw-toothed silhouettes of the Barbican's towers and the stainless steel-faced tower that was once the National Westminster Bank's high-rise headquarters, only the dome of St Paul's itself stands out, clearly defined against the skyline and effortlessly crushing a riverfront scrum of mediocrity from the 1960s and 1970s.

As you walk across, the viewpoint shifts and the dome of the cathedral gets bigger and bigger, until you find yourself drawn into the north bank, where it appears almost vertically above you at the top of a river of stone steps. Stop midstream, and there is the remarkable sense of being afloat on a waterscape as if you were on a tightly rigged racing catamaran.

Spanning a fifth of a mile of water with just two supports is no party trick. Rather than pumping up the structure like a bodybuilder on steroids, the bridge has muscles that ripple under the skin, like a sleek racehorse. And this was to be the trigger for one of the most difficult moments in Foster's career.

It was just after 9 a.m. on a sunny Saturday in June 2000 that the Millennium Bridge first began to wobble. Roger Ridsdill-Smith spotted the first sign of movement as he stood waiting for the start of a sponsored walk. The bridge was beginning to fill with people at the time. 'It happened quite fleetingly, but you could tell it wasn't just a judder; it was a resonant movement. I thought, "That's interesting", but as the numbers thinned out, the bridge calmed down again.'

Then, at lunchtime when the bridge finally opened to the public, the crowds swarmed on from both ends. And that's when the bridge really started to move. All 690 tons of its steel-and-aluminium deck began to sway left and right like a giant executive desktop toy, so much so that pedestrians, suspended above the Thames on slender steel cables, began to clutch at handrails to steady themselves, throwing their weight against the sway in an effort to stay upright. As they did so, the swinging began to get increasingly violent.

Ridsdill-Smith and the police working on crowd control looked at one another. In his mind, Ridsdill-Smith went back over all the calculations, all the safety assessments, all the wind-tunnel tests, even the giant hydraulic tank in Canada used to measure resistance to water. None of them had predicted anything like this. This was simply not supposed to be happening.

All his experience as an engineer told him that the bridge ought to be stable. But he must have seen an image of the great Tacoma Narrows suspension bridge in Washington State in 1940 as it shook itself to pieces, come flashing through his mind.

'We asked ourselves, "Is it dangerous?" You could see that the movement was self-limiting. Beyond a certain point, it simply becomes impossible to get any more people on the bridge. As it gets fuller and fuller, people stop moving and the effect subsides, long before structural safety limits are reached. We knew it wouldn't fall down, but suppose Granny takes a tumble and breaks a hip?'

The next day, Nicholas Serota lent the bridge his security staff from Tate Modern to limit the numbers crossing at any one time. But the wobble didn't go away. The Millennium Bridge Trust hesitated for twenty-four hours before making the decision to close it altogether.

To see such a high-profile design closed down immediately after it had opened was bad enough for Foster. For Arup, the engineers who have made everything from the Sydney Opera House to the Hong Kong and Shanghai Bank possible, it was a humiliation. They could build skyscrapers and nuclear power stations all over the world, but here, in their own backyard, they were conspicuously failing to make a simple footbridge stand still long enough for people to stroll across it.

What made their embarrassment so irresistible to rival engineers, who rushed in to make judgements about what had happened, was that they seemed to have brought it on themselves. The word was that they had allowed an architect, determined to make his mark on the bridge, push them into flouting the sensible limits of design. 'Of course this bridge was going to wobble, just look at it,' was the consensus. With its low-slung outriggers and its very flat profile, the 'blade of light' looked like no other bridge. Stray too far from tried-and-tested traditional designs and you'll get into trouble, was the subtext of much of the debate.

Foster was in a Swiss meadow when he took the call from London telling him that something had gone badly wrong with the bridge. 'It was a terrible moment,' remembers Foster, still shaken by the experience.

At first he wavered about how to respond. Desperate to get the details of what was happening before making any comment, he came back to London immediately. An awkward confrontation with the press ensued in which he ill-advisedly answered their questions in a way that was interpreted as an attempt to shuffle away blame for the problems that the bridge experienced. The trouble, he seemed to be suggesting, stemmed not from a high-profile architect who had been ready to claim credit for the plaudits, but from the engineers whom he now described as the lead consultants. As soon as he had said it, Foster realised that it wasn't the right thing to have implied, and there were plenty of people lining up to tell him so.

Arup began talking to the world's footbridge experts in Japan and Germany. At the same time, they did urgent checks to see if the bridge had been built exactly as they had specified – it had – and then they looked yet again at their own calculations to see if there were any elementary mistakes in the numbers. There weren't. 'It's not what is different about the bridge that caused the problem,' Tony Fitzpatrick, Arup's senior engineer leading the remedial project, claimed. 'Every issue about the bridge that was innovative was properly researched and it worked perfectly. What hit us in the back of the head was that bit of the bridge that was the same as every other long-span bridge. We assumed it would work like other bridges have until now; that was the mistake, but there has to be a first time for everything.'

What Arup eventually discovered was a previously misunderstood phenomenon. Once the number of pedestrians on a bridge passes a critical mass, their footsteps start to make it move; the more they react to that movement to stay upright, the more the bridge shakes. It could potentially affect any pedestrian bridge over a given length. Fitzpatrick believed that there were at least seventy such bridges in Britain alone, with hundreds more around the world.

All bridges are liable to move. Their weight and structure keep them still to a certain extent, but get enough people walking across a bridge and all the natural damping is cancelled out; the next few footsteps will then set it wobbling violently. And it's not a gradual effect. Arup found it was a case of all or nothing. 'Put a thousand people on a bridge and it will seem to be OK. Put eleven hundred on and it starts to wobble,' Fitzpatrick said.

Arup discovered a number of bridges which had suffered from the problem, and every one of them looked different. A high-level suspension bridge in Tokyo, completed in the 1980s, had to have a makeshift damping system retrofitted after its opening; in Canada they came across a hundred-year-old steel truss bridge that never moved a millimetre in its entire life, until the occasion of a firework display to celebrate its centenary attracted so many pedestrians that it began to wobble. Then there was the Pont de Solférino, a graceful arched footbridge across the Seine, which stayed closed after its opening, ostensibly because its surface was slippery. This, too, turned out to be the victim of wobbly-bridge syndrome. According to Fitzpatrick, 'If the engineers involved with some of these cases had been open about their bridges as we are being, the problem would have been resolved long ago.'

The most encouraging find, from Arup and Foster's point of view, was the footbridge linking the National Exhibition Centre in Birmingham to its neighbouring railway station. This was a design clearly untroubled by the least vestige of aesthetic ambition. Yet it, too, suffered from wobbly-bridge syndrome.

Why had none of these cases forewarned Arup? Fitzpatrick's

answer was that they were never reported to the people who write the codes that bridge designers must follow.

Who was really to blame? Following that ill-judged statement uttered by Foster to the mob of reporters besieging his office after the bridge closure, the various members of the design team went out of their way to be nice about each other. Foster now says with hindsight:

> You can only use the word blame in a situation in which somebody says, 'My God, we missed that code, or didn't make that test which anybody else would have done.' That's not what happened here. If you look at the record, much more was done for this bridge than you would reasonably expect. Nobody could ever have anticipated that it would happen to the bridge. In a sense, it is a consequence of its popularity.

Fitzpatrick was clear that responsibility for the bridge was Arup's. 'Norman made it look more people-friendly; he made it more sensual than we would have done on our own, but the concept was an engineering one. It certainly wasn't a case of Norman forcing us to make something work.'

After a £5 million financial settlement for the bridge, work started on the elimination of the wobble. It involved fitting a pair of X-shaped braces under each of the structural bays, along with thirty-seven viscous dampers (the kind of large shock absorbers you might find on a truck), and another fifty tuned mass dampers. These are heavy blocks that sit in baths of oil and are connected by springs to the structure. When the bridge starts to move, the blocks absorb the energy triggered by pedestrians and stop the wobble. It's all been done deftly enough for the additions to look like part of the original design.

*

Designing Beijing's new airport for the Olympics was to bring Foster + Partners face to face with an even clearer demonstration of the political aspects of architecture than that offered by the Reichstag or the British Museum.

Foster's liaison on the project, Commander Chen, an official from the Chinese Civil Aviation Authority, told him when the result of the competition was announced at the end of 2003, 'You have won two airports before in China that you did not get built. This is your third. To secure this one, there are many factors to deal with; mainly they are not to do with architecture.' Which is to say that simply winning a competition in a political landscape as complex as that of contemporary China is unlikely by itself to be enough to realise a project.

To get to build in Beijing, Foster was going to have to call on high-level political support. Tony Blair wrote a helpful letter, neutralising any impulse on George Bush's part to pick up the phone to call the Chinese premier in support of the American contender.

'In any competition for an airport, the shortlist is narrowed to a small group,' says Foster. 'Out of them one scheme is the best, but you could build any of them and it would still be a good airport, otherwise the shortlist would not be like that.'

Once a competition result is announced, there is a whole wave of lobbying by unsuccessful participants. 'The French are formidable as competitors. A trade delegation including the French president went to see the Chinese while we were talking about doing Shanghai airport. "There goes our airport," we thought.'

And there was more than political manoeuvring to deal with. Mouzhan Majidi, who has taken a leading role building all four airports the practice has completed, was up against a preposterously abbreviated schedule. He had from November 2003 until January 2004 to deliver the contract drawings in time for work to start on site after a ground-breaking ceremony in March. The Chinese leadership were determined to have a new airport open in time for the Olympics in 2008, and this was the only way it could be delivered. But whereas the Olympic stadium itself was subject to constraints that led to the retractable roof being sacrificed in an economy drive after construction started, there were no compromises on the airport. Not even the avian flu panic was allowed to hinder its construction. The project took a heavy toll on Majidi. He got the call telling him the practice had won on holiday with his family and immediately afterwards he was summoned to a meeting in Beijing, brutally scheduled for Christmas Day to demonstrate how deadly serious the Chinese were about getting the airport built on time.

With thirty people in China, and the same number in London, Majidi established an office in Beijing, working with the Beijing Institute for Architecture and Planning, the Arup engineers and the NACO consultancy from the Netherlands. At the end of 2003, the existing airport hotel had been commandeered by the construction company that would build the new terminal building. While there were still guests negotiating the lobby, the ballroom was turned into a site office for the Foster team. Their neat ranks of workstations were overshadowed by the mirrored disco ball hanging from the ceiling that nobody had got round to taking down. Some of the guest bedrooms were in use as overflow offices for the squads of consultants planning the structure and managing the building process. Outside the ballroom was a digital clock, counting down the days to the opening of the games in 2008.

In 2008, flying into the completed airport in Beijing from Heathrow's half-derelict Terminal Four meant confronting a whole series of preconceptions. The journey revealed the some-times counterintuitive contrasts between the nature of public life in an advanced capitalist society and what, despite a massive economic transformation since the death of Mao, still declares itself to be a Marxist state guided by a socialist ideology. For all the neon glitter of the new cities on the Pearl River Delta, China is still fractured between extremes of poverty and absurd over-indulgence.

Yet it was not Beijing's Capital International Airport that felt on the edge of chaos but Terminal Four in London, one of the world's richest cities. Terminal Four has become a place where flight disruptions regularly leave thousands of delayed passengers camping outside the departure gates. Security checks organised like cattle pens turn catching a flight there into an ordeal, and maintenance teams fail to keep up with chewing gum-stained carpets.

Britain built Terminal Four in the 1980s, before China had embraced a capitalist economy, but in its architectural quality – the product, incidentally, of the same team that designed Baghdad International for Saddam Hussein – it reflects a stunted level of ambition. It looks as if it belongs to a culture that has lost any sense of self-belief.

Beijing's Terminal Three is an airport built on a vast scale. In terms of sheer floor space, the building is as big as a city, conceived with what can only be described as grandeur. According to some accounts it is, by a considerable distance, the largest single building in the world. And that of course is the whole point of the exercise. For both its domestic audience, and for the world outside, creating the sense of Chinese achievement is crucial. It helps to still dissent at home, and to impress or even intimidate foreigners.

The start of 2008 saw Beijing in the midst of a tidal wave of construction, the result of its conscious transformation into what would unmistakably be the capital of a global superpower. And the airport was its front door.

The successive incarnations of Beijing's airport provide a precise record of the transformation of China as a whole.

The first time that I saw it was in 1992, when its modest size, and its formal planning, reflected a time when air travel in China was still limited to the political elite. It had the flavour of a bus station from the Stalinist era: hard wooden benches, cement floors, and flickering black-and-white monitor screens that rarely worked lined the departure hall. Duty-free shopping was limited to a harshly neon-lit booth selling French brandy in bottles shaped like vintage cars. This was still a time when political tensions over the continuing recognition of Taiwan as the legitimate government of China meant that few Western airlines offered direct flights to Beijing. Decades of cultural isolation had reduced the city to just two real pieces of contemporary architecture: I.M. Pei's Fragrance Hills Hotel and Denton Corker Marshall's Australian Embassy, both built extremely slowly by construction brigades from the People's Liberation Army, struggling to deal with any but the least sophisticated building techniques. The road from the airport was a two-lane black-top choked with trucks bringing winter vegetables into the city.

It's a moment that seems as removed from today's Beijing as the Middle Ages. Yet Terminal One still exists, embedded within the larger airport. After a cosmetic facelift, its sixteen gates have been turned over to domestic flights.

Terminal Two, ready by 1999, represented the Great Leap Forward. China was by this time engaging with the outside world, and was committed to modernising an archaic infrastructure. But it was still struggling to catch up with the outside world, rather than setting the pace for others to follow. It was much bigger that its predecessor, with acres of marble floors and murals representing national tourist attractions, but it felt like a provincial copy of a not very distinguished Western original. There was now a six-lane toll road to take you into town. In a city centre already sprouting skyscrapers, vast neighbourhoods of traditional hutong courtyard houses were being flattened. There were luxury hotels with Australian chefs and cigar bars, and the main streets were beginning to be encrusted with neon advertising. But the cycle-repair stalls eating up the pavement, and the knots of kitchen hands outside the cafés chopping up on trays slippery with poultry entrails, made it still an unmistakably Chinese city.

The preparations for the Olympics brought another level of ambition. Beijing saw the design and construction of an airport much larger than all the five terminals of Heathrow combined, designed to handle fifty-three million passengers per annum, in under four years. That's rather less time than the lawyers spent arguing about whether or not to build Heathrow's Terminal Five.

Beijing may have been planned to be the world's largest and most advanced airport building, but as a construction site it looked like a medieval battlefield, conceived on the scale of epic cinema, rather than the sleek dunescape shown in the glittering computer renderings. Swarming warrior armies clustered around giant cranes, more than one hundred of them, ranged like ancient siege engines across a frontline almost two miles long. The dust swirling across the landscape sometimes made it impossible to count more than a few of them before they disappeared into the acrid haze. Touring the site in a Chinese-made Buick, it was hard at first as a spectator to grasp exactly what was going on. Gradually all the furious activity crystallised into a pattern that began to make some kind of sense. The banners flying from makeshift flagpoles sunk into the mud everywhere carried the names of individual work gangs, each with their own territory. The gangs, moving like disciplined cohorts of soldier ants as they navigated blindly but effectively around the obstacles littering the site, were identifiable by the colour of their helmets. Some were handling new deliveries. Others were preparing them for use. Others shifted barrowloads of nuts and bolts across the site or carried steel bars by hand, two at a time. In the foreground, groups of men in crumpled suits stacked heaps of reinforcing steel, ready to be bent into the hooks that would keep them securely in place when they were finally buried in concrete.

There were dumps of steel everywhere. So much steel, in fact, that it started to become only too clear how the Chinese hunger for the metal after the millennium had pushed up world prices to the point that British construction sites were forced to rediscover the art of building in concrete. There was enough steel there to explain why Australia had reopened iron-ore mines, why ship brokers had taken bulk carriers out of mothballs from their anchorages in the Falmouth estuary, and why manhole covers in Detroit were being stolen for their scrap value.

There were stacks of bicycles amid the welding stations and

forests of concrete columns. Beyond them stood a gigantic concrete raft from which intricate tufts of reinforcing steel sprouted like wild grass. Far in the distance, more clusters of helmeted dots swarmed around craters sunk six floors into the ground. Huge white concrete-mixer trucks wheeled and turned in packs at the lip of the void, marshalled by men with whistles and batons, delivering loads in a continuous stream, day and night. In fact, despite appearances, the project had two main contractors, each starting at opposite ends of the site and working their way across it. The one who finished first would be required to go back and help the second to complete their part of the contract.

There were as many as 50,000 men on the site at its most labour-intensive moment. But when I was there in 2004, from my vantage point, a kind of diving board projecting over the edge of the 150-metre-wide channel dug from one end of the site to the other, I could focus my mind only on two of them. One was dressed in what looked like a second-hand military tunic; the other wore a suit that must once have been his holiday best, but was now covered in stains. Both had yellow hard hats, both wore tennis shoes. The shorter man had a satchel slung across his shoulder, and held a wrench.

At first I assumed that he was the more skilled of the two, and so the leader. They were perched on a scaffolding tower fifteen metres high, rising from the bottom of a trench cut deep into the mud.

The taller man, who looked barely out of his teens, stood with his legs wide apart, feet splayed, one hand fully outstretched, clinging to the nearest secure piece of vertical scaffolding. He had his safety harness wrapped around his waist, but its clip dangled uselessly behind him. Without looking down, he paused to steady himself for a moment, then, with a single effortless movement, used his free hand to swing up another heavy steel scaffolding pole and drop it into the clamp that would keep it secure. His slender body formed a big X as he defined the diagonals in the steel rectangle that framed him, holding the scaffolding in position just long enough for his partner to bolt it into place. As I watched, it became clear that he was the one taking the risks and making the decisions. The task complete, they rested for a minute. Then, without a word, they swung themselves along the scaffolding like tightrope walkers to repeat the entire manoeuvre with balletic grace and precision.

Working without their harnesses, it was a death-defying performance. I couldn't take my eyes off them for fear that, if I did, one would drop the scaffolding pole and fall. They were earning around seven dollars each a day, not enough for the taxi ride back into town.

The site worked in three continuous shifts, seven days a week. Nothing stopped the cranes, the concrete mixers, the welders and the scaffolders. Not even the discovery of fossilised dinosaur bones that turned up in the mud ahead of the bulldozers one day, or a carved ancient stone, saved from the mechanical diggers and re-erected next to a cluster of huts.

The site was still working over the May Day holiday, when the rest of China shuts down for a week. The workers here stopped only for the Chinese New Year, when it got too cold for concrete to set properly. The site came to a standstill and the armies returned to their villages until the thaw came.

During the day they suffered in the dust storms and the summer heat. At night they worked under arc lights. They slept in ramshackle clusters of huts and green army tents in a series of shanty towns scattered around the site. The huts varied in size and shape. Some were made from plywood, with roofs of corrugated clear-plastic sheets, held down by bricks to stop them blowing away. There was no glass in the windows and nothing more elaborate than roofless latrine blocks for sanitation. These men were the legal, the semi-legal and the illegal migrant workers, drawn from China's desperately poor hinterland in their millions by the prospect of jobs in construction and in the factories that the booming cities have to offer. One in every five of Shanghai's population is an illegal migrant. Beijing is not far behind. These migrants are Chinese citizens with fewer rights in their nation's capital than Colombians living illegally in California.

Everywhere you go in Beijing you can see clusters of spray-painted numbers scrawled over walls, on trees and gateposts, under flyovers and on streetlights. In Los Angeles or London they would be gang tags. But there is no graffiti in China. They are the mobile phone numbers of people looking for work.

Beijing is the capital of the world's fastest-growing economy, provoking a titanic struggle between a totalitarian political system and the liberalisation that is the presumed product of its economic transformation. By some estimates, half the world's annual production of concrete and one-third of its steel output was being consumed by China's construction boom. The second ring road that until the 1980s marked the city limits has been followed by the building of a third, fourth and fifth rings. The sixth is under construction. The exploding millions of cars in the city are already enough to wipe out all the improvements in air quality achieved by the expulsion of heavy industry from Beijing's centre. Cars move around disconnected clumps of newly completed towers. The city map looks like a dartboard, with the void of the Forbidden City as its empty bull's-eye. And with the abruptness of a randomly aimed dart, entire new districts appear arbitrarily as if from nowhere.

A city that, until 1990, had no central business district, and little need of it, now has a cluster of glass towers that look like rejects from Singapore or Rotterdam. And these, in turn, are now being replaced and overshadowed by a new crop of taller, slicker towers, the product of the international caravan of travelling architects that has arrived in town to take part in this construction free-fire zone. Rem Koolhaas, Jacques Herzog, Zaha Hadid, Jean Nouvel and Will Alsop are all building or trying to build here. But it is Foster's airport that is the gateway to this new China from the outside world, and the one that everybody must pass through.

At Heathrow, it took twenty years to design and build the airport's fifth terminal. Building Beijing's much larger Terminal Three in just four years is an astonishing feat. It is sometimes claimed that such an achievement is only possible in a society in which labour is endlessly available and cheap, and where trades unions and lawyers have no power. That is to say, a society not so unlike the one that in the nineteenth century used armies of migrant Irish labour to build the canals and railways of Britain's Industrial Revolution. But, in fact, it is not that the building process is slower in Europe, construction itself takes much the same time, it is the management and the decision-making that drags on interminably in Britain.

By spring 2008, when my British Airways Boeing 747 pulled up on the crescent wing of stands furthest from the landside, there was no sign that the warrior armies had ever been here. There was still some dust – that is unavoidable in Beijing – but no mud, and no cranes. The site huts had gone, and in their place was the sharp outline of the new airport: more like a landscape than a single building, a kind of dunescape of glass and steel taking on the form of wind-drifted snow or sand. It was almost impossible to recognise the place as the construction site I had seen three years before. Only after I had negotiated the dazzling arrival hall in the outermost of the three wings of gates, gone through passport control, down into the transit rail system at the lowest level, shuttled off to the luggage hall, and finally emerged out into a humid Beijing afternoon thick with dust, did I experience a sudden flash of recognition. The curving crescent access road up to the main entrance was the same fragment of mud and steel that I had seen in 2004, now come to maturity.

Terminal Three is the largest version that has so far been realised of a new approach to airport terminal design that has a robot train track as its spine. At one end is the transfer station from the rapid transit line into town, and the first of three crescent-like wings that accommodate the gates. The first wing houses the check-in desks and the baggage hall. The additional gates that will one day give this airport a capacity larger than Heathrow are ranged around the two subsequent wings, although in 2008 only the first and the third were functioning.

If Norman Foster has had an impact even more marked than his transformation of London over the last two decades into a city of glass, it is on the design of the airport. The practice has built four so far – first Stansted, then Hong Kong's Chep Lap Kok Airport, followed by the new third terminal at Beijing and Jordan's new airport in Amman. Majidi's first major project on joining Foster was to work on Stansted. Subsequently he moved to Hong Kong to lead the Chep Lap Kok team. Foster has created a new model for mass air travel. It is a model based on simplified architectural spaces characterised by vast internal volumes that are nevertheless suffused with daylight. Conventional airport terminals before Stansted put all the mechanical equipment on the roof, which demanded a heavy, solid structure. Foster's idea was to put the equipment underneath the concourse, making it possible to build lightweight umbrella roof structures that allowed public spaces to be filled with light.

The first in the series, Stansted, was designed for what in those days was still a state-owned monopoly, the British Airports Authority, and run as a public service. Even as it was being completed, Stansted was turning into a revenue-generating retail operation with departure gates attached. In the 1990s, Stansted's structural trees and its lucid diagram set a new standard for clarity. After the monuments of the 1950s, and the subsequent clutter of accretions that left so many airports encrusted with unsympathetic additions, Foster tried to recapture the simple directness of the early days of flying, when travellers were dropped off at the runway and climbed a set of steps into the aircraft. To soothe anxious passengers, struggling to navigate their way to the departure gate, the terminal building was conceived as a transparent box that could easily be understood without reading a single sign. A transit system connected the main terminal to remote stands in two satellite terminals.

Stansted celebrated its opening in 1990 with a black-tie dinner in the vast, empty and still pristine baggage hall. It was an event that felt like a throwback to the Victorian custom of inaugurating great feats of engineering with candlelit banquets attended by men in stove-pipe hats, sitting down in sewers and tunnels to eat pheasant on linen-covered tables. Foster got up to make a speech, and while paying tribute to the determination of the British Airports Authority to complete this massive investment in the future, he attacked the new managers who, even before the airport opened for passengers, were determined to clutter its beautifully clear open spaces with an obstacle course of retailing opportunities.

His fears have come true to an extent which even he would never have predicted. When it opened, the new terminal handled less than five million passengers a year. There was space for sculpture, and for a calm, measured movement from the pavement drop-off in the direction of the departure gate. It was a walk that hardly required any signs to tell you where to go. You moved towards daylight, and towards views of aircraft parked outside. It was briefly the most civilised way to leave and enter the UK. Foster's architecture helped created the impression of a confident new Britain, investing in modern infrastructure.

It is none of those things now. With twenty-four million passengers a year, the airport is overwhelmed by people. The sculpture has been removed. There is no easy transition from the pavement; after the attack on Glasgow Airport by al-Qaeda sympathisers, the terminal entrance is a secure zone defended by concrete tank traps. And low-cost airlines that have started to treat their customers with contempt reduce the building to chaos.

The fate of Stansted is a reminder of the tension between architecture and art, and the fulfilment that one can bring when measured against the other. Architecture engages with the real issues of everyday life, it directly touches millions of lives, and yet the architect's connection with his work is eroded with time to almost nothing. When a building has been in use long enough, whether it works well or not, the architecture mostly becomes invisible. To create an artwork is a more contained, more controlled, more controllable process than building. And in the end, it focuses on the ego of the artist, in a way that architecture never can.

In Hong Kong, Foster's Chep Lap Kok refined the original Stansted concept, setting a precedent for Beijing. In most airports, because they cover such large spaces, the roof is the primary architectural element. Stansted is based on a square grid. Hong Kong brings a more refined series of gentle curved pillow-like forms.

Beijing is the most refined of all, with the roof structure so slender and so attenuated that it is almost at the point of disappearing altogether. It is supported on a restricted number of tapering concrete columns, pylons really, that have a flavour of the huge roof that Foster once proposed building over the Reichstag in Berlin. Inside the terminal the columns are so few and far between that they avoid imposing any kind of structural pattern on the huge space. There is a single external row, which is painted imperial red, in evocation of traditional Chinese colour schemes, an idea that first occurred to Foster for the external structure of the Hong Kong and Shanghai Bank, though it ended up being dropped in favour of a more neutral, and international, grey.

The gentle curves of the over-sailing roof are formed by a steel open grid, some elements of which have been peeled back to open up roof-lights to allow in sparkling flashes of daylight while the glass walls reveal the ranks of aircraft outside. It's a form which some, in another overtly Chinese metaphor, have interpreted as the scales of a dragon.

These are vast, open interiors, elegantly conceived, and a huge technical step forward, along with the Olympic stadium, and the Central China TV building, from anything that China has done before. But of course, China is still China. As you glide along the track of the robot train, you pass the still not completed central pavilion where the gates have yet to come into use, and you can glimpse workers squatting in the empty interiors in their olive drab uniforms, a sharp reminder of the other China. And as you negotiate the spacious and efficiently run departure hall, the elegance of the architecture is occasionally threatened by the profusion of shops and cafés. When the roof is as delicate as this, the kitsch detritus of airport clutter becomes intrusive, although in Bejing there is the scale that Stansted lacks to deal with it.

This is the highly symbolic gateway not only to Beijing, but also to the new China. It represents a country that has undergone change at a pace so rapid that it threatens to become dizzying. The airport shows what China can do at a moment when it is bidding to become as much of a cultural and political force as it is an industrial one. Its next leap forward will come when it will have architects of its own who can design a project like this. Throughout the process, Foster was well aware that in part he had been hired to pass on skills and expertise to his Chinese collaborators.

In contrast to his experiences in Berlin with Chancellor Kohl, Foster had no direct dealings with the party leadership. But he has no doubt that the Chinese premier, Wen Jiabao, took a close personal interest in the project.

In China you never quite know who is taking the decisions. Commander Chen from the Civil Aviation Authority was the highest up we could go in terms of talking to the client. It was clear that he had people that he reported to, but you could only guess who they were. But there was a strong feeling that if the Premier paid a visit to the airport, then if there was a problem with a colour, for example, Commander Chen would bring it up after an elapse of a little time. I had the idea of using a palette of traditional colours, from imperial red to gold, and with the many variations between. And it was after one of those high-level visits that Commander Chen came to us, and said, 'Can't the roof pick up the colour of the Forbidden City?' The design team went and had another close look at the Forbidden City, to try to find a colour that could convey the impact of the many different tones of the terracotta roof tiles used there.

The response was an attempt to create an airport that is at the same time clearly part of the modern world but equally clearly rooted in modern China.

China is a difficult place for a Western architect to make money: fee scales are much lower than in the West, and the architect is expected to do more. And when fees are based on a percentage of construction costs, low-wage Chinese labour makes the contract sum much smaller than it would be in Europe or America. In fact, Foster says that the Beijing job ended up leaving the firm out of pocket. The Chinese had capped the fee and placed a limit on the architect's involvement. When the paid consultancy came to an end, so did the fees. Foster says that he could not walk away from the project that represented so much in terms of his own ambitions. He chose to stay on and help complete the airport. 'We were welcome to stay, and contribute, but in terms of finance, that was it. We elected to stay, because we shared our clients' intent to make the airport the best that they could, and that decision was very well received.' After the Olympics were over, Foster was invited back to Beijing to receive a friendship award in the Great Hall of the People, China's highest decoration for foreigners.

*

It took time for Foster to make an impact in China. Before the Bejing airport there was only a sleek office tower on the Shanghai waterfront, and a string of unbuilt designs, including airports in Guangzhou and Shanghai. Now there is a range of new settlements that are called Eco cities in China, and a scheme in Bejing, in the Caochangdi cultural district. Foster + Partners is building a complex of exhibition spaces and studios on a site between Ai Wei Wei's own studio, and the Three Shadows Centre, established by the photographers RongRong and inri. In Hong Kong he has a continuing relationship with the bank, and the airport. Subsequently there were the plans for the Kowloon cultural district, and there is work in Malaysia and Vietnam. But in the two construction booms of the past decade, China and Russia, Foster has had a higher profile in Russia, even if little of his work has been realised there.

Norman Foster has had a soft spot for Russia ever since he first went with David Nelson in 1990 in the last days of the Soviet Union. He was the guest of Energiya, Russia's newly privatised space agency. They took him to Space City, at Baikonur, to watch the first fare-paying space tourist, a Japanese television reporter named Toyohiro Akiyama, blast off for a week on the Mir space station. Energiya wanted Foster to help them modernise themselves for an uncertain future. In the event, that project failed to materialise, but Foster was fascinated by what he saw in Space City. He went to the museum of the cosmonauts, which he likens to the shrine for a new religion, full of relics and sacred memorabilia that made them look like the martyrs of the early Christian Church.

In Foster's eyes, the Soviet cosmonauts were the first environmentalists. 'They took up the cause of the damage done to the inland lakes of Russia because of what they could see from space. It was their photographs of planet Earth as a serene, beautiful, blue-green globe, caught in the midst of the blackness of space, that triggered the whole earth movement.'

He was fascinated and awed by what he saw of the training regime for the cosmonauts, who had to submit to vast centrifugal machines that pushed them to the limits of human endurance, and to judge by the casualties, maybe sometimes beyond them.

But most of all, he was struck by the difference between the American and the Soviet attitude to space. The Americans were visitors, he suggests. 'The Soviet cosmonauts inhabited space, they truly colonised it, they lived there seven or twenty-four days at a time.'

On the way back from Baikonur he stayed in the Rossiya Hotel, the vast Brezhnev-era hotel under the Kremlin's walls that has been demolished as part of a massive, now-stalled move to remodel the heart of the Russian capital on which he has worked to produce a coherent master plan. He was in Moscow long enough on that first trip to wander through the GUM department store off Red Square. Now, it is a glossy shopping mall dedicated to conspicuous consumption, but in those days it was semi-derelict, its shelves bare of even the simplest goods. Foster remembers the pathos of watching an elderly man with a wad of greasy banknotes lining up patiently to buy a pathetically small toy as a Christmas gift.

By the time that he went back to Russia, Foster was already working on his first project in Kazakhstan – the glass pyramid of the Palace of Peace and Reconciliation. And Russia had emerged from its first post-Soviet economic crisis. The energy boom had made a few Russians extremely rich, triggering a wave of reconstruction. In 2004 Foster went to St Petersburg to see Zaha Hadid collect her Pritzker Prize in the Hermitage, and he came away determined to expand the practice by working in Russia and other new areas.

It was in St Petersburg that he was introduced to Shalva Chigirinsky, the controversial businessman who was to be one of his routes into the volatile Russian property market. Chigirinsky encouraged Foster to take part in an international competition for the renovation of New Holland, formerly a naval base built for the Imperial Russian Fleet in the heart of St Petersburg, as a cultural centre, mixing the careful restoration of the historic areas with auditoria, galleries and a striking open-air theatre. Foster was judged the winner after a public presentation.

More commissions followed. In 2006, Chigirinsky beat two other bidders in a tender to Moscow City Council to redevelop the sprawling site of the 1,000-bed Rossiya Hotel. Foster was asked to work on a master plan that proposed concert halls, galleries, public spaces, retail and residential space, totalling a massive 400,000 square metres. It was the kind of commission that carried both huge risks and even more potential. Russia still lacks transparency in business and clarity about property rights. It's a culture in which business and politics are inextricable. But replanning the Rossiya site was also the chance to give Moscow's most historic sites a new setting, and to create a new civic heart for the city.

Foster's role in the reshaping of Moscow was highlighted when he was the subject of an exhibition in the Pushkin Museum in 2006, the product of a meeting some years earlier with Irina Antonova, the Pushkin's director since 1962. Foster later took part in a state-sponsored competition to create a much larger Pushkin Museum due to be completed in time for the centenary of its foundation in 2012. Pride of place in the exhibition went to a huge model of the 600-metre-high Rossiya tower, yet another design by Foster for Chigirinsky's company, STT. It was conceived as a vertical megastructure that would be the tallest skyscraper in Russia, a city in a single building, with energy-harvesting capacity and a direct connection to the Moscow metro – in short, the realisation of Foster's speculative studies for an ultra-tall tower. An entire wall of the Pushkin was devoted to a massive, seemingly life-size photographic blow-up of the Foster studio in Battersea with its view out over the Thames.

Interviewed during the course of the exhibition, Chigirinsky told the *Moscow News* he had chosen to work with Foster because 'a new kind of consumer is emerging in Russia. People here want to know the world's state of the art, and go one better. In the past, tastes were kitschy, in the "I want more gilt on that ceiling" style. But over the years, people not only got richer, their taste also evolved.'

By the end of 2008, however, the credit crunch put a stop to any speculative project that depended on bank finance. Chigirinsky's plans to build with Foster were no exception, and came crashing to a sickening stop when the Georgian pulled out of the $3 billion Crystal City project, unable to raise the capital. The New Holland project had also come to a standstill. Legal wranglings stalled the old Rossiya Hotel site when Morab, one of the unsuccessful bidders, went to court to contest the tender process, claiming that Chigirinsky had insider knowledge of the deal. Chigirinsky successfully appealed when the decision went against him. Morab appealed in turn, and won, leading to a hiatus. In 2009, the city of Moscow was manoeuvring to take over the project. Work had already stopped on the Rossiya tower. 'Say thanks to Alan Greenspan and George Bush,' said Chigirinsky, blaming the credit crunch.

Foster travelled to Moscow after his first trip to St Petersburg and met the mayor, Yuri Luzhkov. Some time later, he was introduced to Luzhkov's wife, Yelena Baturina, in Chigirinsky's office. Baturina was the first Russian female billionaire. She had worked in a factory before studying at the Moscow Institute of Management, then in the last days of the Soviet Union went to Mosgorispolkom, part of the Moscow local government, where she met Luzhkov, who went on to become the mayor in the Yeltsin years. Baturina has come in for considerable criticism for the way in which her ties with Moscow's mayor have been put to work to help her business grow.

Foster was to find himself caught up unwittingly in one of Baturina's more controversial development proposals, a massive cultural and residential complex in the centre of Moscow, known as the Golden Orange, which provoked a string of disputes that were exacerbated by Russia's fluid understanding of property rights. Chigirinsky asked Foster as a favour to assess the feasibility of a hypothetical structure conceived by Baturina and a Russian architect, and then to see how it might be developed on a specific site. The site eventually targeted by Baturina stood very close to Zurab Tsereteli's bizarre monument to Peter the Great, a giant bronze representation of a three-masted sailing ship, with a huge figure standing on deck, installed thanks to the intervention of her husband the mayor. The site is currently occupied by the Central House of Artists, built in the Brezhnev era, and as unpopular as buildings from the 1970s are in Britain. Nevertheless it is a base for many of Moscow's artists, and it houses the Tretyakov Gallery, which boasts the finest collection of constructivist art in the world. Alongside a garden full of statuary commemorating the fallen monsters of Stalin's Russia, such as Felix Dzerzhinsky, founder of the KGB, dethroned from their original sites, and collected together here as a kind of monumental graveyard, are rooms that house Kazimir Malevich's *Black Square*, and *Composition VII* by Vasily Kandinsky.

Baturina's plan was to accommodate the gallery within her development, meeting the cost with a complex of luxury apartments and five-star hotels. What interested Foster was not the architecture, but the prospect of using the project as a catalyst to regenerate a string of parks running along the river, currently fragmented by roads, in the manner of Olmsted's Central Park. But Baturina wasn't convinced by the idea, and Foster and his team have distanced themselves from the design, which now takes the form of a number of multi-storey spheres, almost in the neo-Classical manner of Étienne Boullée, but sliced open to reveal segments, and connected together with a spiralling twist of peel.

At the Venice architecture Biennale in 2008, the young Moscow architect Boris Bernaskoni was allocated space in the Italian pavilion by the American director, Aaron Betsky for an installation that mounted an acid critique of the Golden Orange project. Bernaskoni flyposted the walls of the gallery with a series of posters. Some rendered Foster's face in a Warhol-style portrait looming over the Moscow skyline. They were interspersed with a particularly phallic banana erupting from the Kremlin walls. On a table in the corner was a collection of letters to President Putin, calling on him to stop Baturina's project. If the site had to be redeveloped, then there should be a less flamboyant, and less ostentatious way to do it. The credit crunch put an end to the project for the foreseeable future.

In fact, of all Foster's work in Russia, the project most likely to be realised in the near future is his careful restructuring of the Pushkin Museum. When Putin was succeeded as Russian president by Medvedev, the government committed the funds for the project.

Foster's work in Russia, and the closely related projects in the former Soviet republic of Kazakhstan, fall into two types. There are sober attempts at contextualism, such as New Holland where a mixed cultural and commercial development is for the most part safely buttoned up behind walls built by Peter the Great, or the effort on the site of the Rossiya to create a setting in the grand manner for the Kremlin that gives a sense of a monumental city fabric in Hausmannian mode. And then there are the wild new projects that aspire to create self-conscious originality and a sense of spectacle: the half-peeled Golden Orange and the Crystal City typify this tendency. Foster has another project under way in this vein: the Khan Shatyry entertainment centre, a 200-metre-high tent, designed to give Nazarbayev's new capital of Astana a social hub with sheltered public spaces in a climate that sees temperatures plummet to thirty degrees below zero. Both the Crystal City and Khan Shatyry can be interpreted as inspired by Buckminster Fuller's dome over Manhattan: utopian visions of a bubble of urbanity in the midst of a hostile climate, though in the form of a vast circus tent rather than a minimalist bubble of air.

Six

The art of the juggler

The choices that an architect makes about the houses in which he lives and the places in which he works are rarely entirely unselfconscious. More likely they are shaped at least in part by the urge to reflect their occupant's self-image.

Like most British architects making their way in the 1960s Norman Foster spent the early days of his career in a sequence of nineteenth-century buildings. But he was already thinking about what he would build for himself when he got the chance. He bought a plot of land in a mews street in Hampstead, and planned a house for it that summed up everything that he wanted to say about architecture. It would have been a tribute to the Maison de Verre in Paris, the icon of the modern movement designed by Pierre Charreau and Bernard Bijvoet in celebration of industrial mechanisms, glass bricks and steel beams. This memory of the avant garde of the 1920s was blended with a flavour of the house that Charles and Ray Eames designed for themselves in Santa Monica in the 1940s, and given a sharp new twist for the 1970s. Like the Maison de Verre, every piece of the Foster house would have been purpose made. Like Charreau, who was fascinated by pivoting mechanical screens and partitions and used them to transform the interior of the Maison de Verre, Foster treated furniture as a kit of interchangeable parts. Like the Eames house, Foster's project was conceived as a kind of proving ground, putting new ideas to the test in laboratory conditions before adapting them for everyday use. The house would have had a single main volume, with a five-metre-high ceiling, allowing for mezzanine levels. The walls would be made from blocks of glass, and the steel structure, punched full of circular holes, would be left on show. Foster's house had the kind of kinship to the Bean Hill housing estate, built by the practice in Milton Keynes at the same time, that a Ferrari has to a Fiat. Between 1978 and 1979, working with the engineer Tony Hunt, Foster built two full-size prototypes of a single bay of the structure, one in steel and the second using aluminium, in the grounds of his weekend home at Compton Bassett.

Foster's one-off house in Hampstead was never built. All that remains is a set of drawings of the interior that show a range of specially designed furniture prefiguring the tables later made for the Foster office.

Bean Hill, with its flat roofs and corrugated black metal skin that looked a lot like the back of a Citroën van, did. Single-storey houses offered the most adaptable layouts and extra outdoor living space. Generously proportioned though the houses were, with courtyard gardens, Bean Hill was not a success. It is still standing, but has been altered out of all recognition. The tenants could not afford their heating bills, and complained about both the industrial image of the houses and the lack of insulation. The flat roofs began to leak and were replaced with sloping ones, a move that might be read as standing for a symbolic triumph of tradition over architectural taste that could have been orchestrated by the Prince of Wales himself.

The project was planned at a moment of rampant inflation, and in an area of Britain suffering a shortage of skilled builders. Foster explored simplified construction techniques and a pre-fabricated timber frame. During the planning stage, Foster's team compared the cost with an off-the-shelf system used for cowsheds, an idea that would not have gone down well with the occupants, had they known.

Foster and Buckminster Fuller worked together on a plan for a solar-powered house taking the form of a dome within a dome, so as to create a highly insulated interior. They were planning to build one each. One would have been at Compton Bassett, the other for Fuller and his wife, Anne, in Los Angeles. Fuller continued to dream of building it even after Anne became too ill to think of moving.

The first home that Foster actually built for himself was an apartment on the roof of his offices in Battersea. It had a spectacular view over the Thames, and a heroic scale. On one pristine white wall, plastered twice over to meet Foster's exacting specifications, Richard Long made an artwork, pasting Thames mud in big streaking arcs across the highly polished plaster. It was a demonstration of Foster's growing interest in contemporary art, both in his personal life, and in his work. Foster's continuing relationship with Long included a commission for the Média-thèque in Nîmes and culminated in a monumental work in the Hearst building in Manhattan.

Over the years, he has been close to many artists. Anthony Caro was a neighbour in Hampstead. Brian Clarke, who made Foster's work into the subject matter of some of his paintings and contributed stained glass to the Palace of Peace in Astana, is a long-term friend. Anish Kapoor was involved in the Ground Zero competition and the British Museum. Foster is also fascinated by the work of Richard Serra. In person, both men have a similar kind of intensity, they understand how to see space, and movement in that space, before it exists.

Foster has thought hard about the relationship between architecture and art. Memorably, he once suggested that the role of public art in contemporary architecture had been reduced to an attempt to put lipstick on a gorilla. Perhaps because they do not speak quite the same language as architects, he is comfortable with artists in a way that he is not always with other architects. But to be an architect is to accept that while your work will transform everyday life, by becoming its background, it is art that will be its foreground. And it is art that serves to define our culture, more than architecture.

Foster followed the Battersea flat with a house in the South of France in pristine white steel and glass. Then in 2000 came an abrupt change. He designed a three-storey apartment building in St Moritz, and acquired one of the flats for his own use. Rather than eat up more precious land in the Engadine, he tried to find a higher-density solution, one that would still give him the qualities of a country home but within a built-up area and suggest ways in which sprawl might be limited on the tightly defined edge of a town. Foster used the traditional materials and craft techniques of the area, not because of local planning controls, but because he had become as fascinated by these skills as he was intrigued by the apparently artlessly engaging quality of the engineering vernacular of the aircraft industry.

The Chesa Futura was one of the first projects that Foster realised after he abandoned his unflinching commitment to rectilinear geometry, and for many it was at first hard to identify it as having come from his studio. From the outside, the Chesa Futura looks like a wooden cloud hoisted up on fat legs, faced with 250,000 wooden shingles. These had been cut by hand, one by one, by a local craftsman in his seventies from one hundred specially selected larch trees. By choosing a material that grew and could be processed so close to the site, the energy needed to utilise it was of course reduced to a minimum.

Shingles cover the walls and roof in a seamless envelope. And if you walk beneath the building, you discover that it has a shingle underbelly too. The parking spaces, storage, and mechanical equipment are concealed underground.

All of the homes Foster built were carefully designed to suggest something very specific about the kind of architect that he wanted to be at various points in his life. But it is his studios that have provided a more direct commentary on his evolving approach to architecture. Setting aside the various spaces that he has made for himself in which to work at home, he has had five studios in the course of his career.

When Foster started talking to IBM's British management in 1969 about building a temporary headquarters for them in Cosham, he knew that his flat in Hampstead was not the best place from which to convince a multinational to hire him. He badly needed somewhere more impressive, and much more professional-looking, even if the practice couldn't afford it yet. Achieving that kind of transformation in perceptions in one form or another is the task that architects have always been asked to take on for their clients.

Tony Hunt, Foster's structural engineer since the Team Four years, had just moved into Bedford Street in Covent Garden.

In those days it was still a daringly exotic address. That was what made it exactly the right kind of place for an architect building inflatable structures for start-up computer companies as Foster had been. Perhaps it also gave IBM the sense that, while Foster was certainly businesslike, he was still in touch with the contemporary world. The Middle Earth, the hippie club in which the Incredible String Band and Pink Floyd had started their careers, was just around the corner in a King Street cellar. In the mornings, the pavements were stacked high with orange boxes from the market.

Foster asked Hunt if he could borrow a couple of rooms for long enough to convince IBM that he was serious. If he didn't get the job, he could always go back to Hampstead. Zeev Aram, the most cerebral furniture store owner in Britain, lent some suitably impressive office furniture and the kind of boardroom table with which to make a statement. Foster hurriedly put up the grey and black RIBA approved architect's name board of the time on the street door, and hung a work of art by Mark Vaux in the reception room.

IBM was impressed enough by what they saw and heard to hire him, and as a result, Foster Associates was able to afford to stay in Covent Garden. The next move came in 1972 when Foster went to Fitzroy Street, just below the Post Office Tower. This time the company created a little slice of Willis Faber on the ground floor of a faceless office building.

Like Willis Faber, the Fitzroy Street office had a black glass front that gave nothing away about what was going on inside, at least not until after dark when the lights came on. Those in the know could spot the Foster office simply from a glimpse of the neoprene-jointed glass façade and the studded rubber plinth on which it sat. For those who weren't, there was a neon sign to spell out the practice's name in letters six inches high. In fact neon had become something of a signature for Foster. He used it for the Olsen Line's Regent Street showroom, and for the Orange Hand store in Hampstead. Inside the office there were bulkhead doors with radiussed corners that made you feel as if you were inside a submarine, a home-made tribute to the steel fabricated by Jean Prouvé. Simply to be seen working in an open-plan office in those days was understood as an act of bravado. It involved pulling down partition walls and dumping all the usual desks and filing cabinets to make room for what were just beginning to be called workstations. Despite Foster's reputation for seeing the world in neutral shades of grey, a lot of Fitzroy Street was painted acid yellow and had mint green carpets, reminders of the searing colours that he had used for the interiors of Willis Faber.

An open-plan office may no longer have much to say about the world of work that is new, but when letters were being hammered out by secretaries in typing pools on IBM golfball electric typewriters that still seemed like a technological break-through, at a time when managers still fought to get corner offices, it was a confrontationally radical stance. Foster wanted to suggest that architecture was more about objective scientific calculation than it was about emotion and sculpture. It was as if the Calvinism of Serge Chermayeff, his tutor from his Yale days, had eclipsed everything that he had learned from Paul Rudolph. Foster made his office look as businesslike as possible. But there was always something else, something more uncon-ventional under the apparent calm of the high-gloss corporate surface.

Reyner Banham described Fitzroy Street as an office in which 'the boss's racing bike hung on one wall, and the male staff came complete with the moustache du jour'. Photographs of the period show Foster's employees dressed like peacocks in their floral-print shirts with huge collars, their tank tops and their flared trousers. And Birkin Haward, who was responsible for some of the most memorable drawings coming out of the office at the time, was always slipping in counter-cultural vignettes in the shape of hot-air balloons and hippies.

It was here that Foster and Partners worked on one of the most impressive of their unbuilt projects. It was for London Transport's redevelopment of the Hammersmith Broadway tube station and bus garage, with a new transport interchange, topped by a ring of offices and shops enclosing a covered public space.

Fitzroy Street was the office in which the team of fifteen people who had won the competition to design the Hong Kong and Shanghai Bank celebrated their victory in November 1979. After the champagne, a delegation from the American manufacturer bidding to make the bank's skin began to look a little restless; it turned out they were waiting to be ushered into the main building, assuming that they had got no further than the lobby.

Foster's next office was in Great Portland Street, and it paraphrased the Sainsbury Centre. The office filled the ground floor and basement of a stone-faced Victorian block with high ceilings, and a clear glass street-front, veiled by white perforated aluminium louvres. The louvres flooded the interior with carefully filtered light, but when they were closed, they made it impossible to make out exactly what was going on inside, night or day. There were automatic sliding glass entrance doors, and a raised perforated grey metal floor, the kind of thing that in those days you only saw in sterile clean rooms built for mainframe computers that were the size of a house. The floor had a hollow mechanical ring as you walked across the office. It felt like negotiating the cargo bay of a Boeing.

By the door there was a specially made table, with lily-pad feet, like a lunar lander, and a gunmetal-finished tubular steel structure that had its roots in the work done on the unbuilt Hampstead house. Years later the Italian furniture company, Tecno, turned the table into a commercial product, as part of an office furniture system. The system never caught on, but the table did succeed in becoming part of the very limited number of pieces of furniture that, like Mies van der Rohe's Barcelona chair or an Eames lounger, can serve to define the tastes of their owners. Most of the time the Great Portland Street version of the table had a large model of Buckminster Fuller's solar house sitting on top of it.

Foster staff who made the transition from Fitzroy Street remember Great Portland Street with affection. At Fitzroy Street, Spencer de Grey recalls office lunches art directed with the same precision applied to the façade of a building. For John Small, who leads Foster + Partners industrial designers, Great Portland Street had lighting that made it feel like a pool hall. There were inspirational images of Prouvé, Eiffel and Fuller on the walls, and architects smoked at their drawing boards in an effort to get the ink to dry faster.

Almost the entire Foster team moved to Hong Kong, where the satellite office building the bank tower eventually grew to more than one hundred people. Spencer de Grey, David Nelson, Graham Philips, Roy Fleetwood and Ken Shuttleworth, Foster's principal lieutenants at the time, all moved to Asia. The exodus was a stark reflection of what the bank represented for the practice. They were building a huge and extraordinarily demanding project on the far side of the world from Great

Portland Street. It was a complex and difficult process, and one that stretched the Foster team to their limits. And at the time there was nothing in London to match the scale of the job. Foster was torn between putting everything he had into the bank, and keeping out of the day-to-day running of the Hong Kong project so that he could concentrate on the next step. The conventional thing to do at the time would have been to move continents. Jorn Utzon shifted his family from Denmark to Sydney to build the Opera House. Richard Rogers lived at least part of the time in Paris to build the Pompidou Centre. But as might be expected from an architect who was already thinking two moves ahead even when he was still a student, Foster chose to stay in London with a rump of his staff, down at some points to a dozen people, while he worried about what the firm would be doing when the Hong Kong project came to an end.

'At the time we couldn't understand why he didn't move to Hong Kong with us,' says David Nelson. 'We had to keep briefing him on what had happened between visits, but in retrospect he was absolutely right.' What Foster always had in mind was the long-term future. When the bank was finished he did not want to find himself back where he had been before he won the Hong Kong competition.

Foster took to descending on the bank team at unpredictable intervals, insisting on changes when he decided that things had taken a wrong turn, while trying to pin down another big commission to secure the future of the office. To fight perpetual jet-lag, he took up running. It was a solitary activity that he used to find time by himself to think, and then as you might expect from a man always driven to excel at everything, it spilled over into competitive marathon races.

Having to deal with the claim that the Hong Kong bank was the most expensive building that the world had ever seen – an assertion that was as hard to prove as it was to disprove – did not help to make Foster more employable. There was a long series of projects such as the BBC Radio headquarters in Portland Place in London, or even more disappointingly for Foster, the aborted German National Athletics Stadium in Frankfurt, that dispiritingly came to nothing. Finally, in 1981, Foster won the commission for a new terminal at Stansted Airport, and a short time later Spencer de Grey came back from Hong Kong to work on the project.

The Foster office bought its first computer while it was still in Great Portland Street, but hardly any of the architects – who sat at their drawing boards, lit by desk lights with red shades, working in ink on paper drawing the four-metre-long cross-sections for the BBC building – had any idea how to use it. Computers were not yet for the creative. David Nelson describes the Foster office that built the Hong Kong and Shanghai Bank as divided between the heavy boots, among which number he saw himself, and the floppy hats. The computer, for a time, introduced a third category: the digitally literate.

Gordon Graham, the chain-smoking and always imperturbably urbane former president of the Royal Institute of British Architects, joined the office after he had helped the bank select Foster Associates. Foster then went on to win commissions to build the Renault centre in Swindon in 1980 and the Médiathèque in Nîmes in 1984. Renault, a vivid yellow cluster of steel umbrellas, was built very quickly, but Nîmes ended up taking almost a decade to finish as the city struggled to find the money to keep construction going. It was so slow that the fees it brought in were hardly enough to keep the office in London afloat. Stansted Airport was moving even more slowly as it ground its way through the intricate coils of the kind of public inquiry demanded by the British planning system.

It was Foster's drawing skills, pitted against formidable competition from Frank Gehry and Jean Nouvel, along with the support of James Stirling, who was on the jury, that won him the Médiathèque project, an art-gallery-cum-library across the street from Nîmes' miraculously well-preserved Roman monument, the Maison Carrée. Martin Francis remembers Gordon Graham using a stopwatch to time Foster in his hotel room while he practised doing a complete set of drawings that showed structure, circulation, and spatial sequences, seemingly instantly. It was an apparently off-the-cuff feat that, when he repeated it the next day, was enough to impress the mayor of Nîmes who was setting out on an ambitious plan to bring the world's most high-profile architects to work in the city. What makes the Médiathèque significant in understanding Foster's work is that it marked a point of transition. Before he built it, rightly or wrongly, he was known as a man with a ruthless approach to history and context. Nîmes was a project in which history and context were extraordinarily important, and which helped shape the way that he worked at the Royal Academy's Sackler Gallery, the British Museum's Great Court, and Boston's Museum of Fine Arts.

Foster himself was becoming an increasingly visible figure, which helped to ensure that the office did not turn into an anonymous set of initials, in the way that many architectural practices of a similar size were moving. Foster was signed up to endorse Rolex watches in a series of press advertisements. He was photographed for the pages of *Vanity Fair*, in the guise of the Hong Kong and Shanghai Bank, when the magazine updated the famous photograph of the architects' Beaux-Arts Ball of 1931 which William van Allen attended dressed as the Chrysler Building. He was even the inspiration for the protagonist of Philip Kerr's thriller, *Gridiron*, about an architect who designs a building that becomes self-aware enough to start killing off its occupants. And Foster found himself moving out of the professional ghetto to work on a series of fashion-conscious projects that made contemporary architecture a part of popular culture in Britain in a way that it had not been for many years. When Katharine Hamnett was at the height of her fame after being photographed with Margaret Thatcher in her political T-shirt dress, she asked Foster to design her first shop for her. There was a project with Doug Tompkins, founder of the Esprit fashion chain. For Joseph Ettedgui he built an elegant flagship store on Sloane Street – subsequently destroyed – that reflected some of the thinking from the Hampstead house.

Finally the office migrated to Battersea, where the Fosters built a complex of their own, mixing flats, offices and workshops.

Foster was at lunch in Chelsea, one day in 1986, and from the restaurant window he and Wendy noticed the empty site across the river, sandwiched between a bus garage and a derelict creek. They went over to take a look, and discussed doing a development on their own account, that would give them an office and also an apartment in the residential development that they planned to put on top of it.

The studio occupies the lower three floors of Riverside. Reversing the pattern established by Paul Rudolph in New Haven, the apartment is four floors above the office. Foster's ambition at Battersea was to create a mixed-use development, putting apartments on top of offices, all with spectacular views of the river.

The main Foster office is a single space on a vast scale. The architects work at pristine benches positioned at regular intervals at right angles to the window wall overlooking the river. One cartoonist represented the arrangement as the slave deck of a trireme. When the office first moved in, the only computers were for the payroll and for the CAD specialists. For the rest of the office, there were drawing boards with parallel-motion rulers, ink, paper and pencils. There is no apparent hierarchy, even if Foster himself spends most of his time at the extreme east end of the studio, closest to the window.

Battersea reflects Foster at his smoothest. Having outgrown high tech, he made an office that looked like the kind of place that could plausibly build a parliament for Germany, or design a superyacht, or a private aircraft. Clients on their way in rise up a sequence of granite steps sweeping directly from the pavement into the studio on the piano nobile above. Foster conceived of it as a workshop in which the client comes to participate in the process of design, rather than to be hidden away in a conference room as the passive audience for a presentation. There are no waiting rooms, no reception seating – an absence which sometimes leaves visitors looking a little puzzled about where to sit or stand as they wait to be invited in.

Wendy Foster did not live to see the studio completed in 1990. She died while building was still going on, leaving Foster with their two sons, by this time in their twenties, and two more adopted children. Shortly before she became ill, Norman and Wendy had followed their friends Richard and Ruthie Rogers in going to America to adopt a child: Jay Foster. Ti, their oldest son, had already persuaded them that an American friend, Steve Abramowitz, whose single parent father had recently died, needed the kind of a stable family home that they could offer. The Fosters immediately adopted him in all but name too.

It could not have been anything but an emotionally turbulent time. Foster had to come to terms with the gaps in both his professional life, in which Wendy had once played such a vital part, and his personal life.

After the grief faded, there were a number of girlfriends. His relationship with Anna Ford got him into the gossip columns for a while, and then came a second marriage to Sabiha Knight in 1991, dissolved less than five years later.

In volume one of the Foster Complete Works series, published in 1990, shortly after his first wife's death, there is a succinct account of the practice's architectural convictions and its principles. It is written by Norman Foster, and in it he movingly remembers that he had not expected to find himself writing what had originally been planned as a text by Wendy. Before she became ill, he had asked her what she was going to say about him. 'I will say that you were a juggler. You throw the balls higher than anybody else, and you let them fall lower before you catch them.' It is as touching an insight into the nature of their relationship as it is into the scale of Foster's ambition. In the end, Foster is driven by the unblinking determination never to duck a challenge. That, and an implacable inability to stop thinking about what else he could be doing next. In some people, this could be described as the compulsive behaviour of a gambler. And indeed, there is something of that addictive quality in his approach to life. Foster takes risks, with his personal safety, with his clients, with technology and with his business.

He has continually been raising the stakes. It is not that he is unaware of danger, but he is at the same time conscious that facing up to a risk can sometimes be a better strategy than trying to avoid it. He carries with him a memory of a long ago attempt to land his glider on a remote airstrip in California. At the last moment on his descent, he spotted a crop duster beneath him, unaware of his presence above, preparing to take off. Running out of height, and options, he considered what to do. Should he ditch in the scrub on the side of the strip, as he had been trained to in countless exercises, or should he head down for the tarmac, and hope that the crop duster would clear before they collided?

After putting off a decision as long as he could, Foster opted for what looked likely to be the catastrophically riskiest option and headed for the runway. He orbited and set up a last minute low approach, hoping that the plane below would take off in time to avoid a collision, or stay on the ground long enough for him to land in front. If the crop duster started to move at the wrong moment, a collision would be inevitable, and almost certainly fatal. He managed to land heavily, just behind the other aircraft as it accelerated down the runway, emerging unharmed. It was only as he looked closely at the scrub on either side of the strip and saw that it was full of metal, from an irrigation system, that he realised that if he had not ignored the lessons of his training and taken the risk of heading for the landing strip, he would certainly have been killed ploughing into a haystack made of jagged steel.

Foster has never been content with what he has already done. He is always looking for something else, taking little satisfaction in a project once it is finished. He is ready to build in countries that others are reluctant to work with. He is prepared, in his seventies, after a heart attack and a fight with bowel cancer, once mistakenly diagnosed as terminal, to match his physical fitness, courage and coordination against former Olympic athletes, men who are thirty years younger than he is. It is some compensation for the fact that he can no longer fly solo after the heart attack. To Elena Foster's considerable anxiety, he risks his life with them on the mountain roads of the Pyrenees, slicing his racing bike through the unstable gap between a vertiginous precipice and an eight-axle fifty-tonne articulated lorry at forty miles an hour. Every year he takes part in the punishing twenty-six-mile Engadine cross-country ski marathon. He suffered frostbite one year when he set off without the appropriate windproof gloves. By the time he had noticed that his fingers were turning blue, he judged it was already further to turn back than to go on and complete the race. It is his world outside architecture that gives him some of his most enduring personal relationships. Getting to the wedding of his ski instructor took priority over work.

As a young architect, he took risks by pushing his clients into letting him try out new building methods, and by attempting to build faster than anybody believed possible, and by ignoring the crutch represented by conventional architectural solutions. Why shouldn't a skyscraper hang between a pair of towers, like a suspension bridge? With what was at the time described as the world's most expensive office tower, the Hong Kong and Shanghai Bank building, Foster proved that it could be done. Why shouldn't biofuels be used to power an air-conditioning system? Why shouldn't giant mirrors be used to bring sunshine deep into the heart of an office tower or a parliament? The Reichstag did both, and successfully showed that Foster was not a wide-eyed fantasist.

Now he is ready to risk his architectural reputation by building work calculated to appeal to the tastes of oligarchs in Siberia who have made huge fortunes at breakneck speed, and lost them again, equally quickly. Would Wendy think that Norman had dropped the ball in Moscow, or in Astana, or North Ossetia? Nobody would say that he had done so at Beijing's airport. A few have said it of the Hearst Tower in New York, even if it prompted Paul Goldberger in the *New Yorker* to dub Foster the 'Mozart of modernism'. But the new city of Masdar in the Arabian gulf state of Abu Dhabi, Pont Millau, Wembley Stadium, and the remodelled British Museum are all achievements that suggest that Foster is still remarkably agile.

Norman Foster is a man who is hard to read. He maintains an apparently inscrutable façade that is as carefully composed and unemotional as that of his own work. Outsiders seldom see what is behind it. When he was gravely ill, nobody knew. But his emotional as well as his professional life was transformed when, in October 1994, he was seated next to a striking woman called Elena Ochoa at a dinner in Toledo. Ochoa, on the face of it, was everything Foster is not: passionate, spontaneous, and never afraid to show her emotions.

Ochoa was an academic with a longstanding professorship at the University of Madrid who ran a private clinic. She had been a Fulbright Scholar at UCLA and the University of Chicago. She spent a year conducting research at Cambridge. But she became well known in Spain for her famously controversial television series 'Let's Talk about Sex', which did not flinch from dealing with every taboo subject, from homosexuality to euthanasia, that conservative Catholic societies are shy of facing up to. The series was influential, contributing to the spread of family-planning clinics in Spain. Foster was impressed. By the beginning of the following year, they were inseparable. Ochoa moved to London in April 1995, and they were married the next year. They have two children, Paola and Eduardo. Ochoa went on to start publishing artists' books, and a photography magazine. In 2009 she opened a new space for contemporary art in Madrid. Her impact on Foster's recent career has been as profound as it has been on his personal life. With her encouragement, Foster has reshaped his practice to operate on an increasingly ambitious global scale, and given it a new structure to ensure that it will outlast him.

Despite a certain impatience with the cautious British way of doing things, Foster operated at the beginning of his career very much in the conventional manner of architectural practice. He was immersed in London's architectural community, in which a fluctuating cast of bright young designers moved from office to office, cross-fertilising them in ways that led to a shared method of doing things in several studios.

Jan Kaplicky for example, worked first for Richard Rogers and then for Norman Foster. Ian Ritchie moved in the opposite direction. Alan Stanton and David Chipperfield also worked for a while in both offices. Ian Simpson went back to Manchester after working for Foster, and started to build a series of high-rises in the city. Architecture in those days was a comfortable world of shared assumptions and values, and a shared way of life, of Saabs and children at progressive schools like King Alfred's, of holidays in the Dordogne, and in many cases, though not Foster's, of voting Labour.

Michael Hopkins, later to design the Glyndebourne Opera House and Portcullis House, the extension to parliament, became Foster's first partner in 1970. They met through Hopkins' wife, Patti, who was still a student at the Architectural Association, where Foster, as a tutor, had been enthusiastic about her work. Hopkins, at the time looking to move on from his job at the office of Sir Frederick Gibberd, wrote to Foster suggesting that they might meet and talk about working together. He offered to make an introduction to his father, a director in Taylor Woodrow, at the time one of the biggest building firms in Britain. Foster was looking to find a partner with the single-mindedness and self-belief to challenge him in the office, in the way that Rogers had once done. Hopkins worked on Willis Faber, and especially on the succession of buildings that the practice designed for IBM in Hampshire. Foster made him a partner, and later gave the same status to two other people in the office, Birkin Haward and Loren Butt (who was not an architect). Foster's relationship with Hopkins was not the same as the one that he had with Rogers. 'With Richard we would get angry with each other, but we both enjoyed it. Michael and I were too comfortable with each other.' In 1976, Hopkins left to establish his own firm with Patti.

With Hopkins gone, Foster rearranged the structure of the office. He became a sole trader again. And it was almost twenty years later, in 1992, before he felt that he was again ready to offer anybody else a stake in his firm. He remained in ultimate control, but he made Spencer de Grey, David Nelson, Ken Shuttleworth and Graham Philips minority partners.

Until the Hong Kong and Shanghai Bank was completed, Foster maintained the conventional mantra that small was beautiful. At one time, he told an interviewer that thirty was the ideal number of people in a successful architectural studio. It meant that the office would always stay small enough to allow everybody to know each other, and everybody to make a visible contribution. Most of all, it was a scale that it was claimed would allow architectural quality to remain, not just the highest, but also the only priority. This was a period when the ingrained ethos of the architectural community was that to become too big, or even just big, would in itself undermine the culture of creativity.

Bigness was understood to impose a constant pressure to accept work that could never lead to architecture of quality. Simply in order to keep everybody employed, work that could never turn out well would have to be taken on. There was an anxiety that, if a creative office grew beyond a certain point, the partners would be distracted from the process of making architecture by the need to devote more and more time to issues of management. Or else they would find themselves obliged to bring professional managers into the practice, effectively ceding control of creative decisions. It was an attitude shaped by an explicit divide between commercial architecture and the other kind. There was a gulf between the expectations and the culture of those architectural firms that built speculative office blocks and shopping centres, and the kind of architects who designed the universities and the art galleries. One was expedient, and depended on minimising costs and maximising revenue-generating square footage. The other had cultural ambition. One looked to establish the concept of authorship for architecture, to develop an individual voice in design. The other was pragmatic about visual expression. It's a division that has all but vanished now. Clients have become bolder in their commissioning strategy and their expectations of what buildings might look like and try to achieve. Architects who, in the past, might never have gone beyond the university campus to look for work, have found themselves being invited to compete to build high-rise office towers. It is a development which is at least in part the result of the growth of Foster + Partners and their work across the architectural spectrum.

While the firm was building the Hong Kong and Shanghai Bank, it deliberately restricted its work abroad, concentrating on its first major overseas project and the first high-rise it had ever built. In those days it turned down other work in Hong Kong. It was avoiding distractions in order to prove itself. But at a certain point, Foster changed his mind about size and decided to take all the opportunities that his early successes offered him. Perhaps it was because he felt that he had achieved all that he could, running a conventional architectural office, and wanted to try another approach. Once he had looked for the approval of his parents, approval that he never had quite as much of as he would have liked. For a while he certainly achieved the approval of his architectural peers, before they grew uneasy about his success. By growing his office, he had the chance to make a mark on a wider world and to succeed in it. And by spreading his workload across the world – Britain accounts for less than 5 per cent today – he hoped to insulate the practice from local downturns.

The shift from wanting to run a small, tightly controlled practice to presiding over something of the size that Foster + Partners has become, can be compared with the restlessness that took him from gliders to helicopters, and from helicopters to fixed-wing aircraft, and from propeller-driven planes to jets. Each is different, but Foster was determined to be equally successful at every version of flight, just as he has been successful at every version of architectural practice that he has attempted.

Architecture has gone through a dramatic scale shift in the last twenty-five years. In the 1970s, thirty people was a large office. Now Foster is far from being alone in having more than a thousand employees; even such a challenging architect as Zaha Hadid employs several hundred people. The effect of size is a phenomenon that may yet turn out to be the most significant change in practice in recent years. Size offers a capacity for research and speculative thinking that smaller offices cannot afford to invest in.

Size also means that an office can work effectively on the most dauntingly scaled programmes, constrained by apparently impossible deadlines, such as Beijing's airport which was completed in four years. But the decision to grow the practice did not come without lengthy discussion. Some senior figures in the studio questioned the need to grow beyond 200. Foster and Majidi didn't want to stop.

The evolution of Foster Associates into Foster + Partners by way of Sir Norman Foster & Partners, has been a step-by-step process. It has been shaped by the development of a management structure that has been adjusted over the years to deal with its growing size. In an organisation of less than two hundred people, everybody can expect to know everybody else, but beyond that more systematic means of achieving central control and offering support are needed. When Foster and Partners had achieved that, and still continued to grow, it passed to the next stage, and needed to go through another restructuring when it grew to more than six hundred people, a size which offers a different set of problems to resolve. Rather than continue trying to run the firm as a single larger and larger entity, the practice reorganised itself in collegiate fashion, as a series of parallel groups. Each of them has a leader, and operates on the whole range of projects, with its own clients, and its own internal loyalties. The change was important, not least for the individual architect to be able to have a sense of belonging to a smaller team.

At the time of writing, Foster + Partners was organised in six groups, but the firm could scale up to operate with more, or if conditions change, cut back to work with less.

The point of this system of groups, rather than organising the firm into specialist departments, is to allow every architect in the company the chance to build at every scale, to make the most of all their skills, and to have the experience of working around the world, rather than to find themselves limited by typology, or by geography or scale. It is an investment in the personal satisfaction of the architects in the practice, in the belief that architects with a fully rounded experience are more likely to sustain the ethos of the office.

The key to maintaining the sense of what is and what is not a Foster + Partners building is the continuing scrutiny of the design board and its guidance to architects throughout the company. The design board – which includes Foster himself as its chairman, Spencer de Grey, David Nelson and Mouzhan Majidi, and now Narinder Sagoo, Armstrong Yakubu and any of the group leaders – scrutinises every project as required, and is ready to insist on a fresh approach if it believes one is necessary. It's a method that has its origins in Foster's past, when as a student at Yale he found himself asked to justify his work in front of a jury of visiting critics and the endlessly demanding chairman of the architecture department, Paul Rudolph. It is a strategy that allows one group to learn from the experiences of another, to retain a unified approach to architecture, and for the firm to maintain a sense of intellectual and aesthetic cohesion. And it has enabled the company to recognise new talent. The groups allow such individuals as Stefan Behling to pursue his passionate interest in sustainability and solar power, and maintain his professorship in Germany, at the same time as exploring the potential for sustainable tourism in Libya. It embraces both more recent recruits, such as Gerard Evenden, as well as veterans like Mark Sutcliffe who first worked with Foster in the Team Four period.

Foster has tried hard to create the conditions that will avoid the firm's work becoming reduced to a formula. He has built one of the strongest international architectural brands, which skilfully combines the aura of an individual approach with corporate reliability, words of course that architects are congenitally disposed to be uncomfortable with. Foster + Partners is coming to resemble not so much any previous large architectural practice, such as SOM, with their federal structures of territorially based offices, or for that matter McKim, Mead and White, or even that of Alfred Waterhouse, perhaps the most successful architect before Foster to emerge from Manchester, but something more like the multiskilled engineering consultancy Arup, where the personality of a strong-minded founder still permeates a large organisation.

In his Hampstead Hill Gardens days, late at night when the phones had stopped ringing, Foster would sit in the office mailing out the invoices and chasing outstanding bills. It was an experience that made him keen to escape from the financial side of architectural practice when he could, and to concentrate on bringing in new commissions and on design.

He looked for managers and financial advisers to take care of the business for him. But none of them could save the practice from repeated financial near-death experiences. The legacy of these has been that, beneath the surface confidence, there is always a certain vulnerability to Foster, who is constantly aware that success can evaporate. He is still scarred by the experience of two Black Fridays, one in the 1980s, the other in the recession of 1992, when he was forced to call in his employees and make multiple redundancies in order to survive. One of the most difficult days was at the end of the Hong Kong and Shanghai Bank saga. 'Everybody assumed that we had made a fortune from building the bank. The reality was different.' He simply did not have enough work to be able to go on employing as many architects as he had been. It meant that some of the most gifted of them suddenly found themselves without a job. It was not an easy moment. Foster's pride collided with his determination to survive at all costs. James Meller, who had made the first introduction to Buckminster Fuller, was among those sacrificed. Foster kept Jan Kaplicky on for as long as he could, keeping him busy on a series of make-work tasks redrawing old projects for potential publication. Kaplicky took redundancy badly. It was almost ten years before he and Foster would speak again as friends, brought together by the artist Brian Clarke, who collaborated with both of them. Foster admired Kaplicky. They shared a passion for models and aircraft that was inseparable from their architecture. But if Kaplicky had not been forced to set up on his own, he might never have managed to build for himself. When Kaplicky died in 2009, Foster joined Clarke and Zaha Hadid to pay tribute in a celebration of his life at London's Design Museum.

The second crisis for the office came in 1992 after the collapse of Reichman Brothers, the Canadian developers of Canary Wharf who went bankrupt owing $20 billion. At the same time, the project for the King's Cross railway lands that the practice was master-planning on a scale to match the massive Canary Wharf office development was also cancelled. By this time, the Foster office in Battersea had grown large enough to employ several hundred people, many of them working on high-rise towers for Canary Wharf that were abruptly cancelled. Inevitably, another round of lay-offs followed.

Foster emerged from the experience determined never to find himself in the same circumstances again. He hired accountants and tax planners and management consultants to propose alternative approaches to running the business. They cost him a great deal of money, and offered plenty of advice, but none of it left Foster + Partners as financially secure as Foster would have liked.

Despite working on some of the biggest projects in the world, Foster discovered his bank was again getting anxious about the state of the firm's overdraft at the height of the post-millennial construction boom. In 2004, the firm's accounts showed a loss. His response was to give his undivided attention to running the business. In his seventies he started to look at his own architectural practice as another kind of unusually urgent design problem. He applied himself to the reorganisation of the financial structure of the firm, in much the same way that he had once looked at the Olsen building in the docks. How could he construct a new kind of architectural practice, one that could outlast him, and at the same time become as profitable as the scale of its projects suggested that it ought to be? And perhaps less easily, but much more importantly, that could make him feel secure enough not always to be anxious that the material success he had worked so hard for would slip away with the next construction industry downturn.

Since 1967 when the dissolution of Team Four left Foster and his first wife as the joint owners of the newly constituted Foster Associates, Foster's practice has had three incarnations. In early 2004 Foster set about devising a fourth version.

I had always believed that business was not for me. We spent millions in fees on advice from the most credible accountants that we gave a mandate to reinvent the company, and they screwed up.

If things had been coasting along, I would never have got involved myself. But they weren't and I realised that it was time to reinvent the business of architecture.

It took almost five years of continuous effort to carry out the strategy that Foster came up with. He transformed a loss-making business into a highly profitable practice. It allowed him to sell a minority stake in the business, while still retaining, along with key staff shareholders, the controlling interest. He would be selling from a position of strength, when revenues and prospects were high, rather than bringing in an outside investor at a moment of crisis. And it would provide the firm with a financial cushion that would free it from a dependence on short-term finance from its bankers.

The company needed a new management structure with a chief executive with the authority to be able to take over the day-to-day responsibilities from Foster himself. There were candidates in the office, senior figures that had been with him since the Fitzroy Street era, who had helped him build the Hong Kong and Shanghai Bank on which every subsequent success had depended, but they were in their fifties and sixties. After much soul searching, Foster took the decision to skip a generation in choosing the new chief executive, in the interests of reenergising the practice and achieving a longer-term con-tinuity in the management of the company. Initially Foster found himself having to face up to the disappointment of old colleagues. However, as the practice grew he succeeded in demonstrating that they had a key role to play ranging across the world to maintain an independent overview of all Foster + Partners' projects.

Architectural practice is always a trade-off between looking after those employees with the fire to run their own firms and trying to persuade them to stay, even when their instincts are to leave as quickly as they can, and those who stay but tend to be skilled followers rather than the natural leaders a practice needs for the long term. Over the years, Foster has had plenty of the former. David Chipperfield, who rebuilt the Neues Museum in Berlin, two-time Stirling Prize winner Chris Wilkinson, responsible for the Gateshead Bridge, and David Marks, who conceived the London Eye, all worked in the Foster office before setting up on their own. Michael Hopkins and Birkin Haward both started their own businesses. Sometimes directors have been poached by commercial rivals to allow them to compete more effectively. Ken Shuttleworth's departure was accompanied by a deft publicity campaign that strained credulity by portraying him as the main author of Swiss Re, the Millennium Footbridge, Hong Kong's airport, the Barcelona communications tower and even Foster and Partners' immensely detailed plans for New York's Ground Zero competition. Shuttleworth's departure did nothing to hinder Foster + Partners' accelerating growth.

David Nelson and Spencer de Grey had both been with Foster for three decades. Without them, the firm could not have been what it had become. But Foster did not see appointing a successor as chief executive from their ranks as the right solution. He wanted to find the best-qualified candidate from a younger generation, who could take a twenty-year perspective. With his controlling stake in the business, the decision was ultimately his. But Foster knew that, to take the organisation with him, he needed to give the staff a say in the selection. There was an elaborate consultation process, from which Majidi emerged as the first choice, not just of Foster, but of the rest of the senior management of the company. Majidi had joined the office in 1987, immediately after graduating from Strathclyde University in Glasgow, where he had grown up.

The change in the company's financial and management structure was devised in such a way as to allow Foster enough freedom from his day-to-day management role in the office to concentrate on design, and on the ambassadorial role that he plays for Foster + Partners. It is a job that involves a huge amount of travel for the presentations and the meetings that a worldwide practice with a high degree of political involvement for its major projects demands. It's the way to win work, and then to be able to make the work get built.

With the group system and the succession in place, Foster set about finding the right investor. He took the message of the returns that were to be made from investing in Foster + Partners to the City of London, and discovered that he enjoyed the process.

> When I wanted to seduce banks to buy into being part of the deal for a minority share, I took them around the studio and showed them how our groups work. I talked about our strategy for diversification that meant that we would not be too dependent on any single country. I took them to the model-making workshop and showed them what we did there.

From a number of possible investors, the London-based invest-ment fund 3i emerged as the closest fit. The fund put up the money in the belief that Foster + Partners had the potential for substantial capital growth. They are represented on the Foster board, whose management have an option to purchase their shares should the chance ever arise.

At the time of the sale, financial analysts calculated that the ten largest architectural practices in the world accounted for less than 1 per cent of the £90 billion spent annually on construction. In any other advanced service industry it would be seen as a derisory proportion for market leaders. Compelling economic logic suggested that the construction industry would rapidly shift to reflect the structure of other businesses. But in the meantime, even a tiny increase in market share could quickly double the revenues of a firm such as Foster + Partners.

The sale was in many ways the most impressive financial deal that he, or any other architect had ever done, one that would push him into the unwelcome scrutiny of the *Sunday Times* Rich List. When the sale of a minority stake became public, it was understood as a move startling enough to shock some of his architectural peers.

In 2007, Foster + Partners came into being, transforming the practice from a company unequivocally controlled by its founder, to an entity with almost seventy individual shareholders, some still in their early thirties, who hold their shares as long as they are employees. After the sale to 3i, Foster + Partners became an architectural giant.

As well as architects, it has engineers, IT specialists, accountants, managers and model makers working for it. Within Foster + Partners, there is not only a team of architects and designers who specialise in researching the potential of new geometries, but also a group of industrial designers who work on furniture, door handles, taps and cutlery. There is a team that helps their clients plan the layout of their offices, and yet another that deals with presentations and proposals.

At the start of 2009 there were twenty-five Foster + Partners offices around the world. Some were temporary, established with the purpose of overseeing a particular building project. Others, in locations in which there is a continuing stream of work, are semi-permanent. Initially all the design work was done in London, but this is beginning to change, and a Foster team member charged with seeing construction through to completion will move to the site when building starts to ensure that the project matches up to the original conception.

The numbers in Battersea fluctuate, but in 2008, when Foster + Partners had a turnover of £170 million and 260 projects under way, ranging from boats, bridges, and aircraft to individual houses, and from skyscrapers to studies intended to shape entire cities, the firm's workforce reached a peak of 1,400.

Foster took steps to protect his rights to his name, and to control the way that his work was used. He opened the Sunday newspapers one morning to find a development of apartments designed by the office marketed with his picture. He was determined that it could not happen without his knowledge again.

The new structure did not mean that Foster + Partners escaped the fallout from the credit crunch. When Dubai's gravity-defying economy came abruptly crashing to the ground, at exactly the same time that Russia, New York and London put every major office project on hold, it was inevitable that even the well-financed Foster + Partners would find itself having to cut back on staff. Other architects had to be even tougher in terms of the percentage of their employees that they made redundant. The sheer size of Foster + Partners meant that the numbers involved were daunting. In the spring of 2009 it had to lay off 400 people in its offices around the world. With its financial partner 3i itself under pressure from its poorly performing share price, there was no room to delay bringing down overheads in a way that was clearly painful for those who lost their jobs. Architecture is the most cyclical of activities. After the financial crisis, Foster + Partners' workload recovered and the practice started recruiting again.

The technical methods used by architects have changed enormously since the 1960s. Ink, tracing paper, drawing boards with parallel motion, and the T-square, have all been consigned more or less to the recycling bin, along with the drawing office smock and the set of French curves that used to hang on every drawing office wall. Imperial measurements have vanished everywhere except America: it seems impossibly archaic now to hear Foster reel off the structural dimensions of the Reliance Controls factory in feet and inches. Lettering is no longer applied to a sheet of tracing paper with a stencil, or rubbed down from a sheet of Letraset.

Painstaking cross-hatching applied, layer upon layer, to build up shadow and texture on a set of presentation drawings is no longer the distraction from thinking about design that it once was. It can be laid down with a keyboard and a mouse in seconds. Digitalisation has had a profound effect on the process of design, as well as on the vocabulary of architecture, in both obvious and much less predictable ways. Architecture has shifted architects away from their reliance on the traditional drawing skills, and made possible new ways in which to visualise and understand space. It has transformed the way that architects communicate their ideas to their clients, and to the builders, contractors and engineers who turn them into physical reality. Until the last decade, very few people who commissioned architecture have been fully able to understand the significance of an architect's plan before it was built, just as very few non-musicians in a concert hall can understand what the music that they are hearing is like simply from being shown a score by its composer. Even an axonometric projection, something architects assume is self-explanatory, baffles most people not familiar with its conventions. But the digital fly-through is not musical notation, or a cross-section, or a mysterious projection convention. For the first time, digital rendering offers a straightforward way to convey to a non-expert what the experience of moving through an architectural space that has not yet been built will be like. The poignant presentation that the Foster practice put together for their submission for the Ground Zero competition in 2003, tracing the journey of a child through the complex, and down into the memorial that they proposed to create within the footprints of the lost Twin Towers, was a resonant demonstration of what is now possible with such techniques.

In the face of such a reduction in the scope for the unexpected and for misunderstandings in the translation from design to built reality, the architect could be said to have rather less room for manoeuvre and for managing and orchestrating the expectations and responses of a client than in the past. The balance of power between architect and client has shifted. The client is in a position to be more detailed and more demanding in his requirements and to be able to play a more informed part in the creative aspects of the design process.

Yet at the same time the impact of digital techniques to convey space and complex forms has not done away with the need for an evaluation of a design through material means at each stage of the design process. Perhaps paradoxically, it has encouraged production of the large-scale physical models that are a particular speciality of Foster + Partners. To explore the physical form of a wall or a window in a prototype before it has been built has been an essential part of the Foster approach since the earliest days. The more architects can speculate freely about what architecture can be, using digital techniques, the more they need to be able to understand the material implications.

As visitors walk into the Foster + Partners studio, they pass an entire wall of models of all sizes stacked up to the ceiling. These reflect past projects, some built, others not, in a way that echoes the clutter of architectural fragments that pack every inch of Sir John Soane's house. They certainly have a seductive charm, but for the architect, these are not toys or sales aids but working tools. They are the means to explore the impact of design decisions, at the scale of both the smallest detail, and at the level of the master plan. Those projects that are in the design development phase are represented by large models aligned along the window wall of the studio, overlooking the Thames. The rest, piled up the ceiling, represent a glimpse of the office's accumulated memory.

The models in the studio are just a fraction of the Foster archive. The rest are in a series of climate-conditioned fine art stores. They contain hundreds of models of all scales, materials and sizes that provide a record of Foster's work, going back to his earliest projects as an independent architect. Before the disastrous fire of 2004 that destroyed so much Brit Art, they were kept in MoMART's bleak Hackney sheds. Amid a clutch of Barry Flanagan hares, and a Damien Hirst, just back from Brooklyn, you could see a giant representation of the dome of the Reichstag, big enough to stand up in, just like one of the great models of St Paul's made for Christopher Wren. Foster's unbuilt scheme to relocate BBC Radio to the site of the Langham Hotel lingered on as a giant model, broken up in sections, and stacked up to the ceiling. There were scores of studies for high-rises in Japan, Germany, Lebanon, Australia and America. There were beautifully detailed designs for remodelling London's South Kensington, for building a new airport in Shanghai, and universities in Malaysia. You could see the original structural model for the Sainsbury Centre at the University of East Anglia, discarded in favour of the even more beautiful version that was actually built when Foster had his last-minute brainwave. There are rough-and-ready foam models, made in the studio, as well as immaculately finished models that were intended to impress clients.

The extensive use of modelling is a thread that has run through every incarnation of the practice. In his days as a student at Yale, Foster's graduation city-of-the-future project stood out for the remarkable quality of the model that he had made. When London's City Hall was under construction, a full-size section of the hand-rail for the ramp that spirals all the way up the interior of the building in a continuous ribbon was made up in the Foster workshop in Battersea, and positioned in the office forecourt. It was there to give the design team a sense of the physical quality of the object that they had designed, to see how it would feel, and how it would look in different light conditions. Such mock-ups and simulations have always been an essential part of architectural practice. Mies van der Rohe, for example, managed to lose his first commission when his client decided that the house he was working on wasn't quite what he wanted on the basis of what he saw from the full-size elevations that were painted on canvas screens and positioned on the site. But even against this background, models are unusually important for Foster, and the precision of his work has its roots in the care with which every possible option is modelled and prototyped before a final decision is taken.

Such an approach to design imposes a demand for model-making skills that, for all the purposeful concentration of the rows of architects at their digital workstations, make some parts of the Foster + Partners building feel more like a particularly elegant factory, full of spray booths and cutting and turning machines, rather than a conventional white-collar workplace. And half a mile away from the main office there is now a vast model-making studio, big enough to work on multiple giant models.

The models reappear in Foster's personal studio, a former chapel attached to his house in Switzerland. One wall is occupied by a vast representation of Beijing Airport. There is a Swiss Re model and one of the Hong Kong and Shanghai Bank, exactly like the model that stands in the office in Battersea. Another version is in the permanent collection of the Museum of Modern Art in New York.

And in an echo of his childhood passion for model aircraft, shelf after shelf in his study is stacked with them.

Digital analysis has changed not just the process of design, but also the way that buildings are made and the nature of the forms that they can be designed to take on. A digital file sent direct from the architect to the factory can form the basis of the pattern-cutting programme that a cladding manufacturer employs to produce the skin for a building. And this in turn allows for far more complex geometries that have become, if not routine, then certainly much more widespread in the last decade. It has allowed architecture to take on something of the character of dressmaking on an epic scale, with the building treated as a structure clad in fabric that needs to be cut from sheet material in the most economical way, as if cutting a pattern for a garment. And just as with a garment, the seams and joints need to be placed with care to create an appropriate form.

If making buildings has become a different process over the last decades, then so has the way in which architects are seen by the world.

There were times, in the 1980s and 1990s, when Foster felt that Britain was not giving him his due. Like many others, he came to believe that he could only get work outside the country. And even when he got it, Britain was ignoring his success – or so he believed. David Chipperfield and Zaha Hadid would have told much the same story about themselves. In fact, it is hard to imagine an architect better known in Britain that Foster. First knighted, then elevated to the House of Lords, Foster has earned every conceivable honour and distinction, including the Order of Merit from the Queen, a distinction that brings with it a dinner every three years with the sovereign; the Royal Gold Medal for Architecture; as well as the Pritzker and Stirling prizes. His new university in Malaysia won the Aga Khan Award in 2007, and he was a recipient of the Japanese Prix Imperium and of the Prince of the Asturias prize.

But as time passes, with every success comes the nagging sense of another generation pressing behind him. Architecture is a profession in which age is not normally a handicap. On the contrary. Philip Webb, who designed William Morris's Red House, once suggested that no architect should be allowed to design a house until they were forty. Frank Lloyd Wright was working on the Guggenheim Museum well past the age of ninety.

In the first decade of this century, Foster's buildings certainly have changed in their emphasis. They have begun to take advantage of the complex forms that are made possible by new techniques of making buildings and analysing them. And they have responded to shifts in scale and geography that are reshaping architecture. He has also become interested in working with other architects. Though in the event the project did not succeed, Foster worked with Gehry on a huge plan for the redevelopment of Milan's trade fair site. It was the first in a series of collaborative projects that has seen Foster work with Jean Nouvel in London and Rem Koolhaas in Dallas.

With the passage of time, the key buildings of Foster's early career – the Sainsbury Centre, the Hong Kong and Shanghai Bank, Willis Faber in Ipswich – look more and more impressive, not less. But the cumulative impact of the torrent of Foster buildings that followed them has changed the way that Foster is now perceived. When he was still running a young architectural practice, every new design that Foster unveiled could be presented as an event. Now that there are so many new designs coming from the office, it is impossible to regard them in the same way that they once might have been. There are still show stoppers, such as the Pont Millau, whose unveiling stilled every critic. But there are other projects that certainly do not stand up to the same level of intensive scrutiny that those pioneering early works do. And there are a few, Birmingham's Sea Life Aquarium, for example, that are best ignored.

There are others that get unjustifiably overlooked in the seemingly endless stream of completed projects emerging on a production line from an office that is now building hundreds of projects at a time. Foster has moved from creating a limited number of masterpieces to running an office that has significantly raised the standard of the ordinary. It could be seen as a much more challenging achievement, and has also allowed for the possibility of some actual failures.

The firm was once regarded as a radical choice, appealing only to a certain kind of client. It is now a reliably innovative one. It's a shift that has allowed Foster + Partners to move centre stage. They have succeeded in making architecture of quality a more mainstream aspiration than it once was in Britain. The challenge for Foster + Partners now is to retain its openness to new fields of inquiry, to keep its sense of freshness and lack of complacency now that it is no longer an ambitious newcomer but a landmark at the very centre of the architectural landscape. In London, Foster + Partners' work is no longer a matter of sporadic individual buildings. There are now so many of them that it is too late to look at them one at a time. Foster's impact is not at the level of one-off buildings, it has taken on an essential part in shaping the overall context.

Walking across Tower Bridge, you can see a city formed to a remarkable extent by Foster buildings and plans. In the foreground is City Hall, and the office development known as More London. Just across the Thames is the Foster + Partners office scheme by the Tower of London. A little way to the west is the Millennium Bridge. On the skyline is the Swiss Re tower, and the crescent-shaped slab that wraps itself around the Lloyds building. Further in the distance is the HSBC tower at Canary Wharf. Elsewhere around London, the firm has built Stansted Airport, Wembley Stadium, the British Museum's new court. On London Wall there are three significant Foster buildings.

It's a crystalline world of glass icebergs, and smooth wavelike forms, of structural gymnastics, and carefully considered landscapes.

Foster + Partners now has the experience of working in every continent of the world, and with every building type, from airports to skyscrapers, from schools to private houses, hotels, bridges and boats. It has the resources to research the issues of energy consumption, transport and prefabrication. The projects that Foster + Partners works on are becoming larger too, which might be an important factor in determining the recruiting policies of architectural offices.

Foster himself suggests that he has become more interested in working at the scale of the city rather than individual buildings. It's a development that has been reflected in the reconfiguration of the meeting rooms on the mezzanine level of the Foster office in London. There are fewer of them, but they are bigger, to allow for the kind of large-scale models required to represent a master plan on an urban scale, and the large groups of people needed to work on them together. Architects must be prepared to work on master plans that can take on the scale of a whole city, or even a region. They are so big now that it is impossible to be entirely precise about their size.

Focusing on narrow architectural definitions of the scale of a project becomes difficult when 100,000 square metres is now the standard unit by which architectural work is measured in some parts of the world. And then there are much larger buildings to deal with. The Central Market in Abu Dhabi that Foster is working on spreads over 500,000 square metres, which is to say ten times the size of the Canary Wharf office development. The new terminal at Beijing Airport covers an almost unimaginable 13 million square metres – an entire city.

When Norman Foster established his office in 1967 there was a sense that architectural reputations were established primarily on the basis of the work that an architect would build within their own country. In the past there might have been a few projects overseas to add an exotic touch to an architectural career, but these were more often than not understood as diversions from the main effort. That is not true now. Architecture is as universal as it was in the Middle Ages, when groups of itinerant masons went from cathedral to cathedral, moving from one construction site to the next. In their constant travel they made gothic architecture in France and Germany and England an integral whole.

Foster + Partners to date has built in thirty-two countries. The staff in London come from a spread of places that is as wide as their workload. The company attracts ambitious and gifted young architects from all around the world to learn, and to get the chance to build.

The first overseas projects Foster Associates worked on were in Norway and in the Canary Islands, both the result of the connection with Fred Olsen, and a natural outgrowth of their domestic practice. It was followed by the Hong Kong and Shanghai Bank, which was perhaps the last manifestation of a colonial connection, with a design being shipped out to what was still a colony from the other side of the world. Foster's role was to supply an expertise and a service that was not at the time locally available.

Since then, the nature of international practice has been transformed. Those early projects reflected a one-way transaction: Britain was exporting expertise while holding the outside world at arm's length. But the more that Foster and Partners worked outside Britain, the more it became a two-way process.

They were exporting their skills, but at the same time they were, consciously or not, finding their view of the world transformed by the places in which they worked, and the kind of projects that they were asked to take on. Once you have built a skyscraper in Shanghai, or an airport in Hong Kong, it is hard to see the world only through the perspective of working with the preconceptions of fitting into the City of London, where architecture can sometimes feel as constrained as dentistry.

The experience of working in cultures in which governments are prepared to countenance radical new approaches to development by trying to connect transport systems in an integrated way, or to drive large-scale projects through a thicket of competing local interests, can serve to reshape a firm's understanding of architectural practice back in Britain. When Hong Kong decided on the closure of the territory's original airport at Kai Tak, and its replacement through the construction of an entirely new one, with runways built on land reclaimed from the sea, connected to the city centre by a brand-new mass-transit rail link, and accompanied by the development of an entire new town, it made the reluctance of London to consider a similarly radical solution to the problem of overcrowding and noise pollution at Heathrow by relocating it to the Thames estuary seem self-defeatingly timid.

The context in which Foster + Partners is now working has had a significant impact on the character of its work. To undertake projects for heads of state in Kazakhstan, or for state-controlled corporations in China, is to be placed in the position of finding ways of meeting the aspirations of cultures with aesthetic expectations very different from those that prevail in Edinburgh, or Barcelona, or London. And it is perhaps the most challenging aspect of the future for the practice. It must find a way to work that will allow a Foster + Partners detached from its roots in London to retain its sense of purpose and meaning. Foster is trying to find ways to address such new building types as the Kazakhstan ecumenical centre, its Palace of Peace and Reconciliation. And to try to find an appropriate form of architectural expression for them is not just a logistical exercise, but a search that goes to the heart of architecture.

Foster + Partners is far too large and sophisticated an operation to be understood as a vehicle for one individual. But Norman Foster is a remarkable architect, and in Foster + Partners he has created an organisation which can carry on the practice of architecture in a way that has the essence of Norman Foster and his personal history and determination at its very centre, in any context.

Norman Foster's Madrid office is on the Paseo de Castellana. Two of his most recent projects have been pinned to the walls. Behind him are the early surveys for a commission to work on the Château Margaux, that will include the first piece of new architecture on the estate since 1810. It sits opposite a series of studies for the expansion of the Pushkin Museum in Moscow that will create a cultural complex larger than either Tate Modern in London or the Museum of Modern Art. A portfolio of photographs shows the array of derelict timber structures surrounding the Pushkin that he is being asked to restore for a project that has the personal approval of Vladimir Putin.

But what Foster really wants to talk about is an entirely new project that has been much on his mind. The question of the affordable house. In conversation with Ricky Burdett, director of the London School of Economics Urban Age programme, he was struck by the figure of $7,500, the sum typically spent on making a self-built basic home in a São Paulo favela, or an illegal Mexico City squatter settlement, or Bogotá, or Mumbai. He was fascinated by the constraints – typically the limits of the size of components that can be fitted into a pick-up truck, and by the potential of using the electrical appliances that even such squatter homes typically have in a more energy-efficient way.

Foster's next mission is to follow in the footsteps of Le Corbusier and Jean Prouve and Buckminster Fuller, all of whom tried and failed to create mass-produced homes. Except that Foster, with his connections with Indian industrialists, international bankers and high-tech manufacturers in America, Britain and Spain, has no intention of failing in mass-producing homes that cost the purchaser no more than a cheap car.

In the sense that patience is commonly understood, Norman Foster is not a patient man. What he does have in abundance is concentration. Juggling the cyclic stick that moves a helicopter up or down, at the same time as moving the collective lever with its twist-grip throttle, and depressing the foot pedals connected to the tail rotor in order to allow a Bell Jet Ranger to swivel on its own axis, is a kind of dance that needs complete control and the complete concentration that is Foster's version of patience. So does assembling an intricate scale-model of a vintage aircraft with glue, razor blades, sandpaper and a watchmaker's glass, or running a marathon, or understanding the essence of a complex design problem.

Foster is quick to boil up into sudden explosions of frustration when the irritating distractions of everyday life suddenly become intolerable. He gets angry with the desk left half cleared, with the studio kitchen less than spotless, with the books shelved in the wrong place, or with the camera that has no batteries. It is an anger that evaporates just as fast as it explodes. He expresses emotion in ways that run counter to the carefully controlled nature of his work. He needs constant stimulation, and change.

He works on a project in intensive bursts, then moves on to the next and the one after that, before returning to the first problem, like an advanced chess player contesting six games at once. He slips in and out of focus; distracted by the next idea that flashes through his consciousness. Concentration, by its nature, fluctuates. In the early days, one associate remembers a presentation with a client and the design team, at which Foster's attention wandered long enough for him to doodle a polo shirt, which he later sent his assistant off to buy, before returning to the project in front of him.

If he is impatient, he is also a man untouched by scepticism, which is a quality whose absence is helpful for an architect. To make a building with any flicker of genuine creative ambition requires its architect to suspend disbelief. It demands the unwavering investment of every ounce of emotional capital that he has in the conviction that his design is actually going to make the transition from paper to steel and glass.

In the face of overwhelming evidence to the contrary, he must live and breathe a design, unconditionally, month after month, without ever, even for a second, betraying the slightest doubt that it will be built. Foster has designed twenty airports, but only four have been built. Out of every eight competitions he takes part in, only one leads to a completed building. And even when it comes to the successful projects where the fees get paid, only one in four produces a building. Yet he must not only design it, but lobby for it, help raise money for it, and do his best to sell it as well. Then he must fight to build it on a rain-sodden, muddy construction site with a contractor who is more interested in finding profitable new ways to use the legal interpretation of the contract than in building the architect's vision.

The process demands the self-knowledge needed to stop the architect from falling into the banal trap of the Fountainhead Complex, losing all touch with reality in the pursuit of a megalomaniac fantasy.

What is not quite so clear is whether the architect needs to be an optimist, rather than a pessimist. Foster could be understood to incline to the latter state of mind.

'There are two kinds of pilot. There is the one who takes off and is shocked and surprised at an engine failure. I am in the second category: I am wonderfully surprised if there is no engine failure after I am in the air,' he says.

Acknowledgements

This is an authorised biography, which suggests a certain intimacy between subject and author. I first met Norman Foster towards the end of the 1970s. He was one of the group of architects and designers that helped to fund the start up of *Blueprint* magazine which I edited back in 1983. He was one of the three architects in the exhibition that Peter Murray and I curated at the Royal Academy. In 1985, I went to see the Hong Kong and Shanghai bank when it was still a construction site, and got a bad case of vertigo on the construction lift slung to the outside of the scaffolding. In the 1990s, I toured Chep Lap Kok airport among the giant earth diggers, before it was finished. In 2006, I had a chance to wander over the site of Beijing's new aiport while a 50,000-strong workforce was living there.

Over the years there have been dinners, and rides in his cars. He flew me to Manchester once, and I clearly remember envisaging the whole-page obituary that would ensue for Norman if we crashed, that might include the line, 'Also in the aircraft at the time was ...'.

This was getting close enough to make some assumptions about the man and the architect, but it has only been since I started work on this book that I have been able to test those assumptions.

This is perhaps not so much a biography, but an account of what it is like to be an architect in a time when cities double in size in a decade, new states set out to present themselves to the world through the glossy presumption of their buildings and architecture has never been more global. It is also an attempt to understand what it is that has driven Norman Foster quite so hard.

Writing it depended on a lot of people who were prepared to talk to me about him, some of whom, such as Jan Kaplicky, are sadly no longer alive. Former associates and employees Alan Stanton, Martin Francis and David Chipperfield talked to me about what it was like to work with him. M.J. Long and Su Rogers discussed life at Yale.

The current Foster + Partners team, notably Mouzhan Mujadi, Spencer de Grey and David Nelson, talked to me at length, and nobody was more helpful and knowledgeable than Katy Harris. I am grateful to my agent, Claire Paterson of Janklow & Nesbit, and to Fernando Gutierrez for designing the book.

References

p. 52 David Greene, *Archigram*, issue number 1, reproduced on the Design Museum's Design Library website

p. 57 Thomas H. Beeby, from the Chicago Architects Oral History Project, The Ernest R. Graham Study Center for Architectural Drawings, Department of Architecture, The Art Institute of Chicago, Copyright 2002

p. 69 William Grindering, from the Paul Rudolph Foundation website

p. 72 Thomas H. Beeby, from the Chicago Architects Oral History Project, The Ernest R. Graham Study Center for Architectural Drawings, Department of Architecture, The Art Institute of Chicago, Copyright 2002

p. 75 Mark Girouard, *Big Jim: The Life and Works of James Stirling*, Chatto & Windus, 1998

p. 78 Dean Keller, letter to the *Yale Daily News*, 1963

p. 80 Paul Rudolph, from the Paul Rudolph Foundation website

p. 85 Serge Chermayeff and Christopher Alexander, *Community and Privacy*, 1964

p. 87 Serge Chermayeff and Christopher Alexander, *Community and Privacy*, 1964

p. 88 Thomas H. Beeby, from the Chicago Architects Oral History Project, The Ernest R. Graham Study Center for Architectural Drawings, Department of Architecture, The Art Institute of Chicago, Copyright 2002

p. 146 Buckminster Fuller, quoted in Nigel Whiteley, *Reyner Banham: Historian of the Immediate Future*, MIT, 2003

p. 146 Nigel Whitely, *Reyner Banham: Historian of the Immediate Future*, MIT 2003

p. 152 Otl Aicher, *The World as Design*, Wiley, 1994

Illustration Credits

Unless otherwise credited, the copyright to all images belongs to Norman Foster

Section One
Foster with bicycle (© Patrick Lichfield)
Norman Foster as a baby
The house in Levenshulme
Family photograph
Foster with his parents
Foster with a bicycle
Images from Norman Foster's sketchbook
Sketch for Bourne Mill
Sketches completed at Yale
Foster and others at university
Foster at a university rag ball
Foster with Richard Rogers and Carl Abbot (© Su Rogers)
Reliance Controls
Creek Vean (© Richard Einzig)
Drawing for Creek Vean
Sketch of Creek Vean
Photograph of Creek Vean (© Camera Craft)
Foster with Buckminster Fuller (© Ken Kirkwood)
Foster with Wendy Cheeseman (© Tim Street Porter)

Section Two
Olsen building under construction (© Tim Street Porter)
Architectural Review cover

Foster with a light aeroplane (© Foster + Partners)
Sketch of Hong Kong & Shanghai Bank Headquarters
Photographs of Hong Kong & Shanghai Bank Headquarters (© Ian Lambot)
Sketch of the Willis Faber building (© Norman Foster)
Willis Faber interior (© Ken Kirkwood)
Willis Faber exterior (© Tim Street Porter)
Sketches for the Sainsbury Centre
Sainsbury Centre exterior (© Ken Kirkwood)
Sainsbury Centre interior (© Nigel Young / Foster + Partners)
Sketch for Stansted Airpot (© Norman Foster)
Stansted Airport (© Richard Davies)
Carré d'Art, Nîmes (© James H Morris)
Foster + Partners London offices (© Rudi Meisel)
Norman and Elena Foster (© Frederic Aranda)

Section Three
Reichstag exterior (© Svenja-Foto / Corbis)
Reichstag interior (© Rudi Meisel)
Sketch for the British Museum
British Museum Great Court (© Nigel Young / Foster + Partners)
Millennium Bridge (© Nigel Young / Foster + Partners)
Millau Viaduct (© Jean-Paul Azam / Getty)
Work in progress on Hearst tower (© Nigel Young / Foster + Partners)
Completed Hearst tower (© Chuck Choi)
View across London (© Nigel Young / Foster + Partners)
Chesa Futura, St Moritz (© Nigel Young / Foster + Partners)
Drawing for Chesa Futura, St Moritz
Beijing Airport photographs (© Nigel Young / Foster + Partners)
Masdar images (© Foster + Partners)

Interior images:
Otl Aicher sketch of NF, 1985 (© Otl Aicher)
Photograph of NF sketching (© Rudi Meisel)

Index

Throughout the index NF has been used as an abbreviation for Norman Foster. Norman Foster's projects have also been annotated with (NF).

30 St Mary's Axe (NF) *see* Swiss RE Headquarters
3i, 276–7, 279

Aalto, Alvar, 67
Abbott, Carl, 74, 75, 89
Abu Dhabi, 1–3, 155, 264, 287
aeroplanes and air travel, 10, 25, 34, 59, 60, 92, 268
  gliders, 119–20, 262
  helicopters, 74, 99–100, 120, 139, 291
Aga Khan Award for Architecture, 284
Agbar Tower, Barcelona, 185
Aicher, Otl, 151–4, 179
Anshen and Allen, 91–2
Architectural Association, London, 51, 52, 73, 90, 96
Archigram, 52
Architects Registration Council, 96
Architectural Forum, 79, 83
Architectural Review, 46, 48, 128, 148
Art and Architecture Building, University of Yale, 68, 70, 72, 77–80
awards:
  Chinese friendship award, 239
  FT Industrial Architecture Award, 105

peerage, 11, 193–4, 284
Royal Gold Medal for Architecture, 141, 284

Bacon, Francis, 127, 128
Banham, Reyner, 52, 65, 146, 147, 148, 253–4
Bank of China, Hong Kong, 163, 175
Batchelor, John, 10–11
Battersea office (Foster + Partners), 89, 249, 259–60, 272
Baturina, Yelena, 243–5
BBC Radio Centre (NF; unbuilt), 100–1, 257, 282
Bean Hill estate, Milton Keynes, 159, 248–9
Beardshaw, John, 36, 37–8, 39–41, 54, 59–60, 97
Beckett, Lionel, 17, 121–2
Beckett, Sid, 17, 122
Beeby, Thomas, 57–8, 72–3, 88–9
Behling, Stefan, 270
Beijing Airport (NF), 224–32, 233–4, 237, 283, 287
Beijing Olympic Stadium, 225, 237
Bernaskoni, Boris, 245

Betjeman, John, 29

Bijvoet, Bernard: Maison de Verre, Paris, 247–8

Bilbao Metro, Spain (NF), 152

Bill, Max, 152

Black, Misha, 92

Blair, Tony, 224

Blue Cross, Blue Shield Buildings, Boston, 76

Branch, Michael, 91, 92

Breuer, Marcel, 56, 126
  Whitney Museum, New York, 159, 181

British Library, London, 75, 211, 216

British Museum, Great Court (NF), 152, 211–16, 250, 258, 264, 286

Browne, Kenneth, 48

Bruijn, Pi de, 200, 201, 202

Brumwell, Marcus, 92, 93, 97

Building Design Partnership, 49

Burj al Arab tower, Dubai, 189

Burnage High School, Manchester, 22–4

Burnham, Daniel Hudson: Monadnock Building, 90

Butt, Loren, 116–17, 266

Calatrava, Santiago, 200, 201, 206–7

Canary Wharf Underground Station (NF), 123

Carnegie, Andrew, 18–19

Caro, Anthony, 249
  Millennium Bridge, 95, 217

Casson, Hugh, 51
  Faculty of Arts, University of Cambridge, 50

Central House of Arts, Russia, 244

Central Park, New York, 245

Charreau, Pierre: Maison de Verre, Paris, 247–8

Château Margaux, Bordeaux (NF), 290

Cheesman, Georgie, 93, 94, 96

Cheesman, Wendy *see* Foster, Wendy (1st wife)

Chen, Commander, 224, 238

Chep Lap Kok Airport, Hong Kong (NF), 234, 237, 275, 276, 289

Chermayeff, Serge, 84–8, 253

Chesa Futura Housing, Switzerland (NF), 250–1

Chigirinsky, Shalva, 241–2, 243, 244

children, 95, 104, 121, 129, 260–1, 265

Childs, David: Ground Zero, New York, 57–8

China, 162–3, 169–70, 175, 227–8, 232–3, 237–40
  see also Beijing Airport (NF)

Chipperfield, David, 265, 284
  Neues Museum, Berlin, 275

Citicorp Tower, New York, 160

City Hall, London (NF), 286

Clarke, Brian, 249, 272

Climatroffice project, 125, 150

Commercial Union Tower, London, 183

Commerzbank Headquarters, Frankfurt (NF), 181, 200

Community and Privacy, 85–7, 88

competitions, 2, 92, 217, 242, 292
  Beijing Airport, 224–5
  City of Tomorrow (Ruberoid Company), 87, 88
  Ground Zero, New York, 186, 275, 280
  Hong Kong Shanghai Banking Corporation, 163–8, 254
  Humana Headquarters, Louisville, 179–80
  Newport School, South Wales, 76, 105
  Reichstag, Berlin, 127, 199, 200, 201–2

computer technology and architecture, 257, 279–81, 283–4

Cook, Peter, 52

Cordingley, Professor Reginald Annandale, 41–2, 44, 47

Creak Vean House, Cornwall (Team Four), 64, 66–7, 93, 97
Crystal City project, 243, 246
Cullen, Gordon, 48
cycling, 24–5, 263

Dan Dare: Pilot of the Future, 3, 9 de Grey, Spencer, 105, 157, 165–6, 211, 214, 255, 257, 266, 270, 275
Denton Corker Marshall: Australian Embassy, Beijing, 227
Design Research Unit, London, 92
digital technology and architecture, 215, 257, 279–81, 283–4
Drew, Jane, 75
Dymaxion projects, 10, 144, 145
Dymsdale School, Manchester, 22

Eagle comic, 3, 8–10, 13
Eames, Charles and Ray, 105, 111, 247–8, 255
East Anglia University (UEA), 130, 138–9
    see also Sainsbury Centre for Visual Arts
education, 33
    Burnage High School, 22–4, 26–7
    Dymsdale School, 22
    Manchester University, School of Architecture, 41–8, 51, 91
    see also Yale University
Empire State Building, New York, 157
employment, 35–6
    John Beardshaw's, 36, 37–8, 39–41, 54, 59–60
    Manchester Town Hall, 27, 28–30, 33, 34–5 national service 33–4, 35
    teaching 95–6, 104, 275 in the US, 68, 91–2
    see also Foster and Associates; Team Four
Energiya, 240
English Heritage, 124, 211–12
environmental issues and architecture, 3,
145, 150, 189, 194–5, 198–9, 240
Erwitt, Elliot, 67, 68
Evans, Eldred, 60, 75
    Newport School, South Wales, 76, 105
    Tate Gallery, St Ives, 73
Evenden, Gerard, 271
Express Newspapers' Buildings, 30–2, 125

Faculty of Arts, University of Cambridge, 50
Faculty of Law, University of Cambridge (NF), 48
Falling Water, Pittsburgh, 89–90
fascism, 55–6, 108, 151, 152, 209
Federal Reserve Tower, Boston, 160
Feng Shui, 166, 170
Festival of Britain, 9, 51
Financial Times, 217
    Industrial Architecture Award, 105
Fisker, Kay, 49
Fitzpatrick, Tony, 221–2
Fitzroy Street offices (Foster and Associates), 252–4, 255
Fleetwood, Roy, 255
Foster, Elena (wife), 8, 120–1, 263, 264
Foster, Lillian (mother), 11, 13, 14, 16, 17, 19, 22, 93, 121–2
Foster, Norman
    childhood, 11–13, 14–15, 19–25
    family and home in Manchester, 4–6, 11–17, 121–122
    children, 95, 104, 121, 129, 260–1, 265
    design of homes, 247–8, 249, 250–1
    hobbies, 24–6, 118, 119–21, 256, 262–3
    character, 106, 149, 203, 261–4, 291–3
    see also aeroplanes and air travel; Aicher, Otl; education; employment; Foster, Elena (wife); Foster, Lillian (mother); Foster, Robert (father); Foster, Wendy (1st wife); Foster + Partners; Foster Associates; Fuller, Buckminster; Hong Kong and

Foster, Norman—*contd*
  see also—contd
    Shanghai Bank; Olsen, Fred; politics
    in architecture; Rogers, Richard;
    Sainsbury, Robert and Lisa; Team
    Four; Yale University
Foster, Robert (father), 11, 14, 16–17, 19,
  93, 121
Foster, Sabiha (2nd wife) see Knight,
  Sabiha
Foster, Wendy (1st wife), 93–5, 96, 104,
  118–19, 129, 143, 157, 165–6, 259,
  260, 261
Foster + Partners, 18, 277–9, 281–3,
  285–90
Foster Associates, 104–18, 268
  financial issues, 271–4, 276–7
  management structure, 274–6
  partners, 265–7
  studios, 251–6, 257, 259–60
  see also Hong Kong and Shanghai Bank;
    Olsen, Fred; Sainsbury, Robert and
    Lisa
Francis, Martin, 116–17, 258
Fragrant Hills Hotel, Beijing, 227
Fred. Olsen Line, Millwall see Olsen, Fred
Fulbright scholarships, 53
Fuller, Buckminster, 143–6, 272
  Dymaxion projects, 10, 144, 154
  NF influenced by, 57, 90, 125, 246,
    291
  NF's relationship with, 141–2, 149–51,
    154–5, 194, 249

Gateshead Millennium Bridge, 275
Gehry, Frank, 217, 258, 285
Germany, 198–202, 207, 208–10
  see also Reichstag, New German
    Parliament (NF)
'Gherkin' (NF) see Swiss RE
    Headquarters, London
Gibberd, Frederick, 23, 266

Gies, Ludwig, 209
Gilbert, Cass
  Union Station, New Haven, 62
  Woolworth Building, New York, 173
Glyndebourne Opera, 265
Goldberger, Paul, 185–6, 264
Golden Orange project, 244, 245, 246
Gomera project (NF; unbuilt), 112–13
Graham, Gordon, 164, 257, 258
Graves, Michael, 173, 181, 211
  Humana Headquarters, Louisville,
    179–80
Great Court at the British Museum (NF)
  see British Museum, Great Court
Great Portland Street offices (Foster and
    Associates), 254–5
Green, David, 52
Greenberg, Alan, 77
Grenfell-Baines, George, 48–9
Grey, Milner, 92
Grimshaw, Nicholas, 106
Grindereng, William, 69
Gropius, Walter, 56, 66, 77, 79, 85, 157
  Pan Am Building, New York, 83
Ground Zero, New York, 58, 186, 250,
    275, 280
Guggenheim Museum, New York, 90,
    186, 285

Hadid, Zaha, 77, 233, 241, 268, 272,
    284
Hall, Ron, 104
Hammersmith Broadway tube station
    (NF; unbuilt), 254
Hampson, Frank, 9
Hancock Tower, Chicago, 173
Harvard University, Boston, 53, 56, 57,
    66, 144
Haward, Birkin, 113, 254, 266, 275
Hearst Building (original by Joseph
    Urban), 187

Hearst Tower, New York (NF), 154–5, 185–8, 249, 264

Heathrow Airport, London, 226, 233

Henry Fellowship, 53–4

Herzog, Jacques, 233

Hitchcock, Henry-Russell, 37, 70

Hitler, Adolf, 151, 152, 200, 210

hobbies, 24–6, 118, 119, 256, 262, 263
  see also aeroplanes and air travel

Hong Kong and Shanghai Bank, Hong Kong (NF), 76, 100, 101, 117, 140, 158, 220, 268, 271, 283
  competition, 156–7, 160, 163–8
  NF's proposals, 168–71
  building the Hong Kong HQ, 171–3
  completed Hong Kong HQ, 174–9, 181–2, 205–6, 263
  Paul Rudolph's opinion, 81, 82
  see also HSBC (UK) Headquarters (NF)

Hong Kong and Shanghai Banking Corporation, 160–3

Hong Kong Club buildings, 160, 181–2

Hong Kong office (Foster and Associates), 255–6

Hopkins, Michael and Patti, 121, 265–6, 275
  Glyndebourne Opera, 265
  Portcullis House, 265

Howarth, Thomas, 43–4

HSBC UK Headquarters, London (NF), 123, 160, 286

Hughes Stanton, Corin, 127–8

Humana Headquarters, Louisville, 179–80

Hunt, Tony, 97–8, 116, 136, 248, 251, 252

IBM, 251, 252, 266

Illinois Institute of Technology, 56

International Finance Centre Tower, Hong Kong, 182

Jacobsen, Arne, 49

Jacoby, Helmut, 126–7

Jiushi Corporation Headquarters, Hong Kong (NF), 182

Johnson, Philip, 56, 65, 66, 126, 147, 173
  Crystal Cathedral, California, 84
  Johnson House 'The Glass House,' 84
  Seagram Building, New York, 56, 83, 90

Kahn, Louis, 56, 65, 76, 90, 91
  Yale Art Museum, 63–4

Kaplicky, Jan, 135, 170, 265, 272

Kapoor, Anish, 215, 250

Kazakhstan, 196–7, 241, 246, 289, 290

Keller, Dean, 78

Kennedy, J.F., 63, 75, 85–6, 91

Kerr, Philip, 259

Khan Shatyry entertainment centre project (NF), 246

Kho Liang Le, 128, 132

Knight, Sabiha (2nd wife), 261

Kohl, Helmut, 206, 207, 208

Koolhaas, Rem, 233, 285

Krier, Leon, 77
  Poundbury, Dorset, 141

Larkin Guaranty Offices, Buffalo, 77

Lasdun, Denys, University of East Anglia campus, 130–1, 138

Le Corbusier (Charles-Edouard Jeanneret-Gris), 11, 15, 18, 49, 75
  work influences NF, 37, 55–6, 82, 291

Lee, Richard, 63

Lever House, New York, 83

Libeskind, Daniel, 58

Lichtenstein, Roy, 11

Lloyds Building, London, 101, 103, 164, 177

London Eye, London, 275
Long, M.J., 74–5, 82
Long, Richard, 249
Loos, Adolf: *Chicago Tribune* Tower, 158
Lowry, L. S., 8, 12
Luzhkov, Yuri, 244

Maison de Verre, Paris, 247–8
Majidi, Mouzhan, 270, 276
Manchester Town Hall, 27, 28–30, 33, 34–5
Manchester University, School of Architecture, 41–8, 51–2, 54, 206
Mao Tse Tung, 163, 175, 226
Marks, David: London Eye, London, 275
Marshall, Gordon, 130–1, 138
Masdar Development, Abu Dhabi (NF), 1–3, 155, 264
Masdar Institute of Science and Technology, 2 mass-produced homes, 144, 290–2
McMorran, Donald: Wood Street Police Station, 101
Médiathèque de Nîmes (NF), 249, 257–8
Meller, James, 150, 272
Mendelsohn, Erich, 84
Millau Viaduct, France (NF), 197–8
Millennium Bridge, London (NF), 11, 95, 143, 216–24, 275, 286
Millennium Dome, Greenwich (O2 Arena) (NF), 123
Millennium Tower projects (NF; unbuilt) Japan, 189–91
London, 191–2
model-making, 25–6, 281–3, 287
Monadnock Building, Chicago, 90
Moore, Charles, 78–9
Moore, Henry, 127, 149, 198
More London Masterplan (NF), 286
Morris, Marcus, 8
Morris, William, 214, 284
Munden, Roy, 164, 166, 170, 175

Museum of Fine Arts, Boston (NF), 258

NACO, 225 national service, 33–4, 35
National Westminster Bank Headquarters, London, 158, 183, 218
Nazarbayev, Nursultan, 196, 197, 246
Nelson, David, 117, 189–90, 191, 204, 240, 255, 256, 257, 266, 270, 275
Neue Nationalgalerie, Berlin, 132
Neues Museum, Berlin, 275
New Architecture Exhibition: Fosters, Rogers, Stirling Royal Academy of Art (1986), 100–1
New Holland Island, Russia (NF), 242, 243, 246
New York Public Library (NF), 18
Newby, Frank, 159
Newport School, South Wales, 76, 105
Nouvel, Jean, 233, 258, 285
Agbar Tower, Barcelona, 185

O2 Arena, Greenwich (Millennium Dome) (NF), 123
Obayashi Corporation Millennium Tower, Japan, 188–9, 190
Ochoa, Elena *see* Foster, Elena
Olmsted, Frederick Law: Central Park, New York, 245
Olsen, Fred, 107, 109, 111, 112, 118, 143, 288
dock amenities, Millwall (NF), 107, 108–12, 113–15, 122, 124, 128, 135
Gomera scheme, 112–13 headquarters, Vestby, Norway (NF), 112, 150, 205
Regent Street showroom (NF), 112, 253
Orange Hand store, Hampstead, 104–5, 253
Ove Arup, 217, 220, 221–3, 225, 271

Palace of Peace and Reconciliation, Kazakhstan (NF), 196–7, 241, 249, 290
Palladio, Andrea, 59, 161
Palmer and Turner, 160
Pan Am Building, New York, 83
Parker, Peter, 75
Pedersen and Tilney, 91 peerage, 11, 193–4, 284
Pei, I.M., 56–7, 66, 126
  Bank of China Tower, Hong Kong, 175
  Fragrant Hills Hotel, 227
  Hancock Tower, Chicago, 173
Pelli, Cesar, 179
  International Finance Centre Tower, Hong Kong, 182
  Petronas Tower, Kuala Lumpur, 189
People's Liberation Army, China, 227
Petronas Tower, Kuala Lumpur, 189
Petronas University of Technology, Malaysia (NF), 284
Pevsner, Nikolaus, 79
Philips, Graham, 255, 266
Pittsburgh Patent Glazing Corporation, 114–15 politics and architecture, 193–5, 198, 199–201, 202–3, 207–11, 224–5, 226, 238–9, 244
Pompidou Centre, Paris (Beaubourg), 81–2, 102, 177
Pont Millau, France (NF), 197–8, 264, 285
Ponti, Gio: Pirelli Tower, Milan, 157
Prince of Asturias Prize, 284
Prince of Wales, 50–1, 77, 100, 141, 193, 217
Pritchard, Tony, 135
Pritzker Prize, 284
Prix Imperium Award, Japan, 284
Prouvé, Jean, 151, 253, 291
Pushkin Museum, Moscow, 242–3, 290
  Extension (NF), 242, 245

Putin, Vladimir, 245, 290

Rand, Ayn, 39, 68
Regent Street Polytechnic (University of Westminster), 51, 94
Reichstag, New German Parliament (NF), 127, 140, 197, 198–204, 206–11, 263, 282
  see also politics and architecture; Wallot, Paul
Reliance Controls Factory, Swindon (Team Four), 76, 93, 100, 105, 106, 111, 122–3
Renault Distribution Centre, Swindon (NF), 10–11, 257
Ridsdill-Smith, Roger, 217, 219
Ritchie, Ian, 265
Rogers, Richard, 41, 53, 58–9, 64, 73–4, 92, 99–100, 143, 193, 194, 265
  collaborates with NF at Yale, 76–7, 91
  88 Wood Street, London, 101–2, 103
  Lloyds Building, London, 101, 103, 164, 177
  New Architecture exhibition (1986), 100, 101
  Pompidou Centre (Beaubourg), 81–2, 102, 177, 256
  see also Team Four
Rogers, Su, 74, 75, 91, 92, 98–9
Rohe, Mies van der, 32, 90, 125, 158, 173, 184, 255, 282–3
  Illinois Institute of Technology, 56
  Neue Nationalgalerie, Berlin, 132
  Seagram Tower, New York, 56, 83, 173, 185
Ronan Point, London, 139
Root, John Wellborn: Monadnock Building, 90
Rossiya Hotel, Moscow, 242, 243
Rossiya Tower, Moscow (NF; unbuilt), 182, 242, 243
Rotis font, 152

Royal Air Force, 34
Royal Institute of British Architects
(RIBA), 163, 164
Rudolph, Paul, 56–7, 71–3, 81–2, 89, 98,
143, 253, 270
Art and Architecture Building, Yale, 68,
70, 72, 77–80
Blue Cross, Blue Shield offices, Boston,
76
Cocoon House, Siesta Key, 66
Foster and Roger's work, 81–2 house
and studio, 68–70
NF's Yale projects, 76, 117, 158
School of Forestry, Yale, 66
Temple Street car park, New Haven,
67
Rufford Hall, Cheshire, 45
Russia, 240–6

Saarinen, Eero, 56, 126
Ezra Stiles and Morse colleges, Yale
University, 65
TWA terminal, Idlewild Airport, 60
Sackler Galleries, Royal Academy of Arts
(NF), 69, 258
Sagoo, Narinder, 270
Sainsbury, David, 142–3
Sainsbury, David, Baron, 11, 193
Sainsbury, Robert and Lisa, 127–30,
132–3, 134, 136, 137, 138, 141, 143
Sainsbury Centre for Visual Arts (NF),
84, 98, 105, 131–42, 198, 282
Samuel Beckett Theatre project (NF;
unbuilt), 149–50
Sandberg, Michael, 157, 162, 163, 165
Scholl family, 151–2
Scott, Peter, 184
Scully, Vincent, 65, 79, 82–3
Seagram Building, New York, 56, 83, 90,
173
Sears Tower, Chicago, 158
Seidler, Harry, 157

Hong Kong Club Building, 181–2
Seifert, Richard: National Westminster
Bank Headquarters, London, 158
Serra, Richard, 208, 217, 250
Sert, Jose Lluis, 57
Shuttleworth, Ken, 255, 266, 275
Simpson, Ian, 265
Sitte, Camillo, 48
Skybreak House, Hertfordshire (Team
Four), 93
Small, John, 255
Smirke, Robert, 211, 213–14
Smithson, Peter and Alison, 147
Society for the Protection of Ancient
Buildings, 214
SOM, 58, 271
Lever House, New York, 83
Space City, Russia, 240–1
Spence, Basil: Coventry Cathedral, 10
sports *see* hobbies
St Paul's Cathedral, London, 217, 244,
282
Staatsgalerie, Stuttgart, 115–16
Stansted Airport (NF), 136, 234, 235–6,
257, 258, 286
Stanton, Alan, 105, 106, 265
Stern, Bob, 77
Stevens, Jocelyn, 211–12
Stirling, James, 32, 55, 70, 75–6, 90, 100,
105, 147
Staatsgalerie, Stuttgart, 115–16
Stirling Prize, 284
Street Porter, Tim, 116
Stubbins, Hugh, 157
Citicorp Tower, New York, 160
Federal Reserve Tower, Boston, 160
Sullivan, Louis, 90
Sussmuth, Rita, 199, 207
Sutcliffe, Mark, 271
Swiss RE Headquarters, London (NF),
103, 154–5, 182–5, 186–7, 191, 192,
217, 275, 283, 286

Sydney Opera House, 49, 164, 220
    symbolism and architecture, 197–9,
    203, 208–10, 238
    see also politics and architecture

Tate Gallery, St Ives, 73
Team Four, 41, 66, 75, 93–4, 95–9, 103,
    106, 266, 270
Team Ten, 93
Television House, Manchester, 38
Temple Street car park, New Haven, 67
Thatcher, Margaret, 101, 259
Thompson, Mike, 107, 109–10, 112
Tigerman, Stanley, 77
Torre de Collserola, Barcelona (NF), 182,
    275
Torre Velasca, Milan, 49
Tower 42, London, 158, 183, 218
Trafalgar Square Redevelopment (NF),
    216
Tubbs, Ralph: Dome of Discovery,
    Festival of Britain, 9
TWA terminal, Idlewild Airport, 60

Ulm School of Design, 151–2
Union Station, New Haven, 62
Unite d'Habitation, Marseilles, 11
Urban, Joseph, 187
Utzon, Jorn Oberg: Sydney Opera House,
    49, 256

Vanbrugh, John: Blenheim Palace,
    Woodstock, 202
Vanity Fair, 258–9
Virlogeux, Michel, 198
Vogue, 67–8

Walker, Derek, 159
Walker, John, 116
Wallis, Barnes, 145
Wallot, Paul: Reichstag, Berlin (original
    building), 199–200, 201, 203

Waterhouse, Alfred, 271
    Manchester Town Hall, 27
    Natural History Museum, London,
    28
Watts, Thomas, 213
Webb, Philip: Red House, Bexleyheath,
    284–5
Weidenfeld, George, Baron, 11, 193
Wembley Stadium, London (NF), 264,
    286
Wen Jiabao, 238–9
Whitby, George: Wood Street Police
    Station, 101
Whitney Museum, New York, 159–60,
    180–1
Wilkinson, Chris: Gateshead Bridge, 275
Williams, Owen: Express Newspapers'
    Buildings, 30–2
Willis Faber and Dumas Headquarters,
    Ipswich (NF), 31–2, 115, 116,
    123–6, 140–1, 151, 253, 266
Wilson, Colin St John: British Library,
    75
Witchita House project, 144
Wood Street, London, 101–3
Woolworth Building, New York, 173
World Trade Center, New York, 158
Wren, Christopher, 101
    St Paul's Cathedral, 217, 244, 282
Wright, Frank Lloyd, 11, 37, 39, 80, 82,
    207
    Falling Water, Pittsburgh, 89–90
    Guggenheim Museum, New York, 90,
    186, 285
    Larkin Guaranty Offices, Buffalo, 77

Yakubu, Armstrong, 270
Yale Daily News, 78
Yale University, 53, 57–8
    NF arrives, 60–1, 62, 63–4, 65–6
    NF collaborates with Richard Rogers,
    76–7

Yale University—*contd*
    NF influenced by Paul Rudolph, 68–9,
      70–2, 76
    NF's student travel and lifestyle, 73–5,
      89–90
    see also Art and Architecture Building;
Chermayeff, Serge; Johnson, Philip;
Rogers, Richard; Rudolph, Paul;
Scully, Vincent

Zunz, Jack, 172